Laughter,
Love
and
a
Barbershop
Song

LAUGHTER, LOVE AND A BARBERSHOP SONG

Behind-the-scene glimpses
of barbershopping at its best,
with stories contributed by barbershoppers
from across the United States and Canada.

Compiled and edited by

FRED GIELOW

★ ★ ★ ★ ★ ★ ★ ★ ★ ★ ★

ISBN: 0-9603938-0-3

Library of Congress Catalog Card Number: 80-65128

Designed by Fred C. Gielow, Jr.
Published by Fred C. Gielow, Jr.
33 Park Drive
Woodstock, New York 12498
U. S. A.

Printed in the United States of America.

To Diane,
      whose love of barbershop music
      and encouragement of my participation in it
      have immensely enhanced and enriched
      my enjoyment of its unique harmony.

To Bob and Tim,
      who exhibited great patience and understanding
      on those all too many occasions
      when my barbershopping commitments
      interfered with family activities and obligations.

To Dad,
      whose counsel and caring
      have meant so much to me
      during the creation of this book,
      and throughout my life.

And to Pete Donatelli, George Nagy, Mike Patti, Bill James,
Mike Myers, Don Barnes, and Anton Gross,
      who have made barbershop quartetting possible for me
      for close to a decade and a half,
      and have thus allowed me to participate
         in a mighty musical joy,
      for which I shall be forever grateful!

Foreword

This foreword was contributed by Walter Latzko, notable barbershopper, renowned barbershop music arranger, and talented, gentle, warm, and now and again witty human being.

Blooming Grove, New York 10914

Dear Fred,

When you asked me to examine the manuscript of this book for review of its syntax, continuity, commas, and spelling of technical terms like "Don Clause," I never dreamed you might also request a foreword. I'm honored, of course, but what could I possibly add to this, the last word on the wonderful world of unaccompanied-four-part-harmony-with-the-melody-most-always-in-the-second-voice-from-the-top singing?

I suppose I could tell how I got started in this musical pastime, but that's bound to be dull and turn readers off before you, Fred, have a chance to turn them on. You see, my humble musical beginnings consisted of the classic strains of Bach, Mozart, Brahms — men of that ilk — men who never dreamed that what they thought to be an ordinary, garden-variety dominant seventh chord was in reality the exalted Barbershop Seventh!

It surely wouldn't be of any historic significance whatsoever to reveal in your book's foreword that my first barbershop arrangement scratchings were of an obscure Dixie tune for the Amherst College DQ (that's Double Quartet). The song title now eludes me, but the lyric had something to do with "honeysuckle vine," "wanta go back," "cho-cho-train," and "levee." (That could be most any Dixie tune you could think of. Or even the all-knowing, all-wise Dave Stevens could think of!)

And likewise, I'm sure it would be of little to no interest to reveal that one of my first public barbershop performing efforts was singing the bass part (albeit second bass, with the Amherst College DQ) in a tender old-time ballad called "Don't Tell Me What You Dreamed Last Night, 'Cause I've Been Reading Freud." Honest, that was the name of it. We could never announce the title ahead of time because it gave away the punch line.

Nor would there by any redeeming value in recalling for your eager readers the good old days of the Arthur (brother of Bob)

Godfrey Show when I was working with the CHORDETTES and how every time they came to one particularly adventuresome chord in a certain ancient arrangement of "When Day Is Done," the guitar player in Archie Bleyer's orchestra and I would look at each other and twitch in unison. This, mind you, was long before our current Arrangement Category got into that elusive thing called "distortion of implied harmony."

Oh sure, I admit that arranging for the BUFFALO BILLS was a bunch of thrills. Not everyone has a chance to hear his notes explode. Nor will I forget that glorious evening at venerable Carnegie Hall when the BILLS, the FOUR RENEGADES, and the Livingston, New Jersey Dapper Dans Chorus rang grand and glorious chords on stage in a show that set the Big Apple on its tin (Pan Alley) ear. Ghosts of the aforementioned Bach, Mozart, and Brahms must have lunged for their quill pens to try their hand at a swipe or tag or two.

But really, Fred, obviously none of this is a mite fitting for a foreword. So, much as I'd like to, I must respectfully decline the honor of authoring such a piece. I'm afraid I just can't think of anything that would be worthy of this, your very fine effort, which I hope will grace a prominent niche on every barber-shopper's library shelf.

Much luck, and why not try Bob Johnson!

Regards,
  Walter

P.S. Please, whatever you do, I beg of you not to show this letter to anyone as I am most reluctant to have it spread around the barbershopping world that I'm backwards when it comes to forewords!

Contributors

For the most part, this book is a collection of super barbershop stories contributed by super barbershoppers. My sincere thanks to:

Sam Aramian	Lindy Levitt
Leon Avakian	Jack Macgregor
Ken Beard	Russell Malony
Jed Casey	Tom Masengale
Keith Clark	Jim Massey
Terry Clarke	Ernie Matson
Tom Cogan	Doran McTaggart
Bill Conway	Ronnie Menard
Buck Dominy	Marty Mendro
Pete Donatelli	Bob Morris
Bob Dykstra	Lou Perry
Dick Ellenberger	Al Poole
Phil Embury	Hal Purdy
Dick Floersheimer	Vern Reed
Dick Hadfield	Bob Royce
Buzz Haeger	Tom Schlinkert
Carl Hancuff	Joe Schmitt
Bud Harvey	Bob Seay
Ken Hatton	Russ Seely
Forry Haynes	Sev Severance
Don Hewey	Jim Sherman
Val Hicks	Huck Sinclair
Tom Hine	Lou Sisk
Jack Hines	Dean Snyder
Hugh Ingraham	Fred Steinkamp
Bill James	Lloyd Steinkamp
Dick Johnson	Tim Stivers
Bob Keener	Don Vienne
Steve Keiss	Jiggs Ward
Freddie King	Harlan Wilson
Frank Lanza	Ernie Winter
Lou Laurel	Reedie Wright

My thanks, also, to Ellie Close, Sylvia Day, Dick deMontmollin, Dick Girvin, Walter Latzko, Chester Lee, Ruth Marks, Art Merrill, Natalie Minewski, and Dan Murphy, all of whom made significant contributions to the book.

Contents

Preface

I am a member of one of the strangest, yet most marvelous organizations in the world. It's called the Society for the Preservation and Encouragement of Barber Shop Quartet Singing in America, Incorporated (SPEBSQSA), but don't let the imposing name turn you off. I don't think you can find a more friendly or more fun-loving bunch of people anywhere!

I've experienced many magnificent moments as part of this super singing society. I've derived a wealth of pleasure and satisfaction in pursuit of a barbershop song. I've learned that barbershopping is an extra special form of joy, created by four-part harmony.

Indeed, barbershopping has been a great and thrilling influence in my life, and I want to share some of my experiences. I want others to share their special moments, too. So this is a book of true experiences about barbershoppers and their harmonious hobby. It's a book that looks behind the scenes of barbershopping into the very heart and soul of this great American creation and tradition.

I wrote to barbershoppers throughout the Society and asked them to record their favorite stories on cassette tape. I also asked them to suggest others with barbershopping experiences to relate. I collected their taped tales, wove them together, and occasionally threw in an anecdote of my own. That's how the book came to be.

Just a word about some printing conventions I've adopted: Quartet names are printed in full capital letters, while barbershop chorus and chapter names are printed with initial capitals only. Wherever the word "Society" (with a capital S) appears, it refers to the Barbershop Society, of course. "International" with an initial capital letter refers to the annual barbershop convention which determines new quartet and chorus champions. When you see "District" or "Division" (with a big D), you'll know the words refer to existing geographical/organizational components of the Society. Stories contributed by other barbershoppers are indented and in *italics*.

On occasion I've used terms that are somewhat unique to the barbershop world, and I haven't belabored a definition or explanation. I assume most readers are familiar enough with barbershop lore and language so that such clarifications are unnecessary. If you consider yourself completely unfamiliar with the subject, however, then I offer my apologies and my recommendation that you seek out an experienced barbershopper for a translation.

This book has been a labor of love. Contributors submitted stories freely and generously. They did so without compensation (none was offered), because they believe in our great avocation. If the book sells, I hope to recover my expenses. After that, I've promised to contribute 75 percent of my net earnings to the Society.

One final comment: It is regrettable that I am able to publish so few of the stories contributed for this book. It is regrettable, too, that I was unable to collect stories from other barbershoppers who I'm sure have equally interesting and entertaining experiences to relate. As I indicated, this book is intended to offer a behind-the-scenes glimpse of barbershopping, so I must leave to another author the challenge of compiling enough stories to present a behind-the-scenes lengthy stare!

Sing and be happy!

Fred Gielow
Woodstock, New York

Laughter,
Love
and
a
Barbershop
Song

CHAPTER 1

They Call Him Barbershopper

They Call Him Barbershopper

We must laugh and we must sing,
We are blest by everything...

William Butler Yeats

ete Bandy and I worked together in the same office years ago, and one day he invited me to join him on a Wednesday evening at the weekly meeting of the Poughkeepsie, New York Chapter of the Society for the Preservation and Encouragement of Barber Shop Quartet Singing in America. I had heard of SPEBSQSA before, had even attended some barbershop shows, and always enjoyed singing, but I wasn't so sure I wanted to attend a barbershop chorus rehearsal and chapter meeting. I told Pete thanks and said I'd think about it.

I did think about it, too. I thought I already had enough activities to keep me busy with work, home, and family. I certainly didn't need another obligation to compete for my time. Not only that, I'd miss some darn good TV programs Wednesday nights. The answer had to be no.

But Pete persisted, and as the weeks slipped by he made a pest of himself with his endless "invitations." I finally ran out of excuses and since Pete was blunt about pointing out how feeble they were to begin with, I finally agreed to go. Actually, we worked out a deal: He'd stop bothering me if I went to just one meeting.

That's all it took! Pete introduced me to a hobby that has been of immeasurable pleasure. My Wednesday nights quickly turned into barbershopping nights and became more dear than even the weekends. I found satisfying singing in the chorus, entertaining programs after rehearsal, casual quartetting and woodshedding after that, and a whole wonderful world of harmony and song. I owe a lot to this "hobby" of mine; hence, to Pete Bandy!

I remember the first time I sang with three other guys in front of the chapter, only weeks after Pete got me to that first meeting. We sang "Down Our Way," an old barbershop chestnut, and I was terrified! Petrified is a better word to describe it. All the blood drained out of my arms and legs and I could hardly move. It was miraculous but I managed to make it all the way through to the end of that forty-five-second epic. It seemed more like an hour and a half.

I was pleased enough just to cross the finish line with the number, so I didn't need any further signs of approbation, but I got them anyway; whoops and hollers like you wouldn't believe. It was a mighty pleasant sensation, in spite of the fact that I knew such demonstrations were staged regardless of the caliber of the performance.

In short order I found myself in another quartet, this one formed to compete in an informal contest with other Poughkeepsie Chapter quartets similarly formed. We sang the "Whiffenpoof Song," and won! And that's the way it went, with one stimulating and rewarding experience after another; chapter shows, chorus contests, singouts, interchapter get-togethers, community service activities, and lots of good old-fashioned singing with three other guys. Then as part of a registered quartet I found another whole world of excitement and challenge. More contests, shows, a brand-new dimension of barbershopping.

I suppose that's the way it is for many music enthusiasts. They come ready-made with a deep-down love of singing, and when they finally happen onto barbershopping, they know they've found a vital missing link in their lives.

Some eagerly search out their first barbershop chapter and may travel as much as a hundred or more miles to the meetings, while others, like myself, may have to be dragged to their first rehearsal session. Sooner or later it seems that cosmic fate is fulfilled and another barbershopper is born!

Lou Sisk reacted a little reluctantly to the bite of the barbershop bug:

My brother, Leo, was a member of the Society and had an old 78 RPM record he used to play at home every once in a while. It was the BUFFALO BILLS. Leo said they were champions, but the record was scratchy and beat up, and I wasn't impressed. Barbershop singing? Ho hum.

When I got out of the Service and got married, Leo was in a quartet called the TOWN AND COUNTRY FOUR, and they sang at our wedding. The reception was kind of hectic, so I didn't pay much attention to them. Besides, I was thinking of other things. I saw four guys with their mouths moving and I almost heard them. Barbershop quartet? Big deal.

A couple of times I even went down to McPoland's Cafe, the neighborhood bar where Leo went with all his cronies late at night after chapter meetings. There was singing, and they had beer and pretzels, but that didn't excite me.

Some time later, Leo began pushing me to buy tickets to an upcoming barbershop show. "Leo, are you serious?" I asked him. "You mean you're going to put those bums from McPoland's Cafe, singing barbershop harmony, up on stage at the Syria Mosque?" That place is a big auditorium for big shows, and it seats about 4000. Leo said he wanted me to spend three bucks a ticket. For Carol and myself it would be six bucks, and then he suggested I take Mom along. That would make nine bucks. Then there was my mother-in-law. Well, what the heck, I thought, so I wrapped myself into twelve dollars' worth of tickets, but I didn't care if I got to see the show or not.

When the time got close, I figured I'd be working late, and that would get me off the hook. I waited until three o'clock in the afternoon before I called Carol. "Gee, it looks like I might be a little late here, so you'd better go ahead alone to the show tonight." I think she wasn't too crazy about going either, but felt obligated.

As it turned out, I got away from work at five, with plenty of time to get home, change clothes, and make it to the show. We sat there lamenting that the evening was lost. Then the curtain opened.

It was the Society's Midwinter Convention show, hosted by the Pittsburgh Chapter, and it featured the CONFEDERATES, International Champs; the PLAYTONICS, Society second-ranking quartet; the PITTSBURGHERS, International Champs from several years before; the WESTINGHOUSE QUARTET, a famous Pittsburgh foursome; the STEEL CITY FOUR; and Leo's quartet, the TOWN AND COUNTRY FOUR, soon to be crowned International Champs. All of a sudden barbershop singing was the most fantastic thing I'd ever heard!

I went to my brother after the show. "McPoland's Cafe it ain't, Leo," I told him. "It's great!" I was completely turned on, went to the next chapter meeting, and signed up to become a member! It took a while for it to get my attention, but when it did, barbershopping quickly became an important part of my life.

Freddie King found barbershopping by looking in a Baltimore newspaper:

When I was sixteen I was in a high school quartet with Jim Grant, Fred Geisler, and a Greek fellow named Bill Horianopoulis. We called Fred "the kid," because he was only a sophomore. For me that quartet turned out to be the beginning of a twenty-five-year sing-in with Jim Grant. One day we saw an ad in the paper: "Go to the Lyric Theater tonight and hear the quartets sing." We thought that meant we could go there and sing for the audience. All excited, we hurried down to the theater. Only standing-room tickets were left, but we bought some and went in.

We grabbed hold of the brass rail at the back of the auditorium and watched intently as the MC walked out on stage. "Ladies and gentlemen," he announced, "to open our show, here is the Baltimore Chapter Chorus." They sang "Lonesome for You, That's All," and "Great Smoky Mountains in Dixie," but their performance didn't do anything to me. As a matter of fact, I thought they were out of tune! I couldn't wait for our chance to get up and sing.

Next to be introduced was the VOLUNTEERS, 1951 Mid-Atlantic District Champions. Four men walked out on the stage and it was the first time I ever heard a male quartet sing. My quartet knew "Sweet Roses of Morn" and "I Had a Dream,

Dear," stuff our high school teacher had given us, but boy, those guys had great music and really laid out some great barbershop sounds. My fingerprints are still on that rail. We nearly fell over backwards! I told Jim I didn't think we were going to do any singing there after all.

When the VOLUNTEERS finished, the MC said, "Now, we go to the distaff side of quartetting..." I asked Jim what that meant. He said he didn't know. That made two of us. Out onstage walked the CHORDETTES. They sang "Running Wild," and we'd never heard anything like it. Over backwards we went!

Then there was an intermission. We went outside, leaned on a wall, and drooled for a while. We couldn't even talk, we were so impressed. When we went back inside, the FOUR CHORDERS from London, Ontario were introduced, and they were one of the most phenomenal quartets ever! I couldn't believe it. The crowd went wild. By the time they finished, we were numb, and the MC had the gall to say, "Coming up next is the quartet you've all been waiting for!" The BUFFALO BILLS charged out onstage, sang "Hi, Neighbor," and over backwards we went again!

We crawled to the next chapter meeting and haven't missed one since!

Bud Harvey found barbershop harmony over the bridge table, but got hooked on it in the most unlikely of locations:

My wife, Barbara, and I used to play bridge every week or so with two neighbors, Tom and Camilla Rosewag. I have what is probably an annoying habit of humming to myself, and one card-playing evening Tom asked if I liked to sing. I said I did, so we started harmonizing over the bridge table with Barbara singing lead, Camilla on tenor, Tom with the bass, and me baritone. Over a period of weeks we learned the parts to a few of the oldies, "Down Our Way," "My Wild Irish Rose," "Roses of Morn," and others.

One day Tom called to tell me there was a barbershop show the next night in Baltimore. He wanted to know if I'd like to go. Absolutely!

It was a great show at the Lyric Theatre, with the BUFFALO BILLS from Buffalo, New York and the SHORT CUTS from Miami. Later we went to the afterglow. Upon its conclusion,

Tom rounded up a lead and tenor from the Catonsville Chapter and we repaired to the men's room for a run-through of my limited repertoire.

We were in the middle of "Shine on Me," when I sensed a change in the voice on my left. I turned to see who had joined us as tenor replacement, and found it was none other than Vern Reed, tenor of the BUFFALO BILLS. I was flabbergasted! That a member of an International Championship Quartet would deign to step in and sing with three peons, including one very novice peon, in the john, after an afterglow, astonished me. That's when I said to myself, "This is my kind of organization! Where do I sign up?"

Apparently the BUFFALO BILLS assumed the role of barbershopping ambassadors. They spread the harmony and they spread the word. Tom Cogan met the quartet and was never quite the same again:

It was one of the highlights of my barbershopping career. The BUFFALO BILLS were featured on the first show I attended after becoming a Society member. Their singing was superb, the audience went berserk, and I was enthralled! I went to the afterglow, then I went to a second afterglow, then a third, and eventually a fourth! But during the third afterglow was when it happened.

Still a newcomer to the world of barbershopping, I was thrilled to be able to sit down and talk with the great BUFFALO BILLS. After a few minutes one of them asked if I wanted to sing a song.

My claim to fame is that I sang baritone with the BUFFALO BILLS! We sang "I'm Alone Because I Love You." If there was one experience that transformed me from an interested barbershopper into a fanatic, it had to be singing that song. The harmony crashed down on me like a tidal wave. It was the most important three minutes of my barbershopping career. I'll never forget it!

If you have never sung in a chorus or quartet, I'm sure it's hard to imagine how such a simple activity can be so satisfying. Whatever can be so terrific about singing four-part barbershop music? Let me try to explain why I think it's so special.

First it's the music itself. A four-part barbershop chord is a huge helping of harmony, and it contains a richness, fullness, and power that surpass by far the caliber and quality of the individual voices producing the chord. The synergism is so great, at times it's awesome!

A second reason is simply the delight of music participation. It's a pleasure to hear barbershop harmony, but I think a far greater pleasure to produce it. To contribute through your own God-given vocal apparatus to a melodic musical expression is both satisfying and gratifying. In a chorus it's magnificent. In a quartet it's overpowering!

Another barbershop singing benefit is the fraternity. For some reason or other, the act of singing creates an extra special bond between people.

A fourth dividend is the joy that is spread with song. Through song a chorus or quartet can impart a smile, a laugh, a great joy to an audience, and when these elements are the mediums of exchange, barbershopping is at its best.

It's curious, but the creation of a series of fleeting sounds can produce lasting pleasures. Performance by-products of laughter, love, and harmony are enduring entities. Indeed, I wonder if that's the magic of barbershop music; that it can communicate a great spectrum of emotion in surprising abundance and intensity.

Barbershop singing may begin as a pastime, but it frequently becomes a passion. It gets into your blood. Phil Embury was one of those whose fascination with the barbershop sound was a passion to begin with:

> *The year was 1939. I came home from a business trip one night, and my wife, Jane, was all excited about a discovery she had made. She found that radio station WLW in Cincinnati had a program called "Sweet Adeline" right after the news at 11:15 p.m. It was fifteen minutes of barbershop singing by a local Cincinnati quartet.*
>
> *I tuned in and heard someone talking about the Barbershop Society. That was when I first heard about Owen C. Cash who had founded the Society the year before. I listened intently to that program and was fascinated with the music. Sometimes the signal faded out. Sometimes there was a lot of static. After all, it's a long way from my home in Warsaw, New York to Cincinnati, Ohio, but the barbershop harmony came through.*
>
> *I wrote a letter to Cash and he wrote back, and sent along a*

membership card. I was officially a barbershopper!

In Kansas City on business a year later, I wondered if it would be possible to meet Cash. I phoned him person-to-person and overheard Mrs. Cash tell the operator he was not at home but would be returning by train the next morning. I, too, was on my way by train to Tulsa, Oklahoma that same night.

The next morning, I checked in at the Mayo Hotel. About noon I phoned again, and for the first time I heard the rich voice of baritone O.C. Cash.

He came right down to the hotel and we had lunch together. He was enthusiastic, happy-go-lucky, and a real music lover. "I'll tell you what we'll do," he said. "Tomorrow is Easter Sunday and I want you to come to church and sing in the choir." I had no idea what hymns were going to be sung, but I was willing just the same.

Sunday afternoon Cash got together the OAKIE FOUR and brought them up to my hotel room. They sang for two hours, all those wonderful old songs like "After Dark," "Coney Island Baby," "Bright Was the Night," "Mandy Lee," "Aura Lee," "Love Me and the World Is Mine," and the harmony was mind-boggling. Oh boy, I thought, this is great stuff! I let those beautiful sounds soak into my consciousness and when I left the next day for Dallas, I knew the barbershop bug had bit me hard.

Harmony spinning around in my head made me feel like I was on a merry-go-round. It was all I could think of. It was my first close-up hearing of a barbershop quartet where I could really absorb the sound. It was terrific!

Jack Hines was almost weaned on four-part harmony. It was part of his family tradition:

There were four of them. They never were in the Society, but they did a lot of singing. My Uncle John had a barn-dance band; square dance, I guess they call it now. He always was somewhat of a musician. He, my Uncle Harold, my Uncle Charlie, and Dad had a quartet when they were in their twenties. Well, Charlie took off and nobody heard from him for a long time. I suppose he moved to some other part of the country; we lost track. Anyway, when I came along they drafted me to sing with them, and that's when I first started singing barbershop.

I was somewhat of a choirboy type at the time, so I sang tenor, and whenever the family got together, the quartet ended up out in the garage, with a bottle of Four Roses for them, and a pot of hot cocoa for me. We sang out there until the wee hours of the morning. We never had a piece of music. I guess everything I learned about singing barbershop I learned as a woodshedder, singing with Uncle Harold, Uncle John, and Dad.

When people talk about woodshedding today, they say you shouldn't move from the note you're singing until you have to. When I was singing with Dad's quartet, it was a case of not moving because I was afraid to! If I put a little something special in the middle of a song, and they didn't like it, I'd get the back of a hand across the side of my head! I learned the hard way!

I remember the first time I ever heard a real barbershop quartet. I was living in New Haven, Connecticut. My dad wanted me to go to the grocery store for some milk and bread or something, so I hopped on my bicycle and started off. It was about six o'clock in the evening. The store was two miles from home.

Along the way I passed Roland T. Warner's Hardware Store, at the corner where the Grand Avenue Bridge crossed the Quinnipiac River. The hardware store was closed, but in the doorway was a quartet singing four-part barbershop harmony. I don't remember their name. They were practicing for an International contest which was going to be held in New York City at the World's Fair Grounds. Ollie Jermine was one of the men, and the tenor was an Irishman, a policeman, but I don't remember the others. They were making beautiful music so I stopped for a while to listen. I put my bike down and sat on the curb. I listened to them practice and enjoyed every chord.

Suddenly it dawned on me it was late, very late. The sky was pitch dark and the grocery store was no longer open. One of the quartetters told me the time: ten minutes after eleven! I didn't have milk or bread and I was afraid my father would kill me when I got home. I jumped on my bicycle and pedaled as fast as I could. Dad was waiting for me and was furious! He wanted to know where I had been for all that time. I told him I'd been sitting on a curbstone in front of Roland T. Warner's Hardware Store listening to a barbershop quartet. Dad thought that was about the most unbelievable story he had ever heard, and he proceeded to beat the living dickens out of me. I paid dearly for that barbershop concert!

Dad was a police detective, and the next morning in the squad room he overheard some policemen talking together in the corner. He heard one of them say something about a quartet rehearsal at Roland T. Warner's Hardware Store. "It was the cutest thing I ever saw," the Irish tenor exclaimed. "A young little kid came along and laid his bicycle down there, sat on the curb, and listened to us for close to five hours!"

Needless to say, Dad felt pretty bad about how he had treated me because he had given me a real thrashing. He was the kind of guy, though, who would do anything but admit he was wrong. When he got home that night he invited me to the ice-cream parlor and bought me a big, hot fudge sundae. It was his way of saying he was sorry.

That was my introduction to barbershopping. I was eleven years old. And let me tell you, that was some fine quartet I heard singing in the doorway of Roland T. Warner's Hardware Store!

They call him "barbershopper." He's no one special, but if he loves the music, thrills to the chords, and finds peace in the harmony, then he's someone very special indeed. From the outside a barbershopper may be hard to recognize, but inside he has a melody on his mind and a song in his heart.

CHAPTER 2

The Barbershop Chapter

these activities are only a means to a more important end: the singing. Russell Malony describes how those long and grueling administrative meetings can sometimes be streamlined:

> *During a Westfield, New Jersey Chapter business meeting, one of the members complained that "Robert's Rules" weren't being strictly adhered to. President Hank Mereness answered the complaint: "Robert doesn't sing in a quartet, so as far as this chapter is concerned, he doesn't exist!"*

So much for the administrative end of barbershopping.

The chorus director is a unique man among unique men. He's the guy who waves his arms in front of everybody, yells at everybody, and tries relentlessly to make a chorus of a crowd. His job is a lot more than arm waving. The chorus director/music director must interpret the songs and explain his interpretations to the singers. He must have a good understanding of music fundamentals and moreover have the skill to teach the music to the "troops." He must be a motivator, to rally everyone together and elicit good-quality singing performances. He must be a disciplinarian, maintaining some fashion of order where chaos would otherwise reign. He must be a diplomat, too, criticizing without intimidating, correcting without embarrassing, leading without dictating. He must even have a personality with sparkle, for without at least a measure of charisma, the chorus members may tend to lose interest over a period of time.

There's yet another characteristic to add to the list: he must also be a showman. Everybody likes to hear good music; everybody loves to see and hear a good show. As you can well understand, being a successful chorus director is no mean feat to pull off! He faithfully fashions each song's tempo and beat, he flails his arms about with fervor, and is probably the single most important musical element of every barbershop chapter.

Obviously, finding a good director is a tough job. Often a tougher job, though, is making a transition from one director to another, without stepping on toes or hurting feelings, while at the same time doing so with full chapter membership support. It's generally a challenging, ticklish, and time-consuming maneuver!

Sam Aramian tells how the whole process can be consummated in a matter of seconds:

> *I was chapter president at the time, and Charlie Rastatter,*

tenor of our quartet, the DESERT KNIGHTS, was director. The quartet was at the airport in Los Angeles, between flights on our way home from a show. We had an hour's layover, so we went to the restaurant to wait for our flight to Phoenix. Charlie began to talk about some of his frustrations with chorus rehearsals. He complained about poor attendance, how slow some chorus members were to learn words and music, how much trouble he had with discipline. Joe Salz, Lloyd Steinkamp, and I listened attentively, as Charlie got hotter and hotter. He worked himself into a lather and finally in exasperation blurted out, "For two cents I'd resign!"

I reached in my pocket and handed him two pennies. "As of now," I said, calmly, "you're through. Next Wednesday Lloyd will take over directing."

Lloyd looked at me in disbelief. Charlie looked at me the same way. Lloyd and Charlie looked at each other. They looked back at me.

"I don't believe what just happened," Charlie said. He stuck the money in his pocket and at the next chorus rehearsal Lloyd was director. He served for four years until he went to work as Field Representative on the Society's International staff.

Once past the serious chorus rehearsing and business portions of a chapter meeting, it's time for the serious fun. "Pickup" quartets may perform, or registered quartets. Sometimes there are guest quartets or other special attractions. There are "disorganized" quartet competitions, Ladies' Night programs, Father-Son programs, interchapter get-togethers, and an endless array of singing gimmicks and entertainment ideas.

Many of these schemes are no more than means for starting off the barbershop merriment. It doesn't take much. Programs are usually designed for singing, but they also give chapter members a chance to clown around and ham it up as well. Often the mirth begins even before it's scheduled. Such was the case on many occasions in the Hollywood, California Chapter, as Leon Avakian recalls:

When I first joined barbershopping, in Hollywood, California, one of the chapter members was Hal Perry, the "Great Gildersleeve!" This "character" came to our chapter meetings perhaps only once a month. He'd sit in the front row and would thoroughly enjoy the rehearsal. When anything silly happened, he'd start to laugh. Even without provocation, he'd liven up the place by unraveling that famous bass-tone laugh of his. He'd start slowly at first, quietly, and his guttural sounds would build in volume until the entire chorus was toppled with laughter. That was the Great Gildersleeve. He had a real talent for making rehearsals a sheer delight.

As lighthearted and frivolous as chapter programs are intended to be, they may still contain their moments of fright, because singing for others can be quite an unnerving process. Under the watchful eye of an audience, what is well remembered can quickly become well forgotten, and in a quartet particularly, where each voice hangs alone on a part, a singer may find his performance squeezed out from under his control. So even in a happy evening of casual barbershopping there can be moments of great stress, as Doran McTaggart learned early in his barbershopping career:

The first time the MERRIMADICS sang, we won a "disorganized" quartet contest in the Windsor, Ontario Chapter, and we were therefore automatically placed on the program for the upcoming Ladies' Night. Since our quartet was scheduled to sing first, we went down to the boiler room to warm up immediately after dinner. I've always had a nervous stomach and I inevitably get a giant collection of butterflies at moments of stress, so I've learned through the years not to eat when I sing or MC a show.

For that Ladies' Night, however, I didn't know any better, and while we warmed up, I felt a sensation which made me fear that my delicious supper might rise to the occasion. I quickly put my hand over my mouth, and at that very instant all the butterflies were released.

It was not a moment that gladdened my heart. I had forgotten my handkerchief, so I asked the guys to lend me one, but just then we were introduced to sing. The other three laughed and scampered off for the stage. The baritone was left alone to solve his problem.

I cleaned my glasses with my shirt tail, combed my hair, and hurriedly joined them. In the meantime they were howling over my predicament. They got a big potato-chip bag, bigger than a trash bag, and put it in front of the microphone, "just in case." It was with that incident that I acquired a reputation. To this

*day, whenever we enter a contest, and it doesn't matter if I'm
directing the chorus or singing in a quartet, they make it a point
to remind me, "Doran, have you heaved?"*

Part of the sport of a disorganized quartet contest is to think up a
wacky name for your foursome. We came up with a dandy for one
contest I sang in. We called ourselves the "Mighty, Invincible,
Carefree, Kindhearted, Engagingly Youthful, Musically Orthodox,
Uniform Singing Ensemble!" We thought that would be a tongue
twister for the MC when he introduced us, and moreover we thought
the initials hand-lettered on our T-shirts in bright red Magic Marker
would be a crowd pleaser, too. I don't for the life of me remember
how we scored, but I guess I'd recall if we'd won. Anyway, besides
memories, I got a new T-shirt out of the contest.

Years later, I was scheduled to take photographs at the hospital in
Hudson, New York. Getting dressed early in the morning, I scrambled around in my T-shirt drawer only to find my supply all but exhausted. Then I came across a nearly unused T-shirt with initials as
bright as ever across the chest. The lettering would be unnoticeable,
I reasoned, if I wore a bright red shirt over it, and that's what I did.

At the hospital it wasn't long before I was dispatched to the
operating room, where an operation was in its final phase. I had to
hurry if I was going to get some pictures for the hospital annual
report. The head nurse met me at the door, ushered me to an
anteroom, and stuffed what looked like a pair of green pajama bot-
toms in my hands. "Take off your shirt and trousers," she directed.
"Put on these pants, and I'll get a top, mask, and foot covering for
you."

There I was, alone in the small room, racing to get ready, with
"MICKEY MOUSE" emblazoned across the front of me in big, bold
letters. There I was, walking out of the small room with my face every
bit as red as the letters. There I was, too, wondering how in the world
I was going to explain my ridiculous attire.

The nurse glanced at my shirt, did a double take, and then looked
at me as if to invite an explanation. I laughed a short, embarrassed
laugh. "There's a story about this..." I began, but it was no use. It
was impossible to explain that one with only a few quick phrases. I
guess she must have thought I was some kind of Walt Disney nut or
something. I might be lucky if that's all she thought!

Though there may be carefully planned chapter meeting programs, big barbershop shows, exciting chorus and quartet contests,

and yearly International Convention extravaganzas, sometimes the best barbershopping comes in none of these forms. Sev Severance tells of his favorite experience:

I was a member of Chicago Number One Chapter, and at the time the chorus director was Frank Thorne, bass of the ELASTIC FOUR, past International Quartet Champions. In those days the chorus rehearsed at the old Hotel Morrison. Frank had seat assignments for each member of the chorus and if you missed three consecutive rehearsals you lost your chair. You had to pass a qualification test before you could be part of the singing and performing chorus again. Anyway, there were about twenty of us who used to hang around woodshedding after each week's regular rehearsal.

One night we were singing up a storm as usual when Frank told us the other members of the ELASTIC FOUR would be stopping by later on in the evening. After a while they straggled in and held a kind of quartet practice. I guess they considered it a practice. We considered it a performance. They hadn't sung more than three or four songs, though, when the door banged open and in came the FOUR HARMONIZERS, also International Champs. They sang some numbers and the door banged open again. There were the MISFITS, still another International Championship quartet! They didn't even get into their third song when the door slammed open again. It was the BELL AND HOWELL FOUR, later to be known as the International Champion MIDSTATES FOUR! Forry Haynes had his guitar, so it was ''gangbusters'' as soon as they started in.

There was laughing and kidding around, and lots of good barbershop music. The quartets sang, one after another, and it went on and on for probably three hours, until 1:30 in the morning. I remember the time because I had to be careful not to miss the last train out of Chicago at the Wells Street Station at 2:00 a.m. The next one wasn't until five. I just made the train by the skin of my teeth, but when I left the Hotel Morrison, the quartets were still going strong.

I've never to this day forgotten the tremendous show those singers put on that night. I've been in barbershopping for close to thirty-five years, and I've never had an evening that gave me more enjoyment.

The interchapter get-together is another unanimously popular barbershop activity. One chapter charters a bus for a trip to another chapter or the members drive, for an extra-heaping helping of singing and shenanigans. Every quartet that can be scraped together performs, and all choruses in attendance sing for the assembled multitude. After such a program, refreshments are dished out along with wild and woolly woodshedding that rattles the rafters!

Such get-togethers are generally carefully planned and scheduled to maximize the harmony and good times, but sometimes they're not. Jed Casey recalls one such spur-of-the-moment interchapter meeting:

> *You never know what's going to happen at the Fairfax, Virginia Chapter. We were renowned for crashing every party and joint chapter venture we heard about. We walked into a Livingston, New Jersey and Philadelphia interchapter meeting once, and it was a fantastic night. Almost as memorable, though, was the trip from Fairfax to Philadelphia.*
>
> *All of us loaded onto the bus at about six o'clock for the 150-mile trip. The vehicle didn't have one of those little rooms in the back, and after an hour or two, most of us were in great need of such a convenience. There was nowhere to stop along the New Jersey Turnpike either, and the ride became more and more uncomfortable. We finally stopped at a very small gas station on the road leading into Philly. There happened to be a plumbing junk dealer next door, and a lot of bathtubs, sinks, and such all over the front lawn. All I can say is that in our haste we felt pressured to put much of the junk dealer's equipment to good use. What a sight it was to behold, with the moon shining full and bright and barbershoppers scampering all about. I suppose that wasn't exactly a memorable barbershop singing experience, but it certainly was memorable!*

Russell Malony tells a tale of a real rip-roaring interchapter get-together:

> *The Westfield, New Jersey Chapter chartered a bus and visited the Manhattan Chapter at Rupert's Brewery. While our chorus was performing, the entire stage collapsed underneath us and everyone went tumbling down. They had some fine quartet and chorus talent there that night, but none of them was*

able to bring down the house quite like the Westfield Chorus!

For an added element of surprise, an interchapter get-together can begin as a mystery bus ride. Except for the few members who make the arrangements, no one knows where the chapter Is going. Don Vienne took a mystery bus ride and found it was a surprise for more than the chapter members:

> *I had an idea that our Montgomery County, Maryland Chapter mystery bus ride might be headed in my direction and not wishing to travel twenty-seven miles to catch a bus that would then retrace my route twenty-seven miles back past my home, I asked if I could meet the bus along the way. I found we were go-ing to visit the Dundalk, Maryland Chapter, so I could meet the bus on Route 29, a short distance from where I lived. A couple of friends and I decided to take this short cut, and just for kicks, Frank Palmer, who was in the ambulance and hearse business, drove to the rendevous in his brand-new Cadillac ambulance.*
>
> *At the designated spot we pulled off to the side of the road to wait for the bus, and we started right in singing. Frank was first to notice the police car behind us. The next thing we knew, the officer was at the side of our vehicle. Frank rolled the window down and the policeman looked in on our song fest.*
>
> *"Is everything all right?" the cop inquired.*
>
> *"Sure, officer," Frank replied. "We're just waiting for a bus!"*
>
> *The man in blue didn't know if he was being insulted or if Frank was just playing cute, but no sooner were the words spoken than a school bus loaded with singing barbershoppers arrived on the scene. We jumped out of the ambulance and piled onto the bus. The officer stood there scratching his head. I looked out the back window and waved as the bus pulled away, and I saw the policeman walk back slowly to his squad car. He reached for the radio microphone, and I can imagine what he reported to headquarters.*
>
> *"Sergeant, you're not going to believe this, but..."*

Those mystery bus rides are generally uproarious episodes, but imagine what a ball it is for chapters that take—are you ready for this—mystery plane rides! Lou Sisk describes what may have been the first of such crazy pilgrimages:

> *It was without a doubt the most lively and exciting five hours in the history of the Pittsburgh Chapter. From the time the Trans-Canadian plane touched down until it was again aloft for the trip back, Pittsburgh's barbershoppers were on cloud nine! What a way to open National Harmony Week!*
>
> *When our Canadian neighbors hit the Monongahela Room at the Penn-Sheraton Hotel, they were greeted with a tumultuous ten-minute standing ovation from more than 250 present. Then it was one chorus and quartet after another until late into the night when refreshments were served.*
>
> *In the Canadian party were two stewardesses, the pilot and co-pilot, the St. Catherines, Ontario Chorus, and the GHOST-AIRES, CRESCENDOS, EMERALDAIRES, CHORD KINGS, and PHONETICS quartets. Also along for the ride were the FOUR SWIPERS from Niagara Falls, New York.*
>
> *For our part of the program we presented the Pittsburgh Chapter Chorus, and the PITTSBURGHERS, SELECTONES, WESTINGHOUSE QUARTET, STEEL CITY FOUR, LEBANAIRES, and the GIBSON GIRLS quartets.*
>
> *Where else but in barbershopping can you find seventy men willing to spend the effort and money for a one-night international journey just to enjoy a few hours of a cappella singing?*

About two and a half years later another mystery flight took off for Pittsburgh. Again, Lou Sisk has all the details:

> *Ninety-one barbershoppers from Dundalk, Maryland; Philadelphia, Pennsylvania; Livingston, New Jersey; and other points east boarded a TWA jet for a mystery flight from Philly on September 14. Delayed by a slight mix-up between the police escort and motorcade leader Larry "Wrong-Way" Autenreith, the honored guests finally arrived to a screaming ovation at 10:15 p.m.*
>
> *From that point on it was absolute bedlam as sixteen wonderful quartets and our Buccannaires Chorus were introduced by MC Tom O'Malley and performed: The PENNSMEN, FREE LANCERS, SOLIDAIRES, MAIN STREET FOUR, DELCO AIRES, DEL CHORDS, DIAMOND STATESMEN, COLONIALS, BON AIRES, SHORT TONES, HI LO TONES, PITTSBURGHERS,*

TOWN AND COUNTRY FOUR, WESTINGHOUSE QUARTET, NORTH CHORDS, and FOR FUN FOUR.

It was after 1:00 a.m. before the singing concluded and we were led back to the refreshment stand. Some time after two, our friends from the Mid-Atlantic District followed their three pilots and three stewardesses out of the door and back to the Greater Pittsburgh Airport, leaving us Pittsburghers limp and numb from an unforgettable evening of harmony and fellowship.

Bob Royce was singing with the MAIN STREET FOUR at the time, and he fondly recalls the experience:

I remember vividly that Tom O'Malley was the MC, and that he wore the most disreputable pair of patent-leather shoes I'd ever seen. They had holes in them, were all scratched up, but still shined under the lights. Tom did an outstanding job as MC. Close to one in the morning, the PITTSBURGHERS sang "When Your Old Wedding Ring Was New," and there were an awful lot of wet eyes in the audience. We were a bunch of emotional, tired guys who had just heard a quartet that was really into a song. It was magnificent!

We were a thoroughly weary crew when we got on the plane for the flight back to Philadelphia. Then on top of that we had a drive of more than two hours to get back to north Jersey. It was close to 6:30 and the sun was coming up when our bass, Dick Floersheimer, sighed. "Boy," he said, "I'm really going to get killed when I walk in the front door. I didn't tell Jeanne anything about our mystery plane ride because she hates it when I fly. I told her we were going to sing in Philadelphia, and she's going to wonder why it takes me until 7:00 a.m. to get home!"

Less than eight months later, the Pittsburgh Chapter itself took to the air. Lou Sisk relates what happened:

"You can't get there from here," or so it seemed to our Toronto-bound party on April 19. Our chartered plane was forced to land at Buffalo, New York because of a heavy blanket of fog over Toronto. After an hour's delay the pilot reluctantly headed north to Canada for a one-in-a-million chance that the fog would be cleared when we got there. It wasn't. Again the

tower refused landing instructions, but the pilot thought he saw enough clearance, and convinced the tower he could make it. We touched down at 11:15 p.m., three hours late. Our tardiness in no way dimmed the spirits of our Canadian hosts, however, nor diminished their great hospitality.

There followed a three-hour wingding, with entertainment supplied by the Pittsburgh area chorus, the St. Catherines Chorus, and the TOWN AND COUNTRY FOUR, RHYTHM COUNTS, NORTH CHORDS, HARMONY LADS, SHORT TONES, and BONAIRES quartets. We travel-weary barbershop ambassadors returned home Saturday morning at 4:00 a.m. with heaps of praise for our Canadian hosts.

When the Huntington, Long Island Chapter called the Boston Chapter about a fly-in interchapter get-together, little did they know what they were starting. At the time, plans were under way in Boston for a "Lou Perry Night" party to honor that dedicated barbershopper who was moving away from the Northeastern District. It seemed natural to combine both events and turn the affair into a district-wide gala soiree! Terry Clarke, of the BOSTON COMMON, tells the story:

Few people know much about Lou, but he's a real musician. He played with some of the jazz all-time greats, including Louis Armstrong, and he arranged music for many of the big bands. He was a trumpet player, got his degree from Tufts University, and is indeed a great musician! It was very fitting that we honored this guy, because he contributed more to barbershopping in the last twenty years than any other person I know.

Back in the 1950's Lou went to a barbershop show in Needham, Massachusetts and heard what was probably one of the worst performances he had ever heard in his life. Nevertheless, he recognized in the music a rich art form. Jazz was an American creation, country-western was American, and he knew barbershop, too, was a precious and typically American phenomenon.

He didn't know the first thing about barbershop music, but he joined the Society and began learning as much as he could. He looked into it, read about it, studied it, got involved in directing, and began singing with probably the worst voice in all the world (please quote me on that). In any event, he began working with the FOUR RASCALS, learning as much from them as they learned from him.

Among other contributions, Lou was instrumental in starting a music education program in the Northeastern District. He invited a bunch of quartet people to his house in hopes of creating some high-caliber, quality quartets. What emerged were the FOUR STATESMEN, the CROSS COUNTRYMEN, and eventually the BOSTON COMMON. We all know what he has done for judging and the influence he has had on the Arrangement category of judging.

Getting back to the party, of all the barbershop festivities I've ever seen, this was the greatest. People came from all over the District. They came from Maine, Vermont, New Hampshire, Connecticut, Rhode Island, and New York. It was like a convention! There were dozens of chapter choruses and quartets.

A small group of us had taken Lou out for dinner that night. We told him the Huntington Chapter was planning a visit, but we wanted the rest of the affair to be a complete surprise. It was. It also turned out to be a surprise for the Huntington Chapter, too. Their New England Airlines flight started off down the runway on Long Island, but then got socked in with fog before it could even get off the ground. The barbershoppers stayed on the plane waiting for the fog to lift, but that became an ordeal. The fog refused to lift.

Meanwhile, all the Boston Chapter members were waiting with their cars at Logan Airport to drive their Long Island guests to the party. Hearing of the flight delay, they got together and gave some impromptu performances in the airport waiting rooms. At 10:30 p.m. when they finally got back to the party, they reported that the Huntington Chapter was hopelessly fogged in. Minutes later we received word that the flight was on its way after all. When everybody thought they'd have to drive back to Logan, the bus driver who had delivered the Worcester contingent volunteered to make the run. There was great spirit all around.

All the while this confusion was going on, the show was in full swing. One quartet after another performed, then a chorus, then another quartet took the stage. The poor Huntington Chapter, due at 7:30, finally rolled in a half hour before midnight.

Lots of Lou Perry arrangements were sung that night. It was really beautiful. Probably the most moving thing that happened was when the FOUR RASCALS sang "Little Pal" to Lou. They sounded better than I've ever heard them. I don't think there was a dry eye in the house. It was incredibly emotional, incredibly beautiful. They also sang "Sweet Adeline." It was one of the most magnificent performances I've ever witnessed. Then the FOUR STATESMEN sang. They were great. We sang We were terrible.

Finally Lou was called up onstage, and one by one the speakers embarrassed the hell out of him. They said absolutely terrible things. It was a roast of roasts! But while the words seemed to have a sharp and biting sting, the messages expressed a distinctly warm and sincere sentiment.

The Boston Chapter had collected $2000 for a going-away gift and gave Lou the equivalent of a good down payment on a new car! Other chapters and a number of quartets also made special presentations. It truly was a great night. An extra large dose of love was expressed. I think everybody deeply appreciated what Lou had done for our hobby, and all that appreciation flowed freely about the room.

Lou got up and gave everybody a scolding for giving him the party. He was very teary-eyed. You'd think at a moment like that he'd get as nasty as all those who had roasted him, but no, all the love in that room was overpowering. He started to weep. (If you know Lou, you know that's a natural reaction for him. He does it every time you hit a nice chord. Hell, we'd sing up-tunes for him and he'd bawl!)

Lou was presented with a lifetime membership in the Society, and the FOUR STATESMEN gave him a lovely plaque. Then the STATESMEN, the FOUR RASCALS, and the BOSTON COMMON joined together to sing Lou's arrangement of "From the First Hello to the Last Goodbye."

The evening concluded with Lou directing us in "Keep the Whole World Singing," and boy, there was a lot of spirit in that! I've never heard it sung with more heart. When we came to the last few chords, tears were cascading down Lou's cheeks, and he yelled out, "Oh, Chrrrist!" Our hearts nearly burst with the emotion.

A strange thing happened. I talked to several people the next day and none of them had been able to get to sleep. Lou said he sat up until 4:30 a.m. Tommy Spirito of the RASCALS said the same thing. I didn't get to sleep until 5:15. It was such a high moment, our bodies were unable to unwind to a state of rest. It was tough to come down from so much intensity and feeling.

It was a high moment for everybody, a truly great affair, like the old-fashioned roasts of years ago before they became popular. None of it was written. It was simply a big, spontaneous display of affection for a beloved barbershopper. It was a roast from the heart!

One of the beauties of barbershopping is that almost anywhere you go in the United States and Canada you can find a barbershop chapter. You can therefore enjoy good harmony on a business trip, visit, or vacation throughout North America. Don Vienne is one of many barbershoppers who does just that:

Our family had the practice of vacationing in the New England area, and one summer we booked a cottage for two weeks in the little town of Rockport, Maine. I noted in the Society's Directory of Chapters that the Knox County Chapter met in a church on Tuesday nights in nearby Camden, Maine. The church was near the center of town, easy to find, so when Tuesday night rolled around, I told my wife I'd be joining the local barbershoppers for the night.

I got to the church at 8:15 and parked with twenty to thirty other cars in the lot. Through the ground-floor windows of the church I saw a large gathering of people. The meeting had already begun. The entrance to the room was in full view of all in attendance and everybody looked up as I entered. It was a little embarrassing to disrupt the proceedings so I quickly found a seat in the back. Several people reached over to shake my hand as I sat down. Barbershoppers everywhere are a friendly lot.

It looked like some sort of business meeting was under way. Somebody was up front talking, but there wasn't any singing. I surmised that the director might be giving a music craft session. I noticed a few women in the crowd and wondered if it was "Ladies' Night." The man up front smiled. "Now," he said, "let's hear from someone else."

A gentleman stood up, went to the center of the room, and faced the group. "My name is Bill," he announced, "and I'm an alcoholic."

It didn't take me a whole lot longer to figure out I wasn't at a barbershop rehearsal at all, but a local meeting of Alcoholics Anonymous.

Having come in late, I felt trapped. I couldn't get up and leave at that point, minutes after I had arrived, so I stuck around for another forty-five minutes. I listened to a parade of eight or nine ex-drinkers tell of their experiences as alcoholics, and then when it came time for refreshments, I had a cup of coffee and made a fast exit!

I later found out that the Knox County Chapter was rather small and the members didn't meet during the summertime.

As I said before, there's a barbershop chapter almost anywhere you go in the United States or Canada. You may not be able to find it, but it's there, somewhere!

Most barbershop activities revolve around the barbershop chapter, and it's there that many of barbershopping's rewards are reaped. There you'll find newcomers who delight with childlike abandon in their newfound discovery. There you'll find old-timers who have sung in dozens of annual shows and still thrill to the sound of a four-part chord. There you'll find people whose only common interest is the love of the music, and that bond alone is a mighty and enduring one.

Lou Laurel sums it up:

I've pretty much run the gamut in this hobby of ours. I've been active in administrative work at the chapter level, in the District, and with the International organization. I've worked with thousands of people in the Society, and I've been involved in a wealth of truly beautiful experiences. I've been quite active, too, in the music side of barbershopping. As director of three International Championship choruses, I've had more than my share of happy times.

I still feel that I get the biggest kick out of this avocation by attending the weekly chapter meeting and by being able to be part of a music program that brings the thrill of barbershop music to the membership, particularly to the new man. If I can help in some small way to bring a little joy to "Joe Barbershopper" at a regular chapter meeting, then I feel I've made a big contribution. I feel that in some way this helps repay the Society for the lifetime of rewarding experiences it has given me.

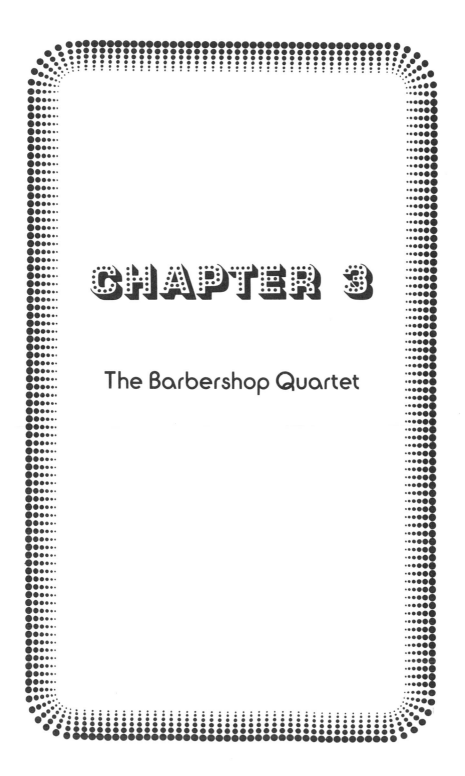

CHAPTER 3

The Barbershop Quartet

The Barbershop Quartet

One song leads on to another,
One friend to another friend,
So I'll travel along
With a friend and a song.

Wilfrid Wilson Gibson

eing part of a fifty- or sixty-voice barbershop chorus can be tremendously exciting and reward ing, but being part of a four-voice barbershop quartet can be even more so! Quartetting is a highly concentrated form of barbershopping. Each voice is indispensable in each chord sung, and the opportunities for expression, creativity, and performing satisfaction are immense. The Society was *founded* as a quartetting organization (SPEBSQSA), so it was recognized at the outset that singing with three other guys is a uniquely exciting endeavor.

An informal "pickup" quartet is a foursome formed for minutes or hours of singing enjoyment, while the more formal "organized" or "registered" quartet is generally carefully created and extensively rehearsed. Though pickup quartets are no more than fleeting excursions into barbershop harmony, many a golden moment has been realized in such singing. On the other hand, many a golden career has been relished in registered quartets, which sing in shows and contests and are more extensive pursuits of barbershopping's rewards.

Quartet Phenomenon

The barbershop magic begins the moment four voices blend together in song. You don't need an audience or auditorium; you need only a tenor, lead, baritone, and bass. With such a combination, anything can happen. Huck Sinclair illustrates:

Before the Society was formed, I sang in a quartet called the CAPITAL CITY FOUR in Topeka, Kansas. We used to sing in the rotunda of the Museum Building at 10th and Jackson Streets. Cars filled up the intersection and snarled to a standstill, but the policeman on the beat sanctioned our street corner serenades. He even passed the hat among the listeners for our benefit. Our lead singer Bud Neal, who later moved to Tulsa, was among those in the group at the first meeting called by O.C. Cash to start our Society. Archie Wilkerson sang both high and loud, and Trim Trimble had a voice that boomed like a church organ. Trim was a World War I casualty, and we had to sneak him and his clothes in and out of the hospital every night we sang.

When I lived in Kansas City, Missouri, I made occasional business trips to Tulsa which was part of my sales territory. Ray Granger was Tulsa's fire chief. I'd let him know whenever I was coming, and he and a couple of other fellows would run right out onto the Sante Fe station platform in the fire truck to meet me. We rode all over town in that fire truck and sang "After Dark" with a two-way radio hookup to the fire station. I introduced that song to barbershoppers in the Society after learning it from another street-corner quartet in Topeka.

Dean Snyder, Past International Historian, relates a story that demonstrates how serious some barbershoppers are in their quest for quartetting:

Back in 1941 there was a great singing weekend at Deac Martin's home in Cleveland, Ohio. Phil Embury flew in from

Warsaw, New York, "Molly" Reagan came from Pittsburgh, and Cy Perkins came by train from Chicago, just to sing barbershop into the early morning hours in Deac's recreation room. There wasn't any audience, just four men blending their voices. They sang for as long as time allowed. As Deac said, "They went back to their planes and train and home again to work the next morning. That's how hungry we were for barbershop harmony in the early days of the Society!"

That's how hungry many barbershoppers are for quartetting today! It seems as though some primal force drives such singers to seek out three other voice parts. It may be for just an evening, or for just a song, but occasionally a chance, informal get-together produces a top-notch quartet. Tom Masengale's quartet was so formed:

The CHORD BUSTERS quartet was born in Skelly Stadium in Tulsa, Oklahoma. As members of the Tulsans, a semi-professional male chorus, we were ushering one night, and after the crowd was seated and the concert was under way, we all headed for the rest room to sing a few quartet songs. There's no better place to hear chords sound and resound than in the echo-chamber-like confines of a rest room.

Four of us recognized something from the very start. We had a natural blend and balance that most quartets work like crazy to achieve, and many quartets never realize. We had it at the beginning, and the CHORD BUSTERS was born.

How a quartet gets its start is often good story material. For example, the FOUR STATESMEN was created when four singers migrated from other quartets to put together a winning combination. Frank Lanza recalls how that fusion came to be:

Before our quartet was formed, we had all been singing quite actively in other quartets. Doc Sause was in the CONNECTICUT YANKEES, Dick Chacos was in the MERRY NOTES, and Don Beinema was in the FOUR OF NOTE. At a barbershop convention in Toronto, three of us (Dick wasn't there) got talking about our Northeastern District quartets, and we realized that none had been International Champions. Wouldn't it be nice, we thought, to be such a quartet! We approached Dick with the idea, and he heartily agreed.

We got together for a few rehearsals at Lou Perry's house. Lou was running seminars and rehearsal/critiquing sessions for barbershoppers interested in forming quartets. Before singing for the group, we agreed among ourselves that no matter what was said, we would sing together and become the FOUR STATESMEN.

After we sang, we heard that a prominent barbershopper/ judge said we sounded like three trumpets and a bass drum! We stuck to our agreement in spite of that critical review, and several years later were pleased to send him a telegram when we won the championship: "Not bad for three trumpets and a bass drum, right, Bob?"

It seems no obstacle, however great, can prevent the formation of a foursome when barbershop harmony is the prize. Lou Laurel tells a story about a singer in his quartet, the DESERTAIRES:

I attended my first International contest in Toledo, Ohio. On Thursday evening, after the quartet quarter finals, a buddy and I wandered around listening with amazement to all the singing going on in the hotel lobby, in the restaurants, and even out in the street. We came across four guys standing on a corner singing their hearts out. We exchanged greetings and introduc- ed ourselves. They were from Hamilton, Ontario. At the time I was living in El Paso, Texas, so we felt that from border to border we had something in common. We stuck together for the rest of the evening and had a great time singing and socializing. As a matter of fact, we spent most of the rest of the convention together.

One of the four and I got to know each other quite well; we just seemed to hit it off right. Besides, he was a very fine tenor. I had recently organized a quartet back home, but our tenor had died in a tragic automobile accident, so I told my friend he should move to Texas to sing with us. We thought that was a good joke. When it came time to say good-bye, we promised to keep in touch by correspondence, and agreed to meet again at the following year's International Convention in Kansas City.

Two weeks after I got home, I received a letter from my new- found friend and, you guessed it, he wanted to know if I was serious about his moving to El Paso. To make a long story short, it took him a year to make all the necessary arrangements, but after the Kansas City convention my friend did not return to Canada. He returned with me to Texas to a new home, climate, and life.

This fervent barbershopper was Bill Spooner and he became lead of the DESERTAIRES. We found another tenor. Who but a dedicated barbershopper would pull up stakes and move more than 1600 miles to a foreign country just to enjoy his hobby?

Some barbershoppers seem to move heaven and earth to get into the right quartet, while others appear to tumble by sheer chance into the ideal combination. That's the way it was with the BUFFALO BILLS. Vern Reed thinks that foursome was inevitable:

It was a childhood dream of mine to be in vaudeville. Most kids wanted to be baseball stars. I wanted to entertain. When I turned seven I started taking violin lessons, and every Friday after school I was backstage at the Shea's Buffalo Theatre for my session with Mr. Ed Jankowski, first violinist in the forty-piece pit orchestra. The orchestra played for all the many vaudeville troupes that visited Buffalo as they toured from coast to coast in those days. When the stage show was over, the performers gathered together and discussed their routines. Often they would rehearse new material, as they constantly updated their acts with the latest songs, jokes, dances, and so on. Since I was backstage a lot, I was exposed to all those show-business people. For a period of five years, I met nearly every act that came to town. You might say I was brought up in the atmosphere of vaudeville.

In my family, too, I was exposed to a lot of music, singing, and performing. Grandparents, aunts, uncles, cousins, and close friends gathered together almost every Saturday night for a social/musical get-together. It wasn't unusual for twenty people to be there. Sometime during the evening my aunt or my mother would sit down at the piano and start playing. Dad was a well-known tenor in Buffalo, and he always started the singing. Out would come guitars, violins, and other instruments, and everyone joined in for several hours of music making. Even though I was a kid, I joined right in and I particularly enjoyed it when we imitated the vaudeville quartets of the day. The scene wasn't unusual. Movies were still silent, crystal sets were a novelty, and families provided their own entertainment.

When I was older, I put down the violin and picked up singing. I first studied with a local teacher, later went to the Eastman School of Music to study with Dr. Arthur Kraft, and then I began to make local appearances on radio and sing solos at church and with various oratorio societies. There was so much going on with music in Buffalo, I was busy singing every day. It was that way with many singers at the time. I was aware of the other three who eventually became the BUFFALO BILLS, but our paths weren't yet destined to cross. In 1942 I went into the Service.

When I was discharged in 1946, the world had changed. Technological improvements seemed to close the curtain on my hopes of performing in vaudeville. Sound movies and national radio networks were snuffing out vaudeville, and a new development, television, appeared destined to become vaudeville's ultimate death knell.

I then had a wife and family, and it became difficult to make the trips to Rochester for voice lessons. My boyhood dreams of singing in a vaudeville barbershop quartet began to crumble when hit with the realities of living in the middle of the Twentieth Century. The prospect of full-time work as a vaudeville entertainer looked bleak. It was just one of those things.

Then Al Shea called one day. "I know we've never met," he began, and he told me about his experiences singing in a Buffalo Chapter barbershop quartet. "We have the same background, so let's get together with two other fellows I have in mind, and see what happens."

The four of us met the following Saturday afternoon and had a heck of a good time. We enjoyed each other as people and made some pretty satisfying sounds. A week later, armed with but three songs, we went to sing on a Ladies' Night program sponsored by the Kenmore, New York Chapter. That was it! We were hooked. The audience enjoyed us and we loved singing for them, and the rewarding life of the BUFFALO BILLS had begun.

Quartet Relations

When four guys decide to form a barbershop quartet there are lots of important things to talk over, many of which have nothing at all to do with voice matching or singing quality. For example, what are the individual expectations of quartet goals and objectives? Some singers want to sing only serious songs—ballads, tear-jerkers, straight and "square" barbershop harmony. Others prefer comedy numbers instead. Some may choose to concentrate on winning contests; others may wish to emphasize show performances.

What about the quartet's activity level? Often singers like to perform two or three or more times a week. Some, though, may wish no more than one or two shows a month. And what about the wives? I wonder how many barbershoppers have given up a quartet or given up all barbershopping because of family factors. It's truly a shame if barbershop harmony must be relinquished in the interest of harmony at home. There should be some way to keep a balance of singing activities and those of work and family.

Still another important consideration is the talent and experience levels of the quartetters. Very experienced singers may be willing to invest months or perhaps years to develop an inexperienced voice, singing skill, and confidence, but it helps if all four men are nearly on a par in those categories.

There's another vital quartet consideration: the individual personalities. I've known beautiful-sounding quartets that had rosy futures, but had to throw in the towel because a couple of personalities, when mixed, reacted like sodium and water! *Boom!*

If a foursome gets past such stumbling blocks, there are still more hurdles to jump. The quartet men must agree on the number of rehearsals, the uniform or costume selection, the fee schedule, who's going to be contact man, who's going to be treasurer, and on and on.

Considering all the elements that must be in harmony for four people of often widely diverse backgrounds to come together and make a successful quartet, it's a wonder there are any quartets at all! Perhaps the answer is that the barbershop desire is so strong, it alone is sufficient to circumvent the obstacles. A quartet is occasionally described as a barbershop marriage. In a manner, it is. A set of vows is either implicitly or explicitly exchanged, and the partnership is subject to all the human weaknesses and frailties of its constituents.

You can therefore conclude correctly that a quartet is a very precious yet perilous and fragile alliance. It can be the source of years of pleasure and fulfillment, but it can also pop unexpectedly like a bubble. The BOSTON COMMON almost went the bubble route early in that quartet's history. Terry Clarke has the details:

> *We were staying at Flossie and Art Dolt's house in New Jersey while we sang on a nearby show. I had brought along four brand-new turtleneck sweaters I'd purchased at Louie's, an exclusive Boston store. I thought the sweaters were beautiful and would be great with the suede outfits we had, and the other guys said they looked nice, but they were more interested in how much I paid. When I told them the price was sixty-five bucks each, the skirmishes began. "You're kidding," one snapped. "That's outrageous!"*
>
> *I couldn't believe we were going to allow something as trivial as the price of four sweaters to get in our way, but sure enough, we were fighting and arguing back and forth. It was the worst argument we ever had. At the peak of the battle somebody bellowed, "That's it! The hell with it!" We didn't talk to each other for the rest of the weekend.*
>
> *The only time we got together was on stage for the show. The performance pulled us together somewhat, but afterward we weren't about to let each other forget the ugly remarks that had been exchanged. Waiting for the plane at La Guardia Airport in New York on the way home, two of us talked it over and decided we were through. No more BOSTON COMMON!*
>
> *Lou Perry brought us back together. Our rift lasted less than four days.*
>
> *Of course we still have occasional differences and difficulties. Sometimes we get peeved with each other. I guess it's only natural. If you live with three other guys for any length of time as all quartetters do, you're bound to have ruffled feathers now and then. We find it toughest when we've been together more than a couple of days at a time. At most conventions, for example, we used to get fed up and all go our separate ways. Particularly at International. We didn't even rehearse. We just showed up backstage and sang.*

Lloyd Steinkamp has a story about quartet relations that sounds more like a TV soap opera than a barbershop incident. He says it's absolutely true:

> *There was a man in our chapter years ago that my quartet, the DESERT KNIGHTS, had trouble getting along with. His*

name was George Stinson. Like many quartets, we were deeply involved in chapter activities. One of us was a chorus director, one was president, one was treasurer, one was show chairman. We were always in the midst of chapter work besides our own quartet work, and that sometimes caused problems because we unwittingly developed jealousies or misunderstandings or personality differences. That's what happened between the quartet and George Stinson.

We were asked to sing on a chapter show and understood we were the headliners. It was a charter show, so we sang for no charge. When we got there, though, we were introduced first, and that was unmistakably a deliberate insult. The MC and perpetrator of the slap in the face was none other than Mr. George Stinson. Well, we finished our bit and hung around for the curtain call. Eventually George ended the show, but the people in the audience started yelling for the DESERT KNIGHTS. By then I was feeling pretty good, and the audience reaction was working a wonderful, curing effect on my damaged pride, so I couldn't wait to jump back up on stage. However, our baritone, Sam Aramian, had figured that our early appearance had fulfilled our commitment, and without saying anything to us, went home! I was furious!

At that time I was working for Sam at the credit union. In his absence the rest of us plotted to get even for his running out on us. We decided on a devilish ruse. The next day when Sam picked me up on the way to work, I would allude to a fist fight between our tenor, Charlie Rastatter, and George Stinson, as a result of Sam's leaving early. We thought Sam would consider how ludicrous such a confrontation would be, would laugh, and then forget about it. That would be the end of that.

At seven o'clock in the morning Sam picked me up. As expected, he asked how the show had turned out. "Well," I said, "I suppose you heard about the fight."

"What fight?" he inquired, biting hard on the bait.

"Oops," I said quickly. "Well, forget it."

"What do you mean, forget it?"

"No," I shrugged off his words, "it's all over now."

"Come on," Sam pleaded, and he pulled the information out of me." What's more, he believed our cock-and-bull story!

During the day our lead, Joe Salz, and Charlie both called and I told them how it went. Charlie said he thought it was a bad idea that I didn't tell Sam it was a practical joke. "He'll be furious when he finds out." That was on Monday.

On Wednesday Sam still didn't know, and was furious, anyway. In the meantime, Charlie had called Sam and reported that I had something to tell him, meaning it was all a gag, but I wasn't going to let the cat out of the bag. With all the vagueness going around, Sam thought we were keeping something from him. That evening Sam and his wife were visiting Hart Shekerjian and his wife. They started talking about the incident and one of the wives said, "I think I know what it is that they don't want to tell you. I bet Charlie's wife, Pat, is in the hospital and she's going to lose the baby." Pat was eight months pregnant at the time. Sam immediately tried to contact Charlie on the phone, got no answer, and became convinced that was what had happened.

Sam was livid! He decided then and there he was going over to George Stinson's house and break his nose! His anger became rage, but just as he was about to go out the door, Sam's son, Terry, who was in on the gag, told his dad not to go, that it was all a joke.

Well, everybody laughed except Sam. After thinking a few minutes, he called Stinson. "George," he said, "you don't like me and I don't care too much for you, but listen to something that just happened..."

The next thing I knew, at eleven o'clock that night, I got a phone call. I picked up the phone and it was Stinson. "Okay, you little flake," he yelled at me. "That bald idiot friend of yours came over to my house and broke my lip and tooth and busted my nose. And when you come down to chapter meeting Friday, I'm going to kill you!" Then he hung up.

I was petrified. I tried to call Joe Salz. His line was busy. After ten minutes he called me. "I just got a phone call from George Stinson," he said. "Sam busted his nose, and oh, my God!" We couldn't reach Charlie because Charlie didn't have a phone. Joe and I were scared silly.

I got in the car with Sam the next morning, and the first thing I did was resign. I felt it was safer if I simply quit my job. I looked at Sam, and his face was all red. I thought it was from anger. Sam was actually biting his lip to keep from laughing.

Well, I exposed the whole story, explained that the whole thing was a practical joke, and all he kept saying was "A joke?

A joke is it? A joke? What kind of a joke is that! Here I busted his face in, and you call it a joke!''

I was terrified. I couldn't think straight. I cried. My whole world was tumbling down around me. When we got to the office I couldn't do any work. I was a mess!

At noon Sam and I went out for lunch. We sat down and I started to grin, just a little. Sam looked up. "What are you smiling about?" he asked.

"I don't know," I said. "My mother told me once that when I die, that very second something will strike me funny and I'll die with a smirk on my face."

A minute later he said, "What's so funny now?"

"Well, I just got a mental picture of big old Charlie Rastatter shadow boxing behind his garage."

Sam started to laugh. "Well, have you learned your lesson?" he asked.

"Now wait a minute, Sam," I said. "Don't tell me that was a joke!"

"Certainly, it was a joke," he said. "I set it all up with Stinson."

"Well, what a rotten trick to play on Joe and me," I said. "That's just terrible!"

It went back and forth. "Oh? What about your dirty joke!"

"Well, that was only because you started it by leaving early. It was your fault!"

When we went down to the chapter meeting Friday night, George was waiting there with two hoods from his agency, but Sam put the kibosh on it. They were going to carry through with the gag and pretend to give us the rubber-hose treatment in a closet at the Knights of Columbus Hall.

Well, we wound up becoming fast friends with George, thank God. But believe me, that was the last time I ever played a practical joke!

Under the stress and emotion of a number of performances, the usual bonds of friendship can become strained. A remark that would normally be overlooked and forgotten is resented instead, and angers flare. Carl Hancuff describes what I mean:

When the SALT FLATS went on our USO show trip, we were constantly together for about twenty-four days. It was a tough

schedule. We put on up to ten performances a day. One per-
formance might be no more than two or three songs, but
another might be a full hour or longer. After a week or two of
that, we were really drained.

I'm not complaining, but the fact is we were thrown together
in tight quarters on a very crowded schedule. We are all
somewhat temperamental to begin with, and sometimes the
conditions were a little unbearable. At Clark Air Force Base
they put all four of us in one little trailer to save money. It was so
crowded, if one guy wanted to stand up, the other three had to
get up with him. Toward the end of the trip tensions were high
and tempers were short. We bit our tongues to make sure we
didn't say something we'd regret. We had some real shouting
matches a couple of times.

Finally, at Okinawa we were put in a building that had one
central room and four big, separate bedrooms. When we check-
ed in and saw that, each of us went to his room, slammed the
door, locked it, and stayed there the rest of the afternoon!

Misunderstandings, resentments, hurt feelings, and personality
conflicts are all an occasional part of the quartet experience. I guess
they're inevitable even though a group may go out of its way to avoid
conflicts. It's a challenge: How can a quartet weave its way through
the emotional interactions of its members without becoming
periodically snagged? If there is a problem, what's the best way to
deal with it when it interferes with the harmony? Jim Massey found
one approach, the talk-it-out session:

I used to sing with a quartet called the MADCAPS, and we
were having trouble with the bass. He was so enamored with
his girl friend, who later became his wife, he didn't have any
time for the quartet. We couldn't rehearse often enough, and
when we did, he'd arrive late with his girl friend, and leave ear-
ly! We were ticked off that he didn't have more respect for our
rehearsals or the quartet in general, and we decided to have a
talk session and let him know how we felt. So we wouldn't of-
fend him, though, we thought we'd have a general gripe
meeting, and the three of us agreed to criticize each other, so
our bass wouldn't feel he was being put upon, although, of
course, that was our intent.

We had our rap session in my office in downtown Dallas, and

I started it off by explaining that I thought it was time we had a clearing of the air. I suggested we discuss whatever griped us about any other member of the quartet. True to our prearranged plan, the tenor, bari, and I started lightly criticizing each other. The bass listened quietly. The plan was in full swing when I began to hear the tenor and bari say things about me that weren't light criticism at all. Some of their comments were downright unfriendly, and I didn't like it! I let go with a couple of zingers at them, and our session heated up. Criticisms turned to insults, our discussion turned into a shouting match, and we had an hour and a half free-for-all, with three of us going at it tooth and nail. The bass twiddled his thumbs. He had nothing to say to us and nothing was said about him. We were too busy with our own mouth-to-mouth combat.

Finally he looked at his watch and stood up. "Well, guys," he said, "if this meeting's nearly over, I'm going to have to go. I promised to meet my girl and I'd better hurry or I'll be late. So long!"

Three of us sat there dazed, as our bass skipped merrily out the door!

Those times of internal quartet tumult are inevitable. One little-recognized but major accomplishment of the long-lasting quartets is simply that they lasted at all! Such tenacity, perseverance, and downright doggedness are not shared by many foursomes. Freddie King says he learned nearly as much about people and their inter-relations from his experiences with the ORIOLE FOUR as he learned about barbershop singing:

Singing with the ORIOLE FOUR taught us everything four men are supposed to know about each other, and we were lucky enough to be young enough to withstand the storm. When four men form a quartet, each brings his own set of personality quirks and idiosyncrasies. In short order those individual characteristics begin to rub against one another and cause friction. Little by little the singers become unenamored of each other and the first crack in the quartet cohesion appears. Rather than discussing their aggravations, they let their feelings fester until the four individuals can't stand one another and the quartet blows up. It usually takes about five years for that to happen.

As I say, in the ORIOLE FOUR we were young enough to withstand an awful lot of hard times, and over the years we learned an awful lot about people-to-people relations. Being able to get along with each other is a crucial talent quartetter must master!

If you consider all the time a quartet spends together, you may begin to wonder how the singers fit so much barbershopping in with their work, home, and other duties and responsibilities. After all, there are only twenty-four hours in a day.

I suppose some quartets reach the point where they find that their singing commitments come first. That may impose hardships on wife and family and often on the work front as well, but it may become unavoidable. If you've agreed to sing on a barbershop show a year or more in advance of the show date, it's tough to back out when the time comes, just because your daughter's tap dance class is giving a recital, or because your wife has the flu, or because of something worse. Vern Reed explains what it means to make such a commitment to quartetting:

The BUFFALO BILLS had one understanding from the beginning. We decided we were either going to make a full and total commitment to the quartet or we weren't going to sing at all. Quartetting obligations were to take precedence over all others except our jobs. We consequently severed the many connections we had previously established with musical and non-musical activities. Our singing schedules quickly caused us to miss anniversaries, birthdays, graduations, and other special family events. We even had children born when we were out of town. Our dedication to the quartet sometimes caused hardship among family members and friends, but our commitment was necessary, worthwhile, and in the final analysis, understandable.

If we said we were going to be somewhere, we did everything humanly possible to be there. I recall when we flew to Bloomington, Illinois for a Sunday afternoon show. As soon as we took off from Buffalo, we ran into foul weather, and the farther west we flew, the worse it became. We circled Chicago for an endless time and finally landed in Cleveland. It was four o'clock. We called Bloomington, but by then the show was almost over and everybody had given up on us. We said we were still on our way, but when we again headed for Chicago, it looked hopeless. I don't know how our pilot landed the plane. The fog was so thick I couldn't see the runway until after we touched down.

We called Bloomington. The showgoers were given rain checks and told to come back at 7:30. We hired a car and groped our way as quickly as possible along unfamiliar roads in the dense fog. It was long past 7:30 when we arrived at the hall. The place was packed. Everyone had been kept busy with community singing and other improvised delaying tactics. There was no time to change into our performing outfits, so we marched right up on stage, set down our suitcases, threw our coats over them, blew the pitch pipe, and did an hour's show.

We missed the last plane out of Chicago for Buffalo and consequently missed work the next day. You can see that if it hadn't been for some very understanding bosses, the quartet would have folded pretty fast for that wasn't the first nor the last travel problem that interrupted business schedules. Moreover, if it hadn't been for some tremendously tolerant and loving wives, forgiving families, and understanding employers, the BUFFALO BILLS could never have even got a start!

Dedication to quartetting is surely not unique to the BUF-FALO BILLS. It was not at all uncommon to see a fellow quartetter hot with fever and struggling vocally with a raspy throat, but smiling bravely and giving the performance his all. It was not unusual to see a singer ashen from lack of sleep with worry about a hospitalized family member, yet putting on a good show. We saw dozens of harried and distraught barbershoppers onstage producing the best they were able, with no apologies to the audience. At some time or other every quartetter has been there. They are all pros, and once on stage it would take a truly sharp eye or keen ear to detect a problem or tension within the foursome.

Such quartet dedication is obviously a hardship on the family. How does a wife contend with a husband whose timetable becomes nothing but barbershopping commitments? Dick Floersheimer tells how his wife handled the situation:

My quartet and chapter activities were often so demanding, and at the same time so stimulating and attractive, that my

*perspective got a little out of kilter from time to time, and I need-
ed a gentle jolt from my frau to return me to reality and the
needs of fatherhood and husbandry.*

*At 5:30 one Sunday morning, the other three quartet
members dropped me at my door after we had just driven back
from a particularly drawn-out show and afterglow. As I tiptoed
through the hall in the dawn's early light, I reflected,
conscience-stricken, that I had been out barbershopping every
night that week! Shoes in hand, I maneuvered stealthily through
the living room and in the dimness saw the sleeping form of my
wife on the sofa. Mercifully, she appeared to be sleeping sound-
ly, a circumstance I had no desire to disturb. As I negotiated the
stairs I wondered vaguely why she wasn't in bed, but I didn't
ruminate on the question too strongly at that hour and under
those circumstances.*

*I quietly attained the bedroom, carefully closed the door,
breathed a sigh of relief, and turned on the light. There on the
pillow on my wife's side of the bed was...my pitch pipe!*

Quartet Rehearsals

How do you get to Carnegie Hall? Everybody knows the answer to
that one: Practice! The same answer applies as good advice to every
quartet that ever dreamed of entertaining more than just the four
singers. Practice, practice, practice!

Quartet rehearsals and chorus rehearsals are rather similar, I suppose. They can be tedious, exhausting, and exasperating, or on the
other hand, exciting, rewarding, and fun. With my first quartet, the
UNLIKELY HOODS, our rehearsals were sometimes more like a dinner club than a musical workout. Pete Donatelli would every now and
then bring along a big zucchini, and he'd prepare it according to his
own special recipe. Our rehearsals at Mike Patti's house were mostly
in the kitchen. When we practiced at my house, my wife, Diane,
usually cooked up a feast. Have you ever tried to sing after a glut-
tony? Too many mashed potatoes will wreak havoc with your sound-
production mechanisms!

Once, we all went to my father's cottage on Lake Michigan for a
series of concentrated and rigorous rehearsal sessions. We had new
music to learn and a good deal of polishing to do on our repertoire.
We boated, swam, played Frisbee, talked a lot, and ate an awful lot.

Come to think of it, we did manage to squeeze in a little rehearsing, but it didn't interfere much with our recreation.

Rehearsals are sometimes just a necessary evil; then again, sometimes they're a ball!

It's best, of course, to have a coach work with a quartet. In that way, there's an impartial listener who can concentrate on the quartet's performance. Without a coach, somebody in the quartet, by mutual consent or otherwise, assumes the role of singer-coach and usually does both jobs poorly. There aren't many barbershoppers, though I've known one or two, who are talented enough to do justice to full-time singing and critiquing simultaneously. Furthermore, if one member of the quartet is constantly criticizing the others, it will eventually affect the group's morale and break down the quartet's bond of togetherness.

Have you ever wondered what rehearsals are like with superstar foursomes? Terry Clarke describes a session with the BOSTON COMMON:

> *Lou Perry hasn't really been a coach to us; he's been a teacher. When we start on a new piece of music, he plays it on the organ, giving each note the time it should have, as arranged. He'll say, "This is the way the man wrote the song." He plays it that way and we learn it that way. We tape-record what he plays and what we sing, and then work with our recorders until the next rehearsal. That's how we learn our songs.*
>
> *When we come back together with Lou, we know our parts. The song is ninety percent completed. Incidentally, when we're learning with a tape recorder we all sing the melody, just like the barbershop craft books recommend. Then we learn our individual parts. We acknowledge that the guy who wrote the song knew what he was doing. He knew music better than we do, so we sing it the way he wrote it, unless we have a pretty darn good reason to make a change. From that point, we put in shading according to what the lead feels, and that's simple enough. We just follow him. So it's the lead with three guys singing along with him. After we're comfortable with the song, we sing it around at afterglows and finally get to the point where we feel it's ready to perform on a show. When we believe in the song we present it accordingly.*
>
> *As I say, Lou has always been a music teacher, not a coach.*

He never tells us what to do. He tells us if we're doing something other than what the music calls for or allows, but he won't interpret a song for us. He explains the musical reasons that make an interpretation inappropriate, but if we ask him to recommend a more apt presentation, he'll say it's up to us. The four of us must then look at the alternatives and discuss what is most appropriate, and in the process we learn music, not just a song. And that's why Lou is a teacher, not a coach.

Lou listens to us and philosophizes with us. Our rehearsals consist of about three hours of discussion and philosophizing and maybe a half hour of singing and working on a new song.

Lou Perry also worked with the FOUR STATESMEN. I like his story about one of their rehearsals:

The FOUR STATESMEN used to come to my house in Boston on Sunday afternoons and we'd rehearse from nine o'clock until six. During one of our sessions I got a call from Jerry Nyhan. I must say that Jerry was considered to be somewhat of a character. He was a marvelous woodshedder and he loved to dig up old songs and teach the parts to a pickup quartet. If you didn't learn your part after three tries, he'd throw you out and find somebody else.

He was a brilliant man, a morphologist from San Francisco. He was so good, in fact, that he was periodically called to the Massachusetts General Hospital in Boston and to John Hopkins Hospital in Baltimore for consulting work.

He used to call me from San Francisco and talk for nearly an hour about barbershopping. Sometimes he'd call just to tell me about a new song he had found or heard.

Anyway, in the middle of the rehearsal with the STATESMEN, he called. "Jerry, where are you?" I inquired. I always had to ask because there was no telling where he would call from.

"I'm in Boston over at the Massachusetts General Hospital and I've got a real dandy of a new song for you."

"That's great," I said. "Can you come over?"

"Yeah, I guess so. How do I get there?"

I told him to take Route 128 and gave him all the directions. I was anxious for the STATESMEN to hear Jerry's new song, because invariably they were dandies, but we waited and waited and he didn't come. It got to be 6:30 and the quartet was

*anxious to get along. Each had a long drive to get home;
one, more than a hundred miles. Finally the telephone rang.
"Jerry, where are you?" I asked.*

"I'm on Route 28, almost in New Hampshire!"

"No, no, Jerry, not Route 28. It's Route 128!"

*I persuaded the boys to wait and at long last there was a
knock on the door. "Jerry," I said, "before you tell me about
your song, let the STATESMEN here sing a fine old number I
dug up and arranged for them." He sat down and the quartet
began.*

*They hadn't sung more than two or three bars when Jerry
jumped out of his chair. "That's it," he shouted. "That's the
song I came all the way from San Francisco to give you!"*

Lou has another quartet rehearsal story, this time about the FOUR
RASCALS:

*I used to coach and arrange music for the FOUR RASCALS.
That quartet was essentially four baritones, and four of the best
woodshedders I ever knew. Since none could read music, they
normally took three to four months to learn a song. I wrote arrangements for them, but I had to be very careful. They'd sing
along to a part they weren't too sure of, and then would woodshed their own arrangement. Sometimes the result was better
than what I had written! Quite a bit of their stuff was a combination of what I had arranged and what they woodshedded.*

*We were on our way to a show in Putnam, Connecticut, and
the RASCALS started woodshedding a song called "Frim Fram
Sauce," one of those 1940's "throwaways," as I call them. By
the time we got to Putnam, they had woodshedded it well
enough to put on the show, and it was an instant hit; so much so
they had to sing it three more times at the afterglow. I'm quite
sure no one in the audience realized it was neither formally arranged nor extensively rehearsed before their performance
that night.*

A rehearsal is generally a private process, not intended for public
consumption. If other people are listening, the quartet discipline
seems to shift and the rehearsal transforms into a performance.
Sometimes, though, an audience is able to witness a rehearsal when
the singers are unaffected by the knowledge that others are within

earshot. Carl Hancuff tells of two such times.

Milt Christensen had a tragic auto accident some years back, and it caused Milt to have great problems with his leg. He had ten operations and some long and painful times. I recall once when we went up to see him. We'd go on the pretense of practicing, but he was so darn weak he could hardly sing through two songs. We wanted to let him know we cared and we wanted to be there with him, so we went up to his room in the LDS Hospital in Salt Lake City.

It was Sunday afternoon. Milt had his TV set on and was watching one heck of a golf match between Arnold Palmer and I don't remember who else. We wanted to sing a little, so we turned the TV sound down and started in. Unbeknown to us, in that sophisticated hospital, nurses can listen in to the rooms of the patients. They had heard us singing and had pushed some buttons to broadcast our practice throughout the entire wing of the hospital. Of course we didn't realize it.

Anyway, as we sang, we continued to watch Arnold Palmer on television. It was an exciting match. Palmer's ball was about seventy yards from the cup. He took a swing and the ball bounced and rolled up and down and back and forth and miraculously fell into the hole. When it did, our room just exploded with expletives! "Did you see that blankety-blank ball go in that blankety-blank blank hole!" We shouted and carried on something fierce.

The door burst open and there stood a nurse with a horrified expression on her face. Her complexion was as white as the rest of her. She gave us a searing reprimand, but the damage was already done. Our expletives had been broadcast to every tender ear in the entire hospital wing!

Probably one of the finest moments in our lives was a time some years back when we went fishing. It was at Williams Lake in Idaho, without a doubt the most gorgeous, absolutely beautiful place I'd ever seen.

Just the four of us had gone there to fish. We had a nice little cabin on the edge of the water. We fished all day and then took the boat across the lake in the evening to eat at a restaurant. On the way back we started talking about one of our contest songs, a ballad. It was a lovely, balmy evening, maybe 9:30 or so, and in a quiet manner in the middle of the lake we sang our song. You know how quartets huddle together and sing.

Well, we had forgotten how sound carries across water, and when we got to the end of the song, the entire lake came alive with applause. It was such a surprising and moving thing; applause and yells of "More, more, more" coming from everywhere. We couldn't see anybody out there and they couldn't see us, but we had sung for one of our best audiences ever! It was a beautiful moment.

Quartet Encounters

I'd say one of the big challenges of singing before an audience is keeping a balance between too much and too little nervousness. Maybe I should call it excitement or enthusiasm or butterflies in the stomach, or something else. But whatever it is, if there's too much, your voice loses support, you lose confidence, and the performance goes down the drain. Too little, on the other hand, and your songs become lifeless and dull; just memorized words and notes.

A song has to be memorized to the point where it can be sung "from the spine," as George Nagy of the UNLIKELY HOODS used to say, but as a singer you must never lose concentration. George knew that principle well, but would occasionally become its victim nevertheless.

On the Poughkeepsie Chapter's annual show one year, the UNLIKELY HOODS decided to use three show-biz gags spaced between the verses of our opening song. One was the old joke about a disbelieving talent agent who was testing a "talking" dog. Pete Donatelli was the talent agent. I was the dog. Meanwhile, George and Mike Myers sang "doo-doos" in the background.

"So, you're Towser, the Wonder Dog who can talk," Pete started off. I panted and nodded my head. "Okay," Pete continued, "I'm going to give you a test. What's on the top of a house?"

"Roofff!" I replied in a bark, panting harder.

"Well, that's pretty good," Pete said. "How would you describe sandpaper?"

"Rough!" I barked back at him.

"Okay. Who holds the record for the most home runs in the American League?"

"Ruth!" I yelped.

"This dog can't talk; he's a fake. Get him out of here!" was Pete's line.

At that point, I was supposed to pause, and with a blank expression, turn to the audience and say, "Was it DiMaggio?"

However, George, with his beautiful bass doo-dooing, had by then lost track of things. His concentration was gone. Noting the lull in the dialogue, he figured it was time to sing his solo lead-in to resume the song. So just as I was about to deliver the punch line, good old George leaped in and launched into the next verse. Well, the joke was lost, the audience was lost, and the quartet had quite a little scrambling to do to get things back on track.

"For heaven's sake, George, what happened?" we demanded as soon as we got off stage.

His answer was succinct: "I was woolgathering," he said in his usual stoical style.

It has happened to me, too. Oh yes, more times than I wish to admit. Sometimes it's simply a matter of misdirected concentrations. In one song we do, I switch from baritone to take the lead part and sing four solo verses, while the other guys sing in the background. The words of each verse are quite similar and it's easy to go astray. More than once I've been thinking about breath support or facial expressions or gestures, and I'm off on the wrong verse. Then comes the hard part.

If it's a verse I haven't yet sung to the audience, I have to mentally shuffle things around so I just sing the verses out of order. On the other hand, if it's a verse I've already bestowed upon the listening crowd, then I have to sing it once more, but in a completely *new* way, so the audience thinks it's *supposed* to be that way. One thing I don't have to worry about is having the rest of the quartet make adjustments with me. Those guys are singing completely on "automatic pilot," and the chances are they won't even notice I'm floundering.

One time the UNLIKELY HOODS quartet was singing for a church group (I think it was) at a dinner meeting in Poughkeepsie. I was singing lead then and was in the middle of a solo part. I have no idea what distracted me, but I remember vividly the abrupt snap back to reality. For some reason I began a verse with a set of words I had never sung before, ever! Coming upon such a predicament brings moments of utter terror to a singer.

The last thing I wanted to do was to bring the whole song to a flaming, screeching stop. Besides inciting embarrassment, such an action tends to push the entire performance over the edge to disaster, to the discomfort of all. So slamming on the brakes is only a last resort.

During my solo panic, all those thoughts were streaming through my brain along with the realization that I did not by any means have a long period of time to ponder my plight. Miraculously, I sang on with a string of words that not only made sense, but was appropriate for the meter and rhythm of the song! On top of all that, the words rhymed where they ought to! I don't know how I did it, and I'm sure I could never do it again, but I did it then. The rest of the quartet stared at me as though I had turned into a warthog or something. I thought I had snatched victory from the jaws of defeat, only to have three quarters of the quartet's expressions reveal that though the song continued, mass confusion reigned!

One goof that particularly tickled my fancy was perpetrated by the PENTHOUSE FOUR. As members of the Poughkeepsie Chapter, they performed at regular chapter meetings every now and then and of course at other chapter events. This particular instance was a chapter meeting and the song was "You Belong to Me." It was arranged as a lead solo, with the tenor, bari, and bass singing background accompaniment and periodically joining in with the lyrics. It's a beautiful song and was beautifully sung. It was a tender, sensitive performance.

However, at the line, "Fly the ocean in a silver plane, see the jungle when it's wet with rain," the lead must have had some fleeting distraction of the thought process, because his words came out (with feeling): "Fly the jungle in a silver plane, see the ocean when it's wet with rain."

There was then his moment of realization that an unrecoverable faux pas had been committed. Audience and performers alike took stock of what that tender phrase meant, but before anyone could react, the lead gestured philosophically and said, "Think about that."

Well, there wasn't much of a chance to do so, because the place burst apart with laughter. The spell of the lovely song had been broken!

Just as sure as there is hope and promise with each new quartet's launching, so, too, is there the inevitable ultimate docking of the Good Ship Lollypop, when the great quartet voyage concludes. Through high seas and stormy weather the quartet craft may steer a steady course, but the end of the journey must come. Though a quartet's final appearance may bring lumps in throats, wet eyes, and sadness, it may, nonetheless, contain some warm and precious moments. The last day of the ORIOLE FOUR was filled with both the bitter and the sweet, as Freddie King recalls:

It was so ironic it was eerie. On the very day the ORIOLE FOUR retired, March 1, 1975, our dear friend and mentor Bob Loose died. That's irony. We sang our last show on that day in Wilkes-Barre, Pennsylvania.

Our wives and several friends were seated in the front row and as we sang we could just barely see them wailing away. We suspected we'd be given the old bum's rush and would have to sing until we couldn't stand up, so we were prepared for that. Sure enough, I think we sang three encores. After that the audience demanded still more. They were pounding on the seats like crowds do at football games, and we were feeling like a million dollars. When we walked out for a final bow, I noticed the MC was gone. In his place was Jim Hackman, spokesman for the Chorus of the Chesapeake. "Jim," I whispered, "what are you doing here?"

"Stand by," he replied. The house lights went up and the entire Chorus of the Chesapeake was sitting there in the auditorium. They marched down the aisle, climbed up on stage, and sang "That's What I Call a Pal." Oh my gosh, I get goose bumps thinking about it!

I'll never forget that night as long as I live. It went on and on and on. We sang some more, and after a while I just got dizzy from it; I really did. It was too much to take. The afterglow went all night long in some hall I can't remember, and we sang everything we knew, some things we didn't. One minute we felt like kings, but the next minute we felt like dodos for calling it quits.

We had to bring it to an end, though, because we weren't working as hard as we worked before winning the championship. We couldn't demean the image of a quartet champion and we couldn't afford to debase what the gold medal stands for, so we retired. It's far better to ride out on the crest of a wave than to crawl out from under a barrage of tomatoes. On March 1, 1975, the tide was up in Wilkes-Barre!

Quartet PR

Public relations, good old PR, is probably ineffectively used, in general, by barbershop quartets and choruses alike. A few groups have excellent promotional campaigns to plug their records or performances, but I suspect most do little to advance their causes. My old quartet, the UNLIKELY HOODS, put together a promotional booklet, but it happened largely by chance.

The UNLIKELY HOODS was my first quartet and it took some time to reach the point where we could charge a modest fee for our singing without being too embarrassed. Over the years there were some personnel changes, and when Bill James left the quartet to be replaced by Mike Myers, it seemed appropriate to let prospective show chairmen know about it. If we were going to write such a notice, why not make it a few pages longer and call it a PR booklet? That's what we did.

It was only two sheets of paper folded in the middle to make eight pages, with a green cover, but it served us nicely. We sent a copy to every chapter in our District and two adjacent Districts, and it landed several jobs for us. In our booklet we used some caricatures Walt Owen had drawn of the quartet. We wrote a brief description of what the quartet was and what we sang, and we wanted to include some photographs. Unfortunately, we were never able to get together for a photo session and when it appeared that situation would prevail indefinitely, we improvised. The first picture in our booklet was simply a gray haze, with the caption: "The UNLIKELY HOODS shown singing and dancing at Carnegie Hall during the Great Northeast Power Failure. What a smashing performance. From left to right are: Pete Donatelli, Mike Myers, Fred Gielow, and George Nagy."

On the next page was a photograph of an automobile which had been totally destroyed in a traffic accident. The caption read: "Another smashing performance by the UNLIKELY HOODS."

The VILLAGE IDIOTS had a good PR piece written by Tom Neal and published in the District newspaper. It was contributed by Bob Keener. Excerpts are:

When a fan recently asked the VILLAGE IDIOTS when the

quartet was organized, one of the members replied, "Someday soon, I hope." In reality, the quartet started out nearly twenty years ago by entering competition in Uniontown, Pennsylvania. After creating chaos and general disorder with their contest rendition of "Bird in a Gilded Cage," the boys were on their way to becoming one of the zaniest and longest lasting quartets on record.

Few people realize that the boys actually did win a contest once. They walked away with top honors at the Cleveland Boat Show Quartet Contest. First prize was a toy boat and 20,000 gallons of toy water. The IDIOTS also finished second at the Smucker's Jam Festival Contest in Orville, Ohio. To show their gratitude, the quartet spokesman announced they all drank Smuckers and intended to order a case apiece. The real story of the VILLAGE IDIOTS' success, though, is the quartet's show career with more than three hundred performances throughout the United States and Canada.

Dan Shramo sings the tenor part and he also holds the record for reaching the highest note ever sung by an adult male. He was singing with a dance band and was standing in front of the trombone player when the event occurred.

Bob Keener is the quartet's lead. After enjoying several noggins of spiritus fermenti at a recent performance, Bob attempted to open his motel door with a cigarette. Imagine his surprise when he reached in his pocket and discovered he had smoked his key.

Baritone Tom Neal is the former director of the Cleveland, Ohio and Euclid, Ohio choruses. Tom is the arranger for the quartet and his work is frequently used in quartet clinics as examples of how to attain a negative score. One of his better known arrangements is "I'm Sorry I Made You Cry, But Your Face is Cleaner."

Willard Kapes, the bass, is known throughout the Society for his pithy epigrams. Only last week Will remarked, "It's impossible to go through a meaningful death experience and still carry a tune."

Sometimes the best of PR efforts can go awry, and sometimes the most carefully chosen words can backfire. In the BROTHERHOOD we spent hours looking for just the right phrase to describe the quartet. We made suggestions, argued over them, fought over them, and finally came to a decision. We chose the catchy saying: "Barbershop harmony you've got to see to believe!"

We thought it would serve nicely on our business card and stationery, and if a chapter chose, on a show program or ad as well. Of course we were wrong. In big, attention-getting letters, one barbershop program boldly announced:

An Evening of Barbershop Harmony
To Benefit the Society for the Blind
Featuring
The BROTHERHOOD Quartet
Barbershop Harmony You've Got To See To Believe!

Fortunately, those most likely to be offended by such a statement were least likely to be reading the program anyway, so I guess no harm was done.

Quartet Contact

One of the little-appreciated yet vitally important jobs in a quartet, or chorus for that matter, is that of the "contact" man. He's the guy who writes all the letters, answers all the phone calls, sends out all the PR materials, makes all the bothersome but essential logistics arrangements, probably worries the most when people aren't on time, and is usually blamed when anything goes wrong. He spends hours with pen in hand or typewriter at fingertip, and his reward never seems to extend beyond a sour tongue licked limp on envelope flaps and postage stamps.

I've held that enviable position for a dozen or more quartetting years, and while it has its many exasperations, it also has an occasional reward. For the most part the job falls into a regular routine. The exchange of correspondence and communications is pretty predictable. Except once it wasn't.

The letter that arrived in my mailbox looked like so many that had come before, and I wrote back like so many times before, but this exchange was destined to veer far away from the normal course and to entrap me in a dialog the likes of which I had never seen, have never since seen, and never expect to see again.

I'm getting ahead of myself. Here's that first letter, just as I received it:

The Merry Go Round Mews
½ Bolling Place
Greenwich, Connecticut 06830
June 25

Mr. Fred Gielow, apparent mainspring of a
   fantastic group calling themselves, of all
   things, the UNLIKELY HOODS, this being
   a remarkable barbershop quartet.
Thirty-Three Park Drive
Woodstock, New York 12498

Dear Mr. Gielow, etc.

I was present last night with two friends at Rippowam High School in Stamford. Let me remark here that I have an honest and quite sincere appreciation of good music. I am not referring to Grand Opera but rather to such items as Pinafore, The Chocolate Soldier, The Merry Widow, Naughty Marietta, Robin Hood, this being the kind of music my Mother loved and taught me to love also. And in another direction, I have independently come to love such work as Fiddler on the Roof, My Fair Lady, The Music Man, and The Sound of Music. For me, one of the high spots of The Music Man was provided by The BUFFALO BILLS. Which I hope will right now establish some degree of rapport.

With this background it is hardly necessary to describe my feelings when the HOODS were on stage. Or why I came backstage during the intermission and bugged one of your associates into giving me your card. My very best to George, Mike and Pete.

Now, the Merry Go Round Mews is a private, non-profit hotel for some sixty-eight retired senior citizens, operated with the idea that there should be something approximating a luxury hotel for people of modest means. The concept was nourished for nearly twenty-five years by Nancy Rockefeller and the cornerstone was laid early in 1969. The joint filled up overnight and there is a waiting list of more than fifty. Naturally, when you assemble sixty-eight seniors, with ages ranging from 70 for me, the baby of the family, to around the corner from 100, you have both a group richly deserving regular entertainment and one generally unable to enjoy it unless it is brought to them. And here is where I shine.

I have, believe me, attracted many notables, but this does not necessarily mean that I am unusually gifted as a program chairman. In most cases I have found a sincere eagerness on the part of my guests to serve when asked, and there have been many that volunteered.

I have had the Commissioner of State Police for Connecticut, Mort Walker, Dick Schaap, and Denise Lor. Through the kindness of a local angel, we were presented with free tickets and transportation to a nearby concert by Hugo Winterhalter. The Yankee Maids have been here and I am promised a return date.

I have commitments from Arnold Stang and John Lahr, Edward Quinn, Stationmaster at Grand Central Terminal, and strong possibilities of snaring Victor Borge and Don Imus.

Certainly, I am trying to impress you because I know the possible results will be well worth it. True, you will not have the apparent incentive toward donating your time that you did for NIRE. But these people also merit consideration and since it isn't but eight miles further from Woodstock to Greenwich than is Stamford and we will expect no more than you gave last night. I realize that you are busy men and do not expect an immediate date. Anyhow, I am booked right through most of July and by the time this reaches you will very likely have to go into August. I enclose a typical program and take the time to add here that I forgot one impressive member of my prospective lineup—Senator Claghorn. And Kenny is due for a surprise in that I intend to run him into a Tell the Truth situation. You see, there is actually a Mr. Claghorn living in Greenwich and he has agreed to drop in and bug Kenny whenever a date is settled.

May I hear from you soon?

Sincerely,
Henry W. Rosenkranz
Program Chairman and outstanding genius
P.S. Don't kid yourself about me being scared to use the same address on the envelope.

His P.S. referred to ''Program Chairman and outstanding genius,'' which, sure enough, was on the envelope. A lengthy and interesting letter to be sure, though a little offbeat, perhaps, so I responded in kind:

July 9

Mr. Henry W. Rosenkranz,
    Program Chairman and Outstanding Genius
The Merry Go Round Mews
½ Bolling Place
Greenwich, Connecticut 06830

Dear Genius,
    Many thanks for your lengthly and interesting letter of June
25, which the postman (with a chuckle) brought personally to
the door, and which the whole quartet has now enjoyed
reading.
    The Merry Go Round Mews (and I'd love to learn the origin of
that name) sounds like a deserving group, and we'd like to perform for you. However, while we are basically a nonprofit
quartet (not necessarily by design, but at least by practice), we
do not wish to become a non-break-even quartet either. We
agreed to perform on the NIRE program for expenses, but this
money ($25.50) won't really cover our costs. We like to support
charities, but just can't afford to do so too extensively. Consequently we'd be willing to put on our regular 25-to-30 minute
performance for one third of our normal fee: $33 plus expenses
on a weekend (Friday through Sunday) night, or $25 plus ex-
penses on a weekday night.
    Let me know if this is agreeable to you, and if so, then we can
decide on a date and time that fit both of our schedules.
    Thanks for thinking of the HOODS.

Unlikely,
    Fred Gielow
    for the HOODS

In practically no time Henry's answer was in my mailbox:

July 11
Dear Fred:
    *As I hinted, I hoped the letter would be provocative enough to
completely arouse your interest, but I suppose you can't win
'em all. On the whole, I don't do too bad, but I had hoped, too,
that you might be inclined to come down and at least see what
kind of a screwball would write that kind of a letter...*

For a good part of the entertainment I can take a pardonable pride, and for a larger percentage I must thank the gracious spirit of so many good people so willing to donate their services, ranging from Mort Walker, already mentioned, to Smokey Ficker, a local boy too and director of the only German Band left in this part of the country, as far as I know...

I can understand your position, but I must, unfortunately also consider my own. I just don't have any budget as yet, and much as I would like to have you here, that's the way it is.

For what it may be worth, I could offer the quartet a damn good lunch and drinks, but that's the limit. May I still hear from you.

Sincerely,
Henry W. Rosenkranz

A spirited and zesty but pleasant exchange of information, I thought. As I wrote the response though, I figured it had finally fallen into the familiar pattern: A request for a "freebie," an exchange of miscellaneous pleasantries, then "sorry, we can't oblige." My letter back was taking on the ring of the old routine:

July 29

Dear Henry,

Thanks for your again-lengthy and again-interesting letter of July 11.

Unfortunately, we will be unable to make a special trip to Greenwich to perform for the MGRM. However, should another quartet job take us in or about your area, we'll try to see if we can work something out.

Sorry we can't make it happen otherwise.

Unlikely,
Fred

Then things began to slide off track:

August 9

Dear Fred:

Thanks very much for your letter of July 29.
I am going to do everything possible to arrange matters so

that you will be able to bring the HOODS to The Merry Go Round Mews.

I have spoken to the entertainment manager at The Greenwich Country Club about having the quartet appear there and he said he would let me know in a couple of days if he can arrange it. It may well be that he would expect you to sing longer than your customary half hour, and since he considered $35 plus expenses quite reasonable, he might be willing to pay a bit more. You can fight that out if you hear from either of us again. I think it was $25 plus expenses you quoted me.

I have another angle, subject to your convenience and pleasure; I intend to keep an eye on the social page of Greenwich Time from now on, and if I see anything that looks promising, such as a wedding, or some other wingding, I will get in touch with the principals and see if they would care for a Barbershop Quartette. I will, of course, wait until I hear from you before I take off.

Sincerely,
   Henry

Now, just hold on! We liked to think of ourselves as charitable, but our charity had limits, and we weren't about to allow those limits to be compromised. If Henry Rosenkranz planned to take advantage of us, I had to set him straight:

                                            August 24

Dear Henry,
   Thanks for your letter of August 9.
   Let me clarify our fee situation. We agreed to come sing for you for $33 plus expenses on a weekend night, or $25 plus expenses on a weekday night. This is one third our normal charge. We would not be willing to sing two jobs in one evening for this reduced, community-service-type fee. Our normal charge is $100 plus expenses for weekends, $75 plus expenses for weekdays (for a single-segment performance of about 25 minutes) and we'd expect to receive this amount for a country club or similar appearance. However, if scheduling could be arranged, we would be willing to sing at the Merry Go Round Mews for no charge, if it accompanied a normal pay job (same day, good timing, reasonably close locations, etc.).

How does this sound?

Unlikely,
    Fred

Henry's letters seemed to be coming every week or so:

August 27

Dear Fred,
    Thank you for your letter of August 24.
    You have clarified your fee situation very well, now let me clarify mine.
    Thursday night, August 24, we were visited by four Robinsons; Scotty, Mary, Lolly, and their collective brother Arthur. They presented Gilbert and Sullivan's H.M.S. Pinafore with Marionettes and a recording of the operetta. The stage, consisting of an aluminum pipe frame, the cloth covering, the scenery, the lighting, the marionettes, everything, they created at their own expense. It took them an hour to set up, an hour and about fifteen minutes for the presentation and another hour to tear down. They considered themselves well paid by both their reception, (they said we are the best audience they ever had) and by a few cookies and glasses of juice that I passed around...
    I can honestly say too, that judging by past experience, you would in all likelihood not have recieved as much of applause as they did. Anyhow, I have suggested to Charley Henniger, who directs The Greenwich Civic Center and who does have a budget, that he get in touch with you. If he does, and you are inclined to use the opportunity to come here and do a turn for free, let me know. Personally, everything considered, I don't give a damn if I never hear from you. You aren't that important.

Sincerely,
    Henry

Oh boy, that one did it! It raised my ire and boosted my temperature over the boiling point. I sat right down and wrote a scorching letter to zing back. I rewrote it and rewrote it agan. Each version simply bristled, so I let a few days go by to cool off. Then I sat down again and wrote as dignified and calm a letter as I was able. I beat a stamp into the envelope and sent it on its way:

September 5

Dear Henry,

A week ago today I received your letter of August 27. Between the lines, or not so much between the lines, I believe I detect a note of anger, or disdain, or indignation, or some such emotion. I am sorry.

You made a request of our quartet and I responded to it. My response was honest and sincere, and I believe it was even generous. It may not be as you desire, but such is life. Neither is the conclusion of your recent letter as I desire, but such is life.

That the four Robinsons have the time, the talent, and the financial resources to perform for you is indeed wonderful. And I am delighted that a warm audience reaction, coupled with "a few cookies and glasses of juice," is more than sufficient to reward them and to elicit their frequent return. They sound like marvelous people indeed. The UNLIKELY HOODS are not so inclined. As I mentioned in an earlier letter, we have but restricted time and money, and our charitable contributions are restrained.

I must say that if my only intent was to turn your request down flatly, I could have done so very rapidly by simply ignoring your initial letter. However, believing your request to be sincere, and wanting to help, I made a sincere offer.

If, however, it is your judgment that 1) our appearance at the Merry Go Round Mews would not be well received ("...you would in all likelihood not have received as much in applause..."), and that 2) our quartet might not be particularly welcome ("...I don't give a damn if I never hear from you."), then perhaps our performance there might not be wise. It's always difficult to do your best job when you feel unwelcome.

So why have I taken the time and effort to explain all this? Well, there are several reasons: You have heard the UNLIKELY HOODS sing; you are part of our audience. You have asked our quartet to perform; you honor us by such a request. And above all, you're a person of feelings and emotions who deserves respect and courtesy; you *are that important!*

Yours very truly,
Fred

How, but with hat in humble hand, could a man answer a masterpiece like that? Surely my graciousness and heart-warming manner would melt his audacity. I eagerly examined the mailbox each day. I didn't have long to wait:

September 9

Dear Fred,

I am admittedly and oftentimes impulsively much too abrasive in my responses. As I was with you.

There is still my point of view, however, and I would like to submit this supportive argument.

Speaking of The Robinsons you say, "They sound like marvelous people." The UNLIKELY HOODS are not so inclined. I misquote you, certainly; deliberately.

I have had hundreds of entertainers here in the last two years, of all kinds and statures; from Mort Walker to The Robinsons, to The Sauerkrauts, and coming up, when her problems permit, Trudy Sampson, a Swiss Yodeler. Mort is admittedly a very busy man and a wealthy one. Neither condition hindered him for a moment when I invited him to appear here for free. To the best of my knowledge, The Robinsons, being still students, can hardly be called affluent. The Sauerkrauts are all professional men with family responsibilities. From correspondence I have had with Trudy, it is quite likely that she too, is only in moderate circumstances. Yet once a month, she regularly travels from her home in Rhinebeck to Mount Kisco to entertain shut-ins at her own expense. On one of her jaunts, she will stop in here. All in all, it seems that the one really insurmountable obstacle is a few gallons of gasoline.

Again I say, but this time considering my first outburst with not the least rancor but still firmly, I don't give a damn if I never hear from you. You aren't that important.

Sincerely,
Henry

I invited him to bury the hatchet and he did, right between my eyes. I was fit to be tied. I let weeks go by but the elapsed time only fueled the furious fires. I finally sat down at the typewriter and let it all come seething out; flame and brimstone, molten rock and lightning:

September 30

My dear Mr. Rosenkranz,

Say it isn't so. Tell me that you are not as despicable and despiteous as your letters lead me to believe. Tell me that you have feeling, that you have compassion, that you have kindness, somewhere beneath that rude, crass, and contemptuous exterior that your written word portrays. Tell me that it's just a cover-up, that the real you is warm, sympathetic, understanding, and human.

Let me reread your words and remember you as crude, perhaps, but not cruel; as presumptuous, but not preposterous; as insensitive, but not insane.

I have now given up all hope of receiving a civil reply from you. I have simply concluded that you are incapable of producing a gracious word without the prospect or the promise of getting things your way, on your and only your terms. Such a pity!

But in spite of all this, I still consider you to be "That important." Now this may sound strange in the face of all your churlish insults. But let me quickly add that I've met a number of wretched and miserable people, and I consider them *all* to be "That important."

As one final note, I should mention that judging exclusively on the basis of your August 27th and September 9th letters, I consider you to be the most wretched and miserable person I've ever met.

With warm regards,
    Fred

For your information, the *American College Dictionary* defines "despiteous" as "malicious, spiteful, contemptuous." It also defines "churlish" as "like a churl, boorish, rude, surly, niggardly, sordid, difficult to work or deal with..."

As I delivered my letter to the post office, I felt terribly ambivalent. I thought he deserved every stinging word, perhaps worse, yet he had reduced me to the point where I was playing the game with his rules. In our verbal duel I was both the victor and the vanquished.

But now, what would be his response? Surely he couldn't better my attack. Would he back off? Would he respond at all? His letter appeared promptly:

October 4

Dear Fred,

I have a fairly friendly association with the one time Stamford superintendent of The Connecticut Company and currently dispatcher at their New Haven terminal. Our association began when I needled him about the actions and behavior of some of the bus drivers under his supervision. One thing led to another and I now have three treasured pictures of old time trolley cars on the wall next to my bathroom door. Quite honestly, when I began this dialog it was my hope for a similar outcome.

I find now, after reading your letter of September 30, that I would after all, like to hear from you further, but before you write, I suggest that you submit both of our latest letters to the inspection of a neutral third party and without identifying them, ask him to judge which is the most offensive. I am referring to my letter of September 9 and yours of September 30.

Sincerely,
Henry

The contest was over. I was out of words to write back to Henry Rosenkranz. Days went by, weeks, and months. Then I had to write again:

December 24

Dear Henry,

Happy holidays, and best wishes for the new year!

I thought you might like to see the quartet's new PR booklet that was just published this month. A copy is enclosed.

What's news at the Mews?

Yours truly,
Fred

His answer was as speedy as ever. It was written on plain white paper with a red-and-green Christmas holly sticker affixed to the upper right-hand corner of the sheet:

December 27

Dear Fred:
What's news at The Mews? What's news is that I received a

*very welcome letter from the spark-plug of The UNLIKELY
HOODS this morning. And that I enjoyed reading the booklet
very much. And for the second time in my advancing years, was
shot with Hydro-Cortisone by Doctor Thomas Rodda; I no
longer creak.*

All in all, it has been a very pleasant holiday season.
Thanks again for your letter.

Sincerely,
Henry

Our bizarre exchange of letters was thus concluded. Who said the
job of quartet contact man is boring?

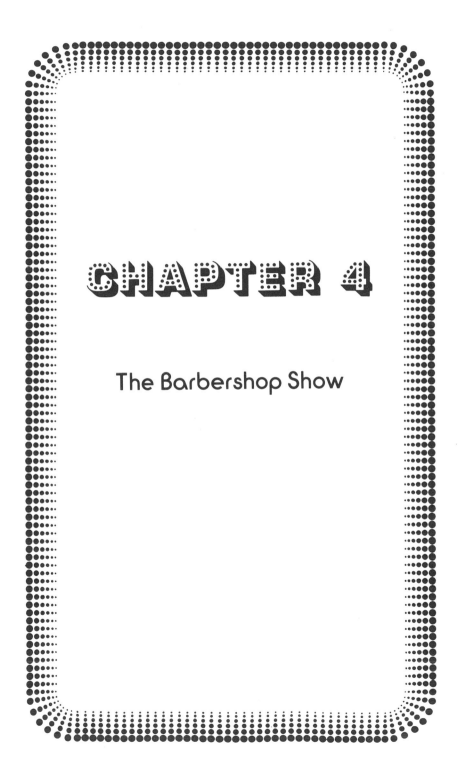

CHAPTER 4

The Barbershop Show

The Barbershop Show

Give us a song to cheer
Our weary hearts, a song of home
And friends we love so dear.

Walter Kittredge

he annual barbershop show sponsored by the local barbershop chapter is a tradition all over North America. Typically, the chapter chorus and a couple of chapter quartets perform, along with a high-ranking or popular "show" quartet. Often a comedy quartet is also on the program. Shows may include complicated skits or grandiose productions or may simply take the form of a parade of barbershop performers. Whatever the theme or organization, shows are entertaining to witness and to participate in, and with any luck will produce sufficient income to support chapter activities for many months to follow, maybe until the next year's show rolls around.

For a guest quartet, the barbershop show itself is but a piece of the weekend's barbershop action. There may be a preglow to sing at, almost certainly an afterglow, and probably an after-afterglow, too. A motel stay is likely, and some hours of travel are inevitable. So, it's not just a barbershop show, it's a whole barbershop weekend adventure!

Quartet Travels

The wild and woolly tales of quartet travels could alone fill a book to overflowing, because singing foursomes seem to have a special propensity for working themselves into trouble, and they then seem to have enough dumb luck or good fortune to work themselves out. A good example is one of my quartet's trips to Canada. Pete Donatelli tells the story:

Surely those who have performed in comedy quartets well understand what a bother it is to lug around all the props. In addition to all the costumes or uniforms, funny quartets carry along a big suitcase of gimmicks that are important in the act. The BROTHERHOOD quartet is no exception, with an "exploding" table, disappearing and reappearing canes, a gangster-type pistol, and many other miscellaneous odds and ends. What better place to store some of these accouterments than in our bass Tony Gross's violin case, saved from his childhood days.

The drive to Boston was uneventful, the flight to Halifax, Nova Scotia was pleasant, and everything was going great. Since it was Saturday, there wasn't much activity at the air terminal, so the passengers quickly filed through the customs check. The quartet, however, had to apply for working papers, so we each had to spend a few minutes going through that relatively easy red-tape procedure. I was finished first and went ahead to the baggage claim area to collect our belongings.

By then everyone else on the flight had gone, so our bags, suitcases, and violin case were all together waiting for us. So was the customs inspector.

He was a pleasant guy and the inspection went smoothly, until we got to the violin case. "You've only got one instrument?" he asked, puzzled.

"We don't have any instruments," I said, thinking that would clarify things.

"What's in the case?"

"Props."

He looked intently at me, as if to measure my veracity. *"We'd better look at the props,"* he said.

The inspector didn't even notice the container of gunpowder we use for our *"exploding"* table. He paid no attention to the handcuffs and chains we use in our gangster routine. Then he came across the starting pistol. The thing hardly ever works and it's probably more trouble than it's worth, but we like to include it in the act just for appearance sake.

The casual manner of the customs man disappeared. He pointed with disdain at the pistol. *"What's this?"* he asked sternly.

"Oh, that's not a real gun," I said, trying to dispel his suspicions. The inspector picked it up cautiously. Then I added quickly, *"It doesn't shoot."* He pulled the trigger.

BOOM! It sounded like a war cannon had gone off.

What I meant to say was, *"It doesn't shoot real bullets,"* but by then it was a little too late to explain that. Echoes of the explosion bounded off all the walls and eardrums in the vicinity and there was a flurry of exclamations: *"Oh, my God!"* *"What the hell was that?"* *"Is anybody shot?"* There was also a call for the Mounted Police!

About that time Mike Myers and Tony Gross had finished their paperwork and had arrived on the scene. As the authorities gathered and the questioning began in earnest, the three of us joined in the explanation. Fred was the last one to be processed, and for some reason the seriousness of the situation eluded him. He thought the whole matter was hilarious! The police were angry enough with embarrassment, and then along came Fred ho-hoing and hee-heeing about the whole affair. It clearly was not a time for any ho-hos or hee-hees!

Finally order was restored and everyone regained composure. The gun was thoroughly examined and found, of course, to have a solid barrel rather than a shootable bore. Nevertheless, the Mounty made his pronouncement: *"We'll have to keep this here. You can claim it when you leave Sunday."*

On the trip back, Air Canada insisted on storing the *"weapon"* with the pilot, who apprehensively returned it to us when we deplaned in Boston.

The experience is now great fun to think about, but at the time it wasn't much fun at all, except for Albert Haverstock, our

*host, who had witnessed the episode from beginning to end
through big glass windows at the end of the customs area. Al is
no featherweight, and when we finally concluded our ordeal
and met, he was still shaking with laughter from head to toe!*

*Some months later we again traveled to Nova Scotia, this
time to sing on the Truro Chapter show. Fortunately, by then
even the customs agents were able to laugh about the matter.*

Something else unusual happened on that Halifax trip. It occurred
Sunday during the customs inspection in Boston on the way home.
Before I get into the details though, I need to mention that some
quartets have a set of travel uniforms for use both en route to shows
and at preglows, receptions, or other hospitality affairs. Other
quartets dress in mufti.

On our trip home from Halifax we were in mufti, and I was wearing
what I considered a very spiffy outfit: denim jeans with a patchwork
of leather pieces on each generously bell-bottomed pants leg, a
matching patchwork-leather vest, a textured-weave shirt, and a pair
of well-heeled shoes, a dapper outfit indeed!

Coming to the customs station, I watched as the people ahead of
me spoke briefly with the agents and were then allowed to pass
through. It was the end of a long and tiring, but thoroughly enjoyable
weekend, and I was anxious to get through the line and on the road
for the still-to-come five-hour drive home. Each of us in the quartet
had about three suitcases or carryables, and finally my turn came to
open the luggage for the inspectors.

Suddenly there were two agents at my side. "You'll have to come
with us," they said sternly. I had nothing to hide and I knew I was
guilty of no crime, but I wasn't particularly anxious to delay our progress home with a side trip to I didn't know where. However, it appeared I had no choice.

With my baggage under my arms I was escorted off. I looked back
anxiously at Pete, Mike, and Tony. They seemed only vaguely aware
of what was happening to me, and even less interested. Then I was
inside a small room. The door was closed. One agent left and another
appeared in his place.

First came the questions. What was my name? Where was I going? Where had I been? What had I been doing? What was in the suitcases? Did I have anything to declare? The exchange was conducted
at a pace which seemed to demand answers before the words or
thoughts had properly formed in my mind. I tried not to stumble over

my responses, but if the situation wasn't disconcerting enough, the weekend's activities had left me at other than my mental best for such an intellectual exercise.

Then it was a search of the luggage, along with more questions. Those questions were flying out at me like bullets from a machine gun. I wasn't at all pleased with the way things were going. I tried to explain that I was a member of a barbershop quartet, that we used lots of strange props when we sang our songs, that the chains, magic tricks, and other paraphernalia were part of our act. As it came out, the explanation didn't sound plausible even to me!

Finally it was a search of me. Off with the vest, the shirt, the pants, the shoes. Hey, I thought to myself, I'm a law-abiding citizen; this shouldn't be happening to me!

Then, as quickly as it all had started, it was over. I was back again with Pete, Mike, and Tony, all of whom reacted with much disinterest over my brush with the law.

Just as I was being released, I heard one agent exclaim to another, "I was sure we had a hot one that time. That getup was a dead giveaway." I don't think I've ever seen a drug smuggler before, but I guess I now know what one looks like!

For some reason I haven't worn that neat denim outfit very much since our trip from Nova Scotia. Come to think of it, I'm dressing more conservatively on all our quartet airplane flights, whether or not they cross international boundaries.

When some quartetters aren't unconsciously getting themselves into trouble, they're going out of their way to find some. It's guaranteed to turn an otherwise dull trip into an exciting one.

They don't give a trophy for the biggest trouble causers, but if they did, I bet the SALT FLATS would have won it, probably very early in their career. Carl Hancuff describes how to transform a simple stroll through an airline terminal into an action-packed melodrama:

> *We had sung a show in Oregon, and were at the Portland Airport en route back home. Milt Christensen had been involved in a real bad accident some time before, so one of the airlines put him in a wheelchair to get through the terminal. I was carrying his crutches.*
>
> *A person just doesn't carry crutches, so I started using them like I was fiercely crippled. I moved right along through the center of the terminal building. It was terribly busy. Out of the corner of my eye I saw Jimmy Wheeler coming toward me, and*

for some reason I knew exactly what he was going to do, so I was prepared. Jimmy kicked the crutches out from underneath me and muttered something about "damn cripple."

I'm pretty good at pretend falls, and I took the wildest spill you've ever seen. I smacked my hands on the tile floor when I hit and it sounded like a rifle going off. Just for realism I let out a mournful cry of distress.

We thought our practical joke was a good laugh, but a couple of passersby didn't. They started to lace right into Jimmy, so I jumped up quickly and explained we were conducting a psychology experiment. Those people were in a downright nasty mood and apparently didn't take too kindly to our prank.

It seems that no setting was too dull nor circumstance too doleful to keep the SALT FLATS from their appontment with foolishness. Carl Hancuff again:

The FLATS were notorious as practical jokers. We loved to do dumb things and pull crazy stunts. The only criterion, of course, was that nobody got hurt or embarrassed too badly.

We were in St. Louis once with an hour layover, so we went to the airport hot dog stand. I happened to get a little ahead of the other guys as we went through the line. They had those tall, round tables to stand at while you eat your hot dog or drink your coffee, but my table was filled when the rest of the quartet got through the line, so they went to another table. When I finished I noticed the place was a mess. Spilled food and cigarette butts, paper and napkins, mustard and catsup were all over everywhere. I started yelling across the room at the other three. "It's disgraceful!" I shouted. "Is this the way you live at home? Are you pigs there, too? Do you live in this kind of filth and then come in here and mess up my place?"

They took the cue and began picking everything up. Somebody turned to Dale Taylor, our baritone, and said, "For heaven's sake, who's that?"

"I don't know," Dale said. "Must be the boss, and boy, is he mad!" They cleaned off the table in a flash.

The funny part was that I made such a fuss, everybody leaped up and pitched in to clean, shine, and polish the place and I mean fast! The five girls behind the counter roared with delight. They gave me the okay signal because we got the whole hot dog stand cleaned up for them in a jiffy.

Even at 35,000 feet, that quartet was up to no good. Carl tells of some high-flying shenanigans:

> *We usually fly tourist, but found ourselves in first-class seats on a flight back from Canada. There weren't many people in the first-class section with us, so we thought we'd try an experiment. We wanted to find out if it was possible to get four grown adults into one of those tiny airplane johns. Those compartments are hardly big enough for one person, but we thought we'd give it a try.*
>
> *The arrangement was this: We'd go into the john one at a time, spaced sixty seconds apart. I went in first; Jimmy Wheeler was the last to squeeze in. We were scrunched up inside there like you wouldn't believe, but we had the door closed and locked. The experiment was a success!*
>
> *Then the door handle shook. One of the passengers wanted to use the facility. We quickly decided on a plan. We'd walk out, one minute apart, and we wouldn't laugh until we got back to our seats. As last in, Jimmy was first out. He closed the door and we locked it. Somebody tried the door again. Sixty seconds later Dale Taylor went out, slamming the door behind him. Again someone tried the door. Sixty seconds later Milt Christensen went out and the same thing happened. I waited a minute, popped open the door, and found a woman standing there with a most distressed expression on her face. "Where in the hell is everybody coming from?" she inquired.*
>
> *I looked her straight in the eye and with a dead-serious voice said, "The john's out on the wing."*

Earthbound rest-room facilities, too, are fair game for quartetting sport. Here's a story from Freddie King about the ORIOLE FOUR:

> *One time we got inside four separate pay toilets. We propped up our feet and let loose with a whole song. We could hear guys mumbling to themselves, "Where the hell is that sound coming from?" The next thing I knew a man's head appeared from underneath the door. I looked down at him straining to look up.*
>
> *"You guys having fun?" he asked.*
>
> *"Yeah!" I said.*

Quartetters who are not inclined to pull practical jokes on total strangers may wish to wait until they reach their destination before they try their tricks. That was a frequent ploy of the BOSTON COMMON, as Terry Clarke reveals:

I guess we're a little unique in the sense that we're so un-conventional. Each of us is pretty individualistic. We don't dress alike when we travel and we like to tease our hosts. When we get off a plane, one of us, usually Rich Knapp, will get lost in the crowd. Three of us will get off, find our host, and then stand and wait. He'll get fidgety after a bit and ask, "Well, where's the fourth?"

I'll look at the plane and say, "He should be in there somewhere. Say, why don't you check?" The poor guy will go aboard and check around and discover the plane is empty. When he comes out, we'll look at each other with puzzled ex-pressions. "Well, I don't understand that at all," I'll say. "He was with us when we got on. Did you check the john?" The poor guy will run back in to check. It's terrible what we do to our hosts.

Sometimes when we get off a plane all four of us will get lost in the crowd. It's easy to spot the host. He has a big barbershop badge hanging on his coat so we can find him, and when no noticeable foursome disembarks, he panics. We always have fun with that. For a while at least.

My quartet, the BROTHERHOOD, pulled that routine once when we flew into the National Airport at Washington, D.C. for a show. Jed Casey and his wife and a half dozen or so other barbershoppers had gathered at the terminal to meet us. Just inside the terminal gate I darted around a corner, up a flight of stairs, and out to the front of the building. Meanwhile, the other three guys were telling our hosts that my wife was ill, so I stayed home.

After fifteen minutes, I had walked all the way around to the park-ing lot. I circled back and jogged across the street to the main en-trance of the terminal, where the whole cortege of barbershoppers had gathered. "Gee, I'm glad I caught you," I said, out of breath. "My wife was better, so I drove. I was afraid I wouldn't get here in time."

I think we had everybody believing the story, briefly, until they figured out I couldn't have made the trip as claimed unless I averaged over a hundred miles an hour! It was a good joke, but it caused a little more worry than we wished. We haven't pulled it again.

When a quartet lands in a faraway place, it's a treat to receive a special welcome. If it's a whole welcoming committee, then a warm bond of friendship is quickly established. Jack Macgregor of the SOUNDSMEN was particularly impressed with the reception his quartet received on the longest trip they ever made for a barbershop show:

> *The trip was to Regina, Saskatchewan, about two hundred fifty miles north of Montana, and we had to travel two days just to get there, with an overnight stop in Toronto. We had written ahead to remind our host that we had eight bags of luggage and we suggested he not meet us with a Volkswagen!*
>
> *As usual, we sang a few songs on the plane, and when we started our descent to land, the stewardess asked if we'd mind waiting so we could sing a song for the captain. Of course we wouldn't mind.*
>
> *One of the Regina Chapter members was manager of the airport and had radioed to the plane to hold us on board until last. When we finally entered the waiting room, there was the entire Regina Chapter singing ''You're as Welcome as the Flowers in May.'' We were completely surprised and a little choked up, too. They asked us to sing a number, but it was tough to do after such a royal reception.*
>
> *Everybody pitched in to carry our multitude of bags and suitcases out to the street and what drove up to meet us but a Volkswagen! We were still laughing when a huge truck pulled up for our baggage. Then they really put the icing on the cake when a big, shiny Cadillac limousine stopped in front of us. It must have been a block long and was just for us!*
>
> *Regina is really in the middle of nowhere, but those barbershoppers made us feel far more welcome than the flowers in May. We felt we were among dear friends, and indeed we were. We had one of our most memorable shows in the gigantic two-thousand seat auditorium in the city's civic center.*

There are a million tales about airplane travels, but there are a lot of automobile stories, too. Bob Dykstra has a couple of good ones:

> *Back in the early days of the HUT FOUR, when we were sta-*

tioned at Fort Riley, Kansas, our mentor and very good friend
was Sam Cohen. When Sam heard about our quartet he took us
under his wing and taught us a lot about barbershopping. He
loved to woodshed, and I'll never forget the hours of singing we
did in his car while he drove us around to shows and contests in
the Central States District. We had no car ourselves, so Sam
graciously did all the driving in his.

We knew how fast or slow we were going because Sam
drove in accord with the tempo of the songs we sang. Sam sang
right along with us, usually on the lead part. If we were in a
hurry, we'd sing up-tempo songs, and he'd drive like the
dickens. Sometimes with a slow ballad we found our speed had
dropped to thirty miles an hour down the open highway. Sam
loved to sing.

I always get a kick thinking about what happened to John
Hansen, our bass. He used to drive a BMW, a funny little foreign
car that had the engine in the back, two big wheels in front, and
two little wheels in back spaced closer together, and it was the
weirdest looking contraption I'd ever seen. But in addition, the
door was the whole front part of the vehicle. The steering wheel
folded out of the way to let the driver in and out.

The HUT FOUR had a singing job in downtown Minneapolis
in the middle of the winter. At the time our uniform was a gay
nineties outfit, which John was wearing on the way to the performance, when he had a fender-bender accident on a slippery
street. Can you imagine the picture? It was the dead of winter.
John opened the front end of his ridiculous-looking vehicle and
stepped out in his garish plaid suit, skimmer hat, and spats. I
wonder if they ever got around to talk about the accident!

The trouble with driving to a show is that it seems endless. My
quartet is so familiar with the Massachusetts Turnpike, we know the
toll takers by first name. Well, not really, but it seems we've spent
months on that stretch of highway, going to shows in Maine, New
Hampshire, and Massachusetts. On the trips going, there's usually
spirited and interesting conversation, but on the trips back, there are
usually three guys sleeping and one wishing he were sleeping.

Jack Macgregor has a cure for those long-drive blues. Install a CB
radio:

We were having a typically uneventful drive en route to a barbershop show, until the CB spoke to us. It was a woman's voice: "Breaker-one-nine to that yellow Torino westbound on this Pennsy Pike. Is that a barbershop sign I saw on your four-wheeler?"

That started quite a conversation. We told her all about the quartet. We even switched to another channel and sang "Hello Cutie" for her. Nothing would do after that but to stop at the next rest station, exchange greetings in person, and sing another song. Our CB conversation must have lasted for ten miles or more.

Freddie King of the ORIOLE FOUR had another scheme his quartet used to while away those endless driving hours:

We got dreadfully bored with all the highway riding we did. Four guys sitting in a car for hours can get to be a real drag, so we invented a game called "Toy Car." You've seen those lithographed prints of automobiles with people riding in them. The people are always looking out the side windows. Even the driver looks out the side window, and that was our game.

On a four-lane superhighway I sat in the driver's seat and we cruised along in the right-hand lane. Bob Welzenbach sat on the passenger side and steered with his hand out of sight at the bottom of the steering wheel. Don Stratton and Jim Grant were in the back making ogling faces out the window. I did the same out the driver's window. We used to go whipping down the road like that and when people in the left lane saw us, they went bananas!

One time we put on the "Toy Car" routine for a whole carful of old ladies and I thought they were going to croak. They were bouncing up and down in their vehicle trying to figure out what was going on in ours. Twenty minutes later they zipped by and did the same thing to us! We laughed so hard I thought we were going to run off the highway!

The BOSTON COMMON has another solution for the monotony of long-distance driving. It's a very simple solution: Speed! Terry Clarke tells how he happened upon this clever denouement:

We were traveling in South Carolina in a rented car we had

> *driven from North Carolina, and we got no less than three speeding tickets along the way. I think Larry Tully got the first, Kent Martin the second, and Rich Knapp the third. In every case we were ticketed for driving just a few miles over the limit; for example, thirty miles an hour in a twenty-five-miles-per-hour zone.*
>
> *I got behind the wheel and floored it. We were bombing down the highway at ninety miles an hour and I said if we were going to get caught, we should really get caught.*
>
> *I was never stopped. We went straight through. The other guys were placing bets on how much the ticket would be, but for all the time I was driving, we never even saw a police car. It sure made the trip go quickly.*

It's rare to go out begging for an encounter with the law enforcers. Heaven knows, there are more than enough unintentional confrontations without actually soliciting more. The CLUB HOUSE FOUR had a real run-in with the police on that quartet's trip to a show in Pensacola, Florida. Tim Stivers has the details:

> *We were going to sing on a Saturday show, but the chapter invited us to come down Friday to join in a big party and oyster roast on the beach. A friend of the quartet and all of the wives accompanied us, so we were a crowd of ten people.*
>
> *A dentist from Pensacola met us at the airport. I think his name was Andrews, and he had made arrangements for us to use a brand new Toronado. It was a beautiful-looking automobile with a sign on the side that said: "Appearing at the Coliseum—The CLUB HOUSE FOUR, from Louisville, Kentucky." Joe Wise said he wanted to drive it, so he, Don Gramer, Schrader Miller, and their wives got in, and the rest of us piled in with the dentist, who led our caravan off to Pensacola.*
>
> *We weren't more than a few miles along the road when there was a siren and a revolving red light. We looked back and saw a state trooper had pulled Joe off the road. We stopped about fifty yards in front of him. The trooper got Joe out of the car. We could easily hear their raised voices, and I envisioned us spending the night in the Pensacola lockup.*
>
> *Then the dentist told me I was supposed to be in the Toronado and the whole thing was a gag. The policeman was a member of the Pensacola Chapter and a sergeant in the Florida*

*State Patrol. He had Joe out of the car and nearly at his wits'
end.*

"What did I do?" Joe asked innocently.

*"Boy," the trooper drawled, "come over here. Come on over
here, right in the middle of this road." Joe walked over to the
trooper who was pointing at the pavement. "Do you see this
line right here? Do you see this line running right down the middle of this road, boy?"*

"Yes, sir," Joe replied.

*"Now, I don't know what a line like this means where you
come from, but here in north Florida that there is a dividing line!
It's not a driving line, boy, it's a dividing line!" He took Joe off to
the side of the road and asked to see his driver's license. A few
moments later he said, "Well, I'm just going to have to take you
all in!"*

Everybody was frantic. "What for?" they wanted to know.

"Post bond," was the answer.

"How much is the bond?"

*The policeman looked over the group. "It's going to cost you
$150."*

*Everybody started digging into pockets and purses. Some-
one held up a twenty-dollar bill. Somebody else had a ten, and
our host, the dentist, walked over to the group and volunteered
to throw in the rest.*

*As the policeman turned to head back to his car, he spotted
the sign. "What's this on the side of the car," he said.*

*Joe proudly piped up, "Oh, we're a barbershop quartet, and
we're going to sing at the coliseum tomorrow night."*

*"Oh, a barbershopper, are you. I've heard of you-all."
Everybody was smiling again. The trooper looked stern. "Yeah,
you-all are the ones that come to town and raise all that hell!"
Joe sank right back down to street level.*

*Finally the big patrolman said, "Well, if you're some kind of a
quartet, let me hear you sing."*

*"But," Joe explained, "our bass is up there in that other car.
We'll have to get him."*

*"Now, wait a minute," the policeman said. "If you can sing,
you can sing! You've got three parts out of four. Let me hear
some music."*

*"Yes, sir," Joe replied. The three of them cleared their
throats and swallowed. Joe took out his pitch pipe. He was so*

nervous he could hardly blow it.

The trooper said, "Sing 'Let Me Call You Sweetheart.'"

So they started. And at just about the end of the first line, the cop joined in with his big, deep bass voice. Joe's expression changed from the depths of degradation to the heights of ecstasy. The four of them had joined in song and all was right with the world!

It was a most memorable weekend for us. We laughed until we nearly cried over our "arrest." The trooper gave us an escort into town and we had a great, great weekend. It was one of the funniest things that ever happened to the CLUB HOUSE FOUR.

Buzz Haeger related an almost identical story about his quartet's visit to Pensacola. Jim Foley was the driver of the car and got the treatment from the trooper, a fellow by the name of Casey Cason. After handing out a real tongue lashing, Casey said he wouldn't arrest Jim on one condition, that they sing "Bright Was the Night" together!

Those off-beat practical jokes can turn out to be a highlight of the weekend, if the show performances turn out to be pretty much routine. Sometimes the pranks are so elaborate that they rival the shows themselves for imagination and complexity. Of course when you toss together two zany madcaps like Carl Hancuff and Lloyd Steinkamp, you know almost anything can happen. Carl tells what did, on one occasion:

The SALT FLATS were going to sing on a show in Arcadia, California, I think it was, and Lloyd was going to be the MC. We had a plan to meet at the airport and the minute Lloyd got off the plane, we threw our grand production into action. A whole bunch of people were in on the act. We had a guy dressed as a cop, a woman holding a baby, and a cast of dozens. As soon as Lloyd walked into the lobby of the Los Angeles Airport, the woman screamed, "That's the man! That's the man! He's the one who fathered my child!"

Of course that caught Lloyd's attention and it also caught the attention of about two hundred travelers who were wandering around the terminal building. When the woman screamed, our cop ran over and grabbed Lloyd and put some handcuffs on him. Now, the SALT FLATS played the part of outraged brothers of the screaming lady, so we started yelling and ranting and raving. We finally made it absolutely clear that Lloyd had to marry the lady or we were going to bust open his head. He agreed to marry her.

A well-known West Coast barbershopper, Ron Pulone, was dressed up in an old preacher's outfit, with coattails, Bible, and all, so we proceeded with the wedding in the middle of the Los Angeles Airport. It was a beautiful ceremony. We threw rice at both of them. We had a bottle of champagne and a dozen and a half Dixie cups, so we all had a toast. The looks on the faces of the people walking by were just priceless! We even sold four tickets to the show that night!

All the fun-making is fine, but every now and then there's a schedule slipup and a trip to or from a show becomes a marathon race. I'm sure every quartetter has felt that empty feeling in the pit of his stomach when a flight is cancelled, or a car won't start, or a meeting time is misunderstood, and the odds of reaching the destination on schedule plummet. Panic and indigestion are the immediate short-term effects while exasperation and frustration may set in for hours or days thereafter.

Imagine the inner agony if, for example, you're scheduled to sing on a show but are tied up serving jury duty. It gets later and later and the trial drags on and on. That was what happened to Ken Hatton of the BLUEGRASS STUDENT UNION:

I was selected for jury duty in Louisville and the case ran for two weeks. Finally on Friday of the second week the case was turned over to us for deliberation, but I was worried because I had to be in Evansville, Indiana that evening to sing at a District Convention with my quartet. Our chorus was going to compete the following day and I sure didn't want any long, drawn-out deliberations.

The defendant in the case was accused of arson, and the way I told the story to the crowd in Evansville, this is what happened: We had eleven people on the jury voting "guilty," and only one guy voting "not guilty," but that "not guilty" vote was mine. We argued and discussed and talked about the evidence. Then I looked at the clock and decided I only had a couple of hours to get myself to Evansville, so I decided, well, the show must go on, so let's hang him! The crowd in Evansville thought that was pretty funny. Needless to say, it didn't really happen exactly as I described it.

Particularly bothersome on a show trip are the schedule misconnections caused by others. Frank Lanza describes the feeling:

> *Just Don Beinema and I were flying back to Boston after a show once, and we had a two-hour stopover at JFK Airport in New York City. We were sitting there kind of slumped over, trying to recover from the show and long night before, when a pilot-type guy came over to us. "Aren't you in the FOUR STATESMEN?" he asked. We said we were.*
>
> *He was a barbershopper from Long Island and invited us to join him in the pilot's lounge. He wanted to get a co-worker to sing a song with us, but couldn't find anyone willing. "Don't worry about your flight," he said. "You've got plenty of time." We started worrying anyway and ten minutes before the departure time we were really edgy.*
>
> *When the pilot realized the time had slipped away, he reassured us. "Don't worry about a thing. I'll get you on that plane if I have to turn it around on the runway!" At the departure gate everything was closed up, but the attendants let the pilot through and he chased and waved and beckoned to the plane's pilot to return. It was to no avail. The plane took off without us and we had to wait another four hours for the next flight.*

The only way to prevent such disasters is to leave plenty of spare time, like the MINIMUM DAILY REQUIREMENT did on one of their flights. Don Hewey describes the foolproof approach:

> *When our quartet was scheduled to sing on its first-ever "outer-island" show at the Maui Mall in Kahului, Maui, the plan was to fly over in the afternoon, do the one-hour show at 7:00 p.m., and return to Honolulu the same night. We decided to get there in plenty of time to enjoy a leisurely dinner before the show. For any of you who have visited our island paradise, you may have heard of the expression "Hawaiian time." That means any time at all is okay, so we wanted to leave lots of leeway in our schedule.*
>
> *We arrived at the airport at 3:20 p.m. Our flight departure*

time was 3:50. It was just a twenty-minute trip to Maui. However, after we checked in we saw our plane being towed to the hangar for repairs and we sang "I'm Going to Maui Tomorrow." The revised, anticipated departure time was 5:00 p.m., still a comfortable schedule for our 7:00 p.m. show.

We walked around the terminal for a while and sang a few songs in the lounge. We returned to the gate at 4:45. Still no plane. Another boarding time had been posted: 6:10. Panic!

Luckily we were able to get on another inter-island flight that was to depart at 5:15, but it had a stop on the island of Molokai en route. Our scheduled arrival time in Maui: 6:10. We got in line at the gate, sang a couple of songs as we waited, and were then notified the flight would be delayed at least thirty minutes. We didn't leave Honolulu until 5:55 for the eleven-minute hop to Molokai.

Molokai was beautiful, but we had to stay there longer than planned. It seems they couldn't retract the stairway back into the plane for takeoff. The pilot and co-pilot were outside kicking at it, trying to get the thing to work.

We were on our way again at 6:30. We decided to change into our show uniforms on the plane. The stewardesses were very helpful and moved passengers around so we could change behind a rear bulkhead without being seen, except by the lovely blonde who appeared when our tenor, Larry McCracken, was changing his pants. You should have seen the looks on their faces! Bass Dave Delzer was putting on his socks as the plane landed in Maui at 6:43, seventeen minutes before show time.

We found our transportation and departed from the airport at 6:51! Halfway to the mall we realized that our lead singer, John Higgins, had left his $450 camera under a seat in the plane. Our driver said he'd try to get it back. We arrived at the Maui Mall at 6:58, in time to hear the announcement that our quartet was stranded in Honolulu. We shouted our Aloha, the crowd applauded, and seconds later, on with the show!

We found out we were competing with the first big football game of the season, so the crowd wasn't too large, but it was enthusiastic. It was the first time a barbershop quartet had ever performed on Maui. Halfway through our show we got the high sign that the camera had not only been found, but had been delivered to the mall by airport security people.

Our performance ended at 8:00 p.m. and by 8:15 we were on

our way back to the airport for an 8:45 flight to Honolulu, the last one that night. At the terminal we sang for the good people who had retrieved John's camera. We sang a few more songs at the gate and then were told our flight would be delayed twenty minutes. Not again!

We left Maui on Hawaiian time, singing all the way, and landed back in Honolulu at 9:30. Realizing we hadn't eaten since noon, we headed for our favorite restaurant, where, with sustenance and a second wind, we sang for another hour, finishing off with a couple of fantastic tags in the underground parking garage at 1:30 a.m.

Before we had left Maui, we were booked for a return show in December. We all agreed that when the time came, just to be safe, we'd leave the day before for the twenty-minute flight!

There's always a last-ditch alternative when commercial flights are missed: the private, chartered airplane. You can choose the time, you can choose the destination, and you can pay dearly for that flexibility, but on occasion a chartered flight is the only possible alternative. Tom Schlinkert tells of one such occasion:

The ROARING 20's always seemed to have more than its share of missed planes and missed schedules. I think that while I sang with the quartet we missed a total of four flights, and at least one of those instances was noteworthy enough to relate. Our tenor, Donald Gray, was a systems analyst with Proctor and Gamble in Cincinnati and he had to work the night shift for a couple of months. That meant, of course, that he slept during the day. He lived alone in an apartment and had a housekeeper come in to clean up during the daytime, but he learned to sleep through the vacuuming. He did have trouble with telephone calls until he solved that one by taking the phone off the hook. I think you can see the plot developing.

One Friday afternoon we were supposed to catch a flight to Salisbury, Maryland for a Friday night and Saturday night show. Don went to sleep in the morning, as usual, and he set the alarm to get up in plenty of time to catch our afternoon plane. But now the twist. When the housekeeper did the vacuuming, she pulled out the electrical plug of the alarm clock and forgot to put it back. Don had a nice, long sleep.

The other three of us snuck away from work as we usually did for Friday evening shows, and went to the airport to meet Don. He wasn't there. We tried to call his apartment. The line was busy. We jumped in the car and raced twenty-two miles to his apartment. We pounded on the windows and doors and finally woke him up. He muttered and sputtered and mumbled, but by then our plane had taken off for Salisbury.

The local charter service said a plane was available to take us to Salisbury and we could get to the show on time if we got to the airport in forty-five minutes. Off we went. We met the pilot and quickly took to the air.

I had never flown in a small aircraft before. It was a six-seater, with only enough room to stuff our baggage and ourselves inside. I thought it was strange there was so much vibration, but figured that was just the way they were. A half hour out of Cincinnati the pilot radioed back to the tower. He said we were having engine problems. I wondered if we'd ever make it back in one piece. The plane was rattling like crazy. Nothing looked better than little Lunken Airport when we approached the runway and landed safely.

In the hangar the pilot opened a compartment on the side of the plane and started fooling around with the spark plugs. He found lead deposits had built up from the leaded gas. He scraped off the buildup with his pocket knife and in thirty minutes we were ready to go again. I wasn't so sure I wanted to give it another try, but there was no other way to get to Salisbury, so we piled back in the plane and took off.

We had the presence of mind to dress alike in the event that somebody lost our baggage on the commercial flight, but lost baggage was then the least of our worries. The pilot figured we wouldn't get to Salisbury until after the airport closed at 9:00 p.m. He radioed ahead and got in touch with a barbershopper's wife, who got word to her husband. He had the airport reopened for us and the runway was lit up like a Christmas tree when we flew in at 9:05. The show had started at eight. We jumped out of the plane into the barbershopper's car and took off for the auditorium. There we dashed up the back steps and ran backstage. "Ladies and gentlemen," the MC said, "from Cincinnati, the ROARING 20's!"

We went directly out onstage without any warm-up and did the show. Nothing to it!

It sounds as though all those frantic-panic-rush-rush stories have happy endings. Miraculously, the quartet makes it to the auditorium at the last possible instant, the singers dash onstage, and live happily ever after. There are those true fairy tales, but there are also those other grim tales of close-but-no-cigar races. Dick Johnson recalls such an experience.

When I was singing with the VARIETIES quartet, we were confronted with quite a problem. We were booked on the Dubuque show one weekend, but found, unfortunately, it was the same weekend our baritone, Bob Menter, was scheduled to direct his chorus in Sweet Adeline competition in St. Louis. We didn't want to renege on our commitment to Dubuque, and Bob couldn't let down his chorus, so we decided to do both.

We arranged for the chorus to compete first in the contest to give Bob enough time to change clothes, leap in his car, and drive to the airport where a chartered plane would fly him to Dubuque. Meanwhile, the three of us would drive to the Dubuque Airport where we would rendezvous at 6:00 p.m.

We were at the airport at six sharp. The weather began to close in. As we waited it got worse and worse, so we thought we'd go to the school auditorium and let the chapter know that three-fourths of us had arrived. It was eight o'clock and the show had begun when we got there. We had still heard nothing from Bob.

The show chairman kept switching around the script of the show, hoping our baritone would appear. Finally they put on the headline quartet, whose performance ended at quarter to ten. Still no Bob Menter. In true barbershop spirit we decided that the show must go on. The three of us walked out onstage and sang "Have You Ever Been Lonely." That was exactly how we felt and probably how we sounded, too. We had a lot of patter, told a lot of stories, and sang our regular show material, sans baritone. It was hilarious.

At the finale when we were introduced, we walked out from stage right and at that moment from stage left came the most bedraggled, dripping wet hunk of humanity we'd ever seen. It was Bob Menter in his old and soaked wool suit. He looked and smelled like a drowned rat. We bowed together, then three of us hauled our drowned rat offstage.

Bob said he made it to the charter plane on time, it took off without any trouble, and he had a beautiful flight until he was about twenty-five feet in the air. Then the weather turned to soup. He said it was so thick he couldn't even see the propeller on the front of the aircraft. He insisted that the pilot head for Dubuque anyway, but the airport was closed and the plane was diverted to Cedar Rapids, seventy miles away. Bob rented a car and drove to Dubuque, making the trip in about sixty minutes. Checking in at the airport, he was told to proceed directly to the high school, but he didn't know which one. He found there were five high schools in and around the city. On a wild-goose chase he found three schools locked tighter than a drum before he found us in the fourth.

To make amends to the chapter, we offered to go back to Dubuque the following year for no fee, just expenses. Since then, we've checked our show dates rather carefully.

Here's a story from Bill Conway about a PITTSBURGHERS' beat-the-clock experience:

We had one of the best times ever with the SCHMITT BROTHERS on a show in Sheboygan, Wisconsin, and it was a great afterglow, too. We didn't get to bed until 4:00 a.m. Since we had reservations on a flight out of Milwaukee at 11:15 the next morning, we figured we'd get up at 7:00, go to church at 7:30, get back to the hotel for breakfast, pack, and be ready to leave at 9:00. I thought Jiggs Ward had made arrangements for a seven o'clock wake-up call. Unfortunately, he thought I had scheduled the call.

When the phone rang, I awoke with a start. It was already 9:00 and our host was waiting for us in the lobby. You never saw such a scramble. Our host brought coffee and we dressed, packed, and drank coffee still half asleep. We checked out at 9:30. It was a seventy-mile drive to Milwaukee, then a twelve-mile drive through the city to the airport.

Tearing along the highway as fast as the previous night's six-inch snow allowed, we counted the miles and the minutes going by, when we came to a railroad crossing of the Pere Marquette. We skidded to a stop and watched helplessly as a train of a hundred cars blocked our path. Worse yet, the train wasn't moving! We had to catch our flight to make a singing engagement at the William Penn Hotel in Pittsburgh that night, but we thought that train was going to be our Waterloo!

A state police car pulled up behind us and we told the troopers of our trouble. We even told the train conductor, who was walking nonchalantly along the track. He said it wouldn't be much longer; we'd have to wait until he got back to the caboose. When the train had cleared the crossing, we had lost fifteen valuable minutes. The state policemen went ahead to lead the way, but could only take us as far as the Milwaukee City line. Inside the city limits was outside state police jurisdiction. Thoughtfully, though, the troopers had radioed ahead and the city police met us and escorted us across town. They also radioed the airline to hold the flight.

We didn't go into the terminal building at all. Our police escort led us right out onto the runway. The plane's engines were running and it was all ready to take off. Attendants grabbed our luggage and we scrambled aboard. The flight was then fifteen minutes late.

As soon as we were airborne, the stewardess announced to the passengers the cause of their delay, and to thank everyone for their patience, we put on a short in-flight show.

We had an awful lot of people to thank for helping us catch that plane. Fortunately, once we got to Pittsburgh, we had plenty of time to catch our breath and calm down our knotted stomachs!

It's neat that so many people will go so far out of their way to help a quartet get to a show. After all, barbershopping isn't exactly a life-and-death matter, but people sometimes seem willing to jump through hoops if it would help get some singers onstage. Here's Buzz Haeger's you're-late-for-a-very-important-date story about the FOUR RENEGADES:

We were asked to sing on a Friday night Salt Lake City show, but three of us couldn't leave work until 5:00 p.m. We planned to make a beeline for the airport, jump on a commercial flight to Denver, make an immediate connection to another airplane, fly to Salt Lake City, and dash in for the show. We knew it would be tight, so we changed into our World War I outfits in the rest room at the back of the airplane on the flight from Denver. One by one we went traipsing down the aisle in our uniforms, with our wrapped puttees and metal helmets and everything. The other passengers must have thought we were nuts. Maybe we were.

When we got to Salt Lake City, they had a police car waiting for us at the airport. All the side streets were blocked off through the center of town and our squad car raced along like a rocket ship. I think we're the only four guys who ever went through the center of Salt Lake City at ninety-five miles per hour, and I'm telling you that was a hair-raising experience! When we got to the auditorium we ran backstage and out into the spotlight to do our show.

If it seems that fate is always throwing up roadblocks for a quartet racing to a show, listen to the story Harlan Wilson tells about a SUN-TONES trip. Although it appeared that fate was fouling up matters all along the way, in fact it withheld a disaster:

To sing on the show sponsored by the Montevideo, Minnesota Chapter, we had to fly into Minneapolis and then drive a hundred twenty-five miles almost to the other side of the state to get to the auditorium. We were behind schedule, it was snowing like mad in Minnesota, flights were delayed, and our plane landed late, about six o'clock. The show started at 8:00. Our host met us with a ten-year-old Cadillac that looked like it wasn't going to make it out of the parking lot.

Heavy, thick snowflakes were falling and we couldn't see anything except high white walls on either side of the road. The banks must have been five feet deep, and the Cadillac didn't appear up to the challenge.

After a grueling drive at very high speeds, we reached the town of Montevideo safe and sound. When we arrived at the auditorium, almost as if that were a cue, the left rear tire on the car went flat as a pancake. If it had given way any time before, we undoubtedly would have missed the show.

That trip to Montevideo has been a tough one for more than one invited quartet. Dick Johnson's foursome, the VARIETIES, was plagued with a whole sad string of problems, weather just one among them:

When our bid to sing on the January Montevideo show was accepted, we were delighted. We knew it would be an exciting barbershop weekend and we looked forward to it for months.

Days before the show, however, our baritone, Bob Menter, suf-
fered a severe back problem, and his doctor refused to let him
travel. We had to call and cancel. I think a substitute quartet
was found, thank goodness, but we were awfully disappointed
to miss the performance.

A few years later, we were again asked to sing on the
Montevideo show. As the date neared, we were all super-
cautious so we wouldn't have any back troubles, colds, or other
maladies that might prevent our singing on the program. Then
we were hit with the worst blizzard in Chicago's history. It was
the first time ever that O'Hare International Airport had to be
closed down. I had four feet of snow on my front porch! None of
us could move, thousands of motorists were stranded, the en-
tire Midwest was paralyzed, and we had to call again and
cancel. Strike two. The chapter was able to get the GOLDEN
STATERS to fly in from Los Angeles and sing the show, but we
were unable to get there from Chicago.

You can imagine our surprise when we got a third invitation
to sing on the Montevideo show. We were then the CHORDS
UNLIMITED and we were bound and determined to make it
there, come hell or high water.

Three of us flew from Chicago to Minneapolis where we met
our fourth, John Erickson, who was visiting his folks. For the
long ride west, we three rode in a rented car, while John fol-
lowed with his parents in their car.

The first few flakes of snow didn't bother us. But then shortly
it was a flurry. Soon it was a full-fledged storm. Then it was an
arctic blizzard! The snow got thicker and deeper as we drove
and it wasn't long before we got a frantic horn-beeping, light-
flashing signal from behind us. John said his parents' car
couldn't make it through the blowing wind and snow. They
turned around and headed back to Minneapolis. John got in
with us and off we went into the white.

The weather was incredible. We found a maintenance crew
along the highway. They said the authorities were about to
close the road and unless we had just a short distance to go,
we'd have to turn back. We told them we had to go all the way
to Montevideo, but no, we weren't turning back! No strike three
for us! We had to make it to Montevideo! They said we didn't
have a chance.

We drove on and the storm was the most horrendous blizzard

I've ever seen. It was as if somebody had poured white paint on the windshield. We couldn't see a thing. The four of us had our noses glued to the windows. All we could see was the faint silhouettes of utility poles on either side of the road.

At every intersection the snow had drifted into towering mountains blocking both lanes of the thoroughfare. At the first big drift, Bob got out of the car to appraise the situation. Then he got back in, revved the engine, and bashed his way through. At the next drift he got a little braver. After a while we were smashing through snow drifts without even slowing down. I kept hoping there wasn't a snowplow on the other side!

We kept going but the conditions got worse and worse. It was dreadfully cold, the windows were all fogged up, and we were shivering and worried, but we managed to make it to the out- skirts of Montevideo just as it began to get dark. There I saw a sight I'll never forget. The sheriff, state troopers, volunteers, and the Civil Defense were all out in their parkas and heavy boots and gloves. Barricades were up, red lights were flashing in the snow, and they were stopping all traffic trying to leave the city. Everyone had to turn around and go back home. The road was closed. I'll never forget the look of astonishment as they glanced over their shoulders and saw our snow-laden Dodge coming into town. Our vehicle had made it through the blizzard with four bleary-eyed, rosy-cheeked, exhausted men inside.

We went to our motel, registered, and collapsed. George Peters called our host and proudly announced that the CHORDS UNLIMITED had arrived!

"Nice to have you here," he said, "but, unfortunately, the show has been cancelled. The weather is so bad, nobody can get to the auditorium. People aren't even allowed out on the highway."

Actually, the show wasn't cancelled, merely postponed until the following day when the DEALER'S CHOICE made it to Montevideo (after some trials and tribulations of their own), and we had ourselves one heck of a good time together!

Oh, those happy-go-lucky trips to barbershop shows. Why is it that a simple plane ride or automobile drive can turn into such a monumental expedition for a quartet? I think it's often the barber- shoppers themselves who change the ordinary into the bizarre, the commonplace into the catastrophe, and the routine into the utterly ridiculous. As Terry Clarke once remarked, "When you all meet at the airport you're transformed into kids again." Every experience becomes a grand game. Every opportunity for fun becomes an encounter with joy. Every moment of laughter becomes a glorious moment of shared delight.

Take the NOTE-WITS, for example. All they have to do is pick up their belongings at an airport baggage claim area and presto, instant comedy. Fred Steinkamp narrates the episode:

Our lead, Dick DeVany, likes to be as efficient as possible. For an overnight stay, three of us will take a garment bag plus small traveling case for shaving needs, pajamas, underwear, and so forth. Dick sees this as rather inefficient and simply stuffs everything into his garment carrier. When you consider that we have three changes of costume for our performances, you can appreciate that the garment carriers are crammed to begin with. Then if you knew how flimsy Dick's case was, you could guess what happened on one of our trips, a flight to Canada to sing on the Montreal Chapter show.

We had sixteen pieces of luggage with us on that trip, our own plus those of our wives, who accompanied us. When we got to the baggage claim area, the luggage was being spewed out of the chute onto a carrousel. I'm sure you've seen the machines that do that. We watched and waited and picked off our belongings one by one. Dick looked for his bag in vain. We watched and waited, but Dick's garment carrier did not make an appearance.

Then the machine began to spit out a whole assortment of small items: some underwear, socks with holes in them, a torn shirt, a toothbrush, a shaver, a whole shower of personal items floated down. They all belonged to Dick. He jumped on the carrousel to retrieve his things and looked like Sir Edmund Hillary ascending the Matterhorn! He stuffed his scattered belongings into his coat pockets, while the rest of us watched and giggled with glee.

We finally got ourselves together and went outside to find our host. We expected a van or bus or maybe a caravan of cars to carry everything, but our host had a meager two-door Plymouth. We loaded all of our belongings into the vehicle and squeezed ourselves in, too, for the drive to Montreal.

One of the best-known and most highly respected sayings in the entertainment business is "The show must go on," and many of the quartet stories you've now read stand as brave testimony to that rule. Barbershop performers overcome great odds at times to abide by it. Their dedication and commitment to their audiences and the chapters that hire them are legendary. Only rarely will a turn of events cause a quartet to miss a performance. Buzz Haeger describes such a turn of events:

When the FOUR RENEGADES were hired to sing in Altoona, Pennsylvania, we prevailed upon a good friend of mine, Irv Seren, to fly us there for the show. At the time I was not instrument-rated and the weather demanded an experienced pilot. There were heavy clouds and lots of rain. When we got near Pittsburgh, we received an unusual radio message from air traffic control: "How would you guys like to save two lives?"

Visibility in Altoona was down to zero, so we knew we'd have to land somewhere else, rent a car, and speed over to do the show. We also knew we were already behind schedule, but you don't turn down a request like that!

We were told a single-engine airplane was in trouble. It was flying at 11,000 feet, on top of the clouds in bright sunshine, but the pilot didn't know how to get the craft down through the heavy cloud cover. The Pittsburgh controller had the other plane and ours on radar, and he directed us to head west toward Ohio. We climbed up into the sunshine and in a short time made visual and radio contact with the plane in distress. Irv instructed the nervous pilot how to get down through the clouds, and we led the way, making an oval descent pattern. Irv talked the pilot all the way down, until we could see the outer marker at the Akron-Canton Airport. When the other pilot saw the runway, he made a beeline for it.

It was raining lightly as he landed. We landed behind him. He was instructed to turn off at the first taxi strip, but the guy was flustered and turned back out on the runway in front of us. We had to zigzag on the wet pavement to miss him and we lost control, ran off the runway, down an embankment, and into a fence. The other pilot pulled off the runway onto the taxi strip and right then and there ran out of gas! He couldn't even get his plane to the terminal.

With a broken propeller and the delay, we obviously couldn't

make the show, so we phoned the Altoona Chapter and ex-
plained what happened. Then with nothing better to do for the
evening, we sang a show of our own in the airport restaurant.
Everybody there had a ball, except the pilot of the other plane.
He was an airplane dealer from Canada on a return flight from
Memphis with a customer. His license was revoked, but I guess
he was lucky to be alive.

The following year the Altoona Chapter again asked us to
sing on their show. On that occasion we flew in my airplane, the
weather was great, I piloted, and we had a great show!

A quartet goes for the show, for the singing, and for the barbershop fraternity, but it's not infrequent that the trip to the show is half
the fun. It's also not infrequent that the trip is all the grief!

Before, Between, and After the Shows

Your quartet has been invited to sing on a two-night barbershop
show in West Overshoe, Montana. You get there on time for the Friday night performance, the show goes well, there's a small party
afterward, then it's to bed. Now it's Saturday morning. You get up at
10:15, get dressed, and have breakfast. Then what? The Saturday
night show isn't until eight. You've got a whole day to kill. What is
there to do to while away the hours in West Overshoe, Montana?

Well, that usually isn't a problem, because one or more chapter
members volunteer to host your quartet, and you spend a pleasant
day sightseeing, playing golf or tennis, attending parties, or engaging
in whatever other activities may present themselves.

I look back on many happy memories of experiences between
shows, of delightful dinners before shows, and even of pleasant
times with gracious hosts after shows. A BROTHERHOOD trip to sing
on the Greater Canaveral Chapter two-night show at Cocoa Beach,
Florida comes to mind. We were hosted handsomely! During the day
Saturday, Tim Hanrahan gave us a grand guided tour of the Space
Center at Cape Canaveral, and on Sunday before our flight home,
Tom Cecil invited us to join him for a sail on the Banana River. What a
weekend! With hosting like that and barbershop singing too, none of
us wanted to leave, particularly when we had to return to New York's
mid-March snow and cold!

I'll never forget the super hosting we received in Pasadena,

California, or our "big splash" canoe trip down the Little Miami River near Hillsboro, Ohio, or our Opryland visit in Nashville, or the parties in Alexandria, Virginia, or the countless kindnesses during North-eastern District show weekends. We are indebted to many gracious hosts for much thoughtfulness and hospitality.

Barbershoppers bend over backward to make a singer's stay pleasant. They loan you their cars, feed you feasts, and treat you to their finest tourist attractions. While the kindness is always appreciated, every now and then the results fall a little short of expectations. Carl Hancuff recalls the good intentions of a Hawaiian host:

The SALT FLATS quartet was booked in Hawaii twice, and on one occasion our hosts took us deep-sea fishing. It sounded like a great idea, but it didn't exactly turn out that way. First of all the boat bounced up and down like a cork. It was bouncing in three different directions at the same time. Secondly, we weren't getting a single nibble on the end of our fishing lines. Finally, we were so drugged with Dramamine, we really didn't care if we caught a fish or not!

Our guide put out eight lines for us, and hooked them to clothespins clamped to the side of the boat. If a fish pulled a line, the clothespin would break, a bell would ring, and the action would begin. We numbered the clothespins so we knew whose line was whose and we waited. We bounced and we waited. For hours we bounced and waited. It got so boring our tenor, Jim Wheeler, decided to cop out and go to sleep.

We thought we'd have to do something to get some action, so we reeled in one of the lines, tied a red bucket to it, and let it out again. On cue, the pilot revved the motor, the boat speeded up, the clothespin popped off, the bell rang, and we all jumped up and yelled. "Jim, come on! You've got a fish! Gosh, it's a big one! Hurry up!" We strapped him in the seat and got his fishing pole attached. He was still drowsy. He didn't realize it was the boat's speed that prevented him from pulling in the line. His eyes were as big as silver dollars. He thought he was wrestling with ten tons of whale.

Slowly it began to dawn on him. He turned around and issued a real classic of a statement: "Gentlemen," he declared, "if there's a fish on my line, it's on this end!" We presented him with the only good catch of our trip, what we called the "Red Buckette," a very rare fish, indeed!

I doubt that Carl Hancuff's quartet ever needed much hosting. They obviously were well able to entertain themselves:

> *One time we tried to incorporate the use of a fake arm into our act. It was one of those rubber hands that goes up about as far as the elbow. It was terribly realistic. We had lots of fun taking that thing with us.*
>
> *Sometimes getting off a plane, I'd wear the thing and it would cause my right arm to hang down about eight inches below my left. I'd keep a straight face and walk a few paces in front of the rest of the quartet. They would check out the expressions on the people's faces and would explain that I had just won a national bowling championship.*
>
> *In our hotel room once, we piled up the covers and pillows in a heap, like there was somebody sleeping in the bed, and we stuck the arm out with a half-burned cigarette in it. As people came in to visit, we talked in hushed tones. They whispered politely, too, but never asked who was asleep.*
>
> *The funniest thing we did with the arm was stick it down the toilet in the hotel room so only the hand showed. We put the lid down and placed a note between the fingers. It said "Help!" Then we left. I understand the maid nearly had a stroke on that one!*

Even poor accommodations couldn't dim the spirits of the mischievous SALT FLATS. Carl Hancuff again:

> *We were singing in California, I don't remember where, on a Friday-Saturday, two-night show. I think our host's brother-in-law must have been the guy who ran the motel where we stayed because it was an A-number-one flophouse. Actually, the motel consisted of a bunch of cheap mobile homes strung out in a row, and they were bad! But we take the accommodations we're given.*
>
> *Saturday morning I was up early, feeling good. I showered and got dressed. Half the quartet was in one trailer, the other half in another, so I decided to pull a trick on the other two guys. I noticed the windows didn't have locks on them, so I quietly tiptoed next door, put my hand on the window, opened it quickly, stuck my head in, and yelled "BOO!" at the top of my lungs.*
>
> *It seems I had forgotten that the other two guys weren't next*

door at all. Instead, a man and woman were in there, and fortunately they were just sleeping. But when I shouted "Boo!" the woman shot out of bed with the most ear-splitting scream I'd ever heard.

When I realized what I'd done, all I could think of to say was "Oh, God, I'm sorry! Oh, God, am I sorry! Oh, God! I am sorry!" By then the other three guys in the quartet were awake, and when they saw what happened, the rats locked the doors and wouldn't let me back in! I was sure that nine feet of madman was going to charge out of the trailer and rip me to shreds, but he didn't. Maybe he was too scared. On the other hand, maybe he had a heart attack and expired on the spot. After I had paid dearly in embarrassment, the guys finally let me back inside.

When a couple of guest quartets are invited to sing on the same show, then there's a chance for double the tomfoolery. Carl Hancuff describes what can happen:

We've always admired and respected the WESTERN CONTINENTALS and had a lot of fun with them. Their beautiful singing and our hell-raising made a good combination and we found ourselves on a lot of shows together. We pulled tricks on each other and thoroughly enjoyed each other's company.

Both quartets were staying at the Westerner Motel in Arcadia, California for a two-night show, and on Saturday afternoon we were relaxing, recuperating from the previous night's festivities. Our baritone, Dale Taylor, and I decided to take a little snooze. We stripped down to our Jockey shorts, climbed in our beds, and were on the edge of unconsciousness, when I heard a key slip into the lock on our door. The room was dark and the covers were pulled over my head, but I could open one eye and see what was going on. The door opened slowly, and there was Paul Graham, baritone of the WESTERN CONTINENTALS. He was pulling a green garden hose into the room. It didn't take me long to figure out what was going to happen. On a given signal somebody was going to turn on the water and we were in for a drenching!

You've got to bear in mind that Paul is a fastidious dresser. He and his wife run a beauty salon and he knows everything there is to know about good appearance. He has fine clothes, knows how to wear them, and his hair always looks beautiful.

I just lay there as Paul cautiously dragged in the hose and got it ready. He's going to yell, I thought to myself, and somebody's going to turn on the water, but the water won't come out immediately. It takes a while to travel the length of the hose. I remained absolutely still. Soon he had the hose pointed straight at me.

Paul let out a blood-curdling scream and I knew the water was on its way. I leaped out of bed and grabbed at the hose. I'm bigger than he is and I caught him completely by surprise. I yanked the hose out of his hands, swung it around, and aimed it at him.

The expression on Paul's face changed from fiendish glee to utter horror. "No, no, no!" he shouted, as he backed up into the closet. Yes, yes, yes, I thought to myself, you started this. The water came out in a heavy stream, and I nearly drowned the son of a gun, pure silk shirt and all!

In addition to all the silliness before, between, and after barbershop shows, there are also occasional crises. Word can come from home about an accident, death, or other disaster, and a quartet is severely tested with the "show must go on" principle. Here's another story from Carl Hancuff:

We were in Stockton, California for a show, and Dale Taylor and I were lying in our beds watching television in our motel room when the phone rang. It was my wife, Mitzi, calling from Salt Lake City. She asked if Dale was with me. He was. "Don't let him know it's me," she said. "Pretend I'm your brother calling." I made our conversation sound accordingly.

"Don't let on," Mitzi continued, "but they have just taken Danny to the hospital. He's very ill and the doctors are trying to diagnose it. They think it might be spinal meningitis. They'll know definitely in about two hours and I'll call back then." Danny is Dale's son.

I continued with my put-on conversation for a few minutes longer and then hung up. I let a few more minutes go by and told Dale I thought I'd see what the other guys were doing. I raced over to tell them the sad news.

We knew we had to complete the show. It's corny and trite, but the show must go on. We had to worry about getting an earlier flight home, though, and we wondered if we should ask the chapter to excuse us from singing at the afterglow. We tried to find a flight out at midnight or thereabouts, but could get nothing. We knew that once we told Dale, he'd probably go to pieces, so we thought we'd better get some food in him. He wasn't hungry. We insisted.

Table service was extremely slow, and we weren't halfway through the meal when the phone call came. It was spinal meningitis.

The four of us excused ourselves from our hosts and went back to the room. We all cried. There was nothing that could be said. We stood in a circle facing one another, with our arms around each other, and we prayed. We each said a part of the prayer. We each shared in the tragedy and sorrow.

After the show Dale had to suffer through the rest of the night, because the earliest flight wasn't until six in the morning. The story has a happy ending, though, because Danny recovered one hundred percent, with no permanent effects. The doctors said such complete recovery was rare, only possible because the disease was detected early.

Those kind of experiences make a bond among four guys in a quartet that in many cases is even stronger than family ties. You know so much about each other and understand each other so intimately. Over a period of years an internal quartet love emerges and matures. It's very close. It's very beautiful and warm. It's probably the most precious treasure you can derive from a quartetting relationship.

A quartet works together, plays together, gets itself in and out of trouble together, and with a common bond of four-part harmony, develops a unique oneness. Four personalities, often wildly diverse personalities, merge to create and assume the identity of a single entity, the barbershop quartet.

After a while, the group almost thinks as a unit. On stage and off, each member responds to the thought process of the others. It's an interesting phenomenon to experience. Let me give you an illustration:

My quartet, the BROTHERHOOD, had just arrived in Utica, New York for a barbershop show and were checking in at the Holiday Inn. There was a little confusion at the registration desk because a drunk was causing trouble in the restaurant and the clerk had to call the police. Moments later the men in blue arrived. We were still signing in and getting our keys. Two big cops shoved open the front doors and glanced quickly about the lobby. One with a nightstick in hand walked slowly toward us at the desk.

It was like a carefully rehearsed routine, though it was completely spontaneous. Mike Myers, Pete Donatelli, and I all together motioned toward bass Tony Gross and said, "There he is, officer. He's the one you want!" The police closed in.

You should have seen the expression on Tony's face. His eyes were large with disbelief at our betrayal and he was uncharacteristically speechless. Unfortunately, we weren't able to keep our composure and we burst into laughter. Realizing that our identification was in jest, the police pressed on to attend to the drunk. I don't think Tony was particularly amused, but the rest of us have chuckled over the incident ever since and we've marveled at the unanimity and timing of our mutual inspiration.

Yes, it's a lesson in togetherness. Quartetters travel, perform, rehearse, eat, and even sleep together. Now, there's an interesting topic. Good sleep-in stories abound, but the one I like best comes from Pete Donatelli:

> *As was our custom to save expenses, we FREE LANCERS had a single motel room with two double beds for one of our overnight stays. Nelson Lawhon and Vern Leonard slept in one bed, Bob Seay and I slept in the other.*
>
> *Sunday morning, after a long evening of show, afterglow, and after-afterglow, Vernon and Nels got up early and went to breakfast, leaving Bob and me fast asleep in bed. Neither of us heard the maid's knock on the door. With no answer, she unlocked the door and entered the room. Just then Bob and I awoke suddenly.*
>
> *The maid looked piercingly at the other bed, with its covers tossed aside. She frowned, then glared at us. "You ought to be ashamed of yourselves!" she snipped, and stormed out of the room in a huff. It was a few moments before we were able to get our thoughts together enough to figure out what she was talking about!*

For popular quartets, one of the side benefits of singing on shows is the chance to travel to new and interesting places and dine at some pretty super restaurants. A dining experience can be a particularly pleasant part of a singing weekend's festivities. I believe it was Jon Lowe of the SUSSEX COUNTS who told me it wasn't unusual for his quartet to spend the better part of their singing fee on meals. I understand they frequently forked out more than a hundred bucks for a single dinner, and apparently many quartets enjoy making a meal into a gourmet feast!

Such events not only please the palate, they also offer more opportunities for practical jokes. Here's a great dinner tale from Carl Hancuff:

> *We were in Eugene, Oregon for a show, and we stayed at a beautiful hotel which had a fantastic restaurant. We were eating there and noticed a big-name opera star seated three or four tables away. While he waited for his entree, Milt Christensen started singing the first line from the song "The Sound of Music." At the end of the line, when he reached the last word, he purposely sang flat, about a half note. We saw the opera guy's head jerk. It clearly irritated him, but he just sat there. Milt sang it again and he flatted again. This time the opera star turned around and looked at us.*
>
> *When Milt did it a third time it was too much for the opera singer. He came over to our table and introduced himself to all of us. Then he looked Milt straight in the eye. "Sir," he said, "I want to compliment you on your terrific singing voice, beautiful quality, great tone, but..." He paused. "That last note..." He frowned. "You're flatting ever so slightly."*
>
> *Milt registered surprise and embarrassment and volunteered to try it again. This time he sang the last note sharp, and the opera star was exasperated. Milt quickly tried it once more and sang it just right. The guy was first pleased, then apologetic. He said he hoped he hadn't embarrassed Milt and he politely excused himself and returned to his table.*
>
> *Before we left, we walked over and burst into a big, beautiful four-part barbershop song. The opera singer realized he'd been taken, and he laughed harder than anybody else in the place. He was a super nice guy about our practical joke.*

Not all between-the-show experiences are jokes, laughter, and gaiety. Buzz Haeger describes a most sobering moment when the FOUR RENEGADES ran into some real danger:

We had a most memorable trip to Guantanamo, Cuba, to sing for the sailors and marines stationed there. The show was a success and we even got a grand tour of the Guantanamo base. There's a big fence around the military installation with guard houses along it and we felt like we were in a prison. When our lead, Ben Williams, walked over toward the fence for a better view of the terrain beyond, one of the military men hollered at him, "Stop where you are!"

Ben stopped and the fellow barked another order. "Turn around very slowly and face me, but don't take another step." Ben did as directed. "You're in the middle of a mine field," the sergeant told him, "so if you don't want to get yourself blown to pieces, follow my directions exactly!" He managed to get Ben out of the mine field, and our hearts out of our throats!

I mentioned the importance of hosting earlier, how it can make a quartet feel welcome, how it can buoy up a quartet's spirits after a long or difficult trip, how it can even make a difference in a quartet's performance. I guess like most performers, quartetters are sensitive, creative creatures, and warm, friendly, supportive hosting can help a lot to elicit a peak performance on stage.

By good hosting I don't mean fancy or expensive parties, big dinner feasts, or other social extravaganzas to treat a guest quartet like visiting royalty, although such gestures might be appreciated and enjoyed. Rather, I mean letting the guest quartet know it's welcome, that it's something special. Sometimes good hosting may be letting a quartet alone to rest up after a tough trip. Sometimes it may indeed be going out to a restaurant for a good meal. Sometimes it may be a preglow party at a chapter member's home where the singers can meet local barbershoppers, get comfortable, and perhaps sing some songs. I think the best hosting is simply being sensitive and responsive to a quartet's needs.

The quartets I've sung in have enjoyed some pretty grand hosting over the years. I must in all honesty add that we've also run into some rather rotten hospitality at times, but sour experiences are only infrequently found. The general rule is warm hospitality, like that offered by Jed Casey and his wife. As Jed will tell you, the hosting game can be great sport, too:

We considered ourselves lucky years ago to be able to contract the services of a young quartet from Miami. The group wasn't well known at the time although it had competed in a couple of International quartet contests. We booked them in Philadelphia just before the International contest there, and darned if those guys didn't win it! We got ourselves the SUN-TONES at a bargain price.

We've become good friends with them over the years and have had them on our Fairfax show four or five times. When they first came to sing on our show we had a dinner party for them. Actually, it was an afternoon-brunch type of affair at about 4:00 p.m. My wife had made a large sheet cake with frosting and beautiful decorations, and it said "Welcome SUN-TONES." There was only one thing unusual about it. The cake was made out of wood. We had nailed three one-by-sixes together and had frosted it!

Bob Franklin, SUNTONES lead, won the honor of cake cutter, and he commented at great length about how beautiful it was. Then with grand ceremony he proceeded to try to cut into it. You can imagine his surprise when the sheet cake first seemed just tough, and then turned out to be Georgian pine! There were lots of pictures taken, a lot of laughter and hilarity, and Bob made reference to it on both the show and afterglow.

The next year, close to show time, the Fairfax Jubil-Aires received a case of oranges from the SUNTONES. It was sent as thanks for having the quartet on the previous year's show. We all thought it was a wonderfully thoughtful gesture. One of the chapter members was munching on an orange as he carried the case into our rehearsal meeting. It looked juicy and tasty. The crate was addressed to me, so I opened it. The oranges weren't juicy or tasty at all. They were plaster! The next time we saw the SUNTONES we ribbed them about their one-upmanship.

Years later we again had the SUNTONES on our show, and just for the occasion, my wife made another sheet cake. When the SUNTONES arrived in the afternoon, we told them we had a special dessert treat for them. They were naturally suspicious, so we took them out to the kitchen and showed them the cake. We let them stick a toothpick in it, taste the frosting, even stick their fingers down in the cake. No doubt about it, it was a real cake!

After dinner when it was cake-cutting time, we made a switch. We substituted an identical copy, which, of course, was constructed of solid Georgian pine. Bob Franklin took the knife, everybody got their cameras ready, and sure enough, he did it all over again! It was another "gotcha" on Bob. We had quite a time with the SUNTONES.

We were able to give them a real send-off the first time they flew to Fairfax for our show. By coincidence one of the secretaries where I work was heading for Miami for vacation on the same day so she was at the Miami airport when the SUN-TONES got there to catch their flight. The secretary wore a "good luck" banner over her shoulder and gave them each a carnation. The quartet said it was the finest send-off they ever received.

That year we instituted a program we've used ever since. We sent flowers to the wives of the SUNTONES to thank them for allowing us to make them husbandless for the weekend. We wanted them to know we appreciated the sacrifice they made, too, for our show.

When curtain time nears and the excitement of another show begins to build, quartetters react in different ways. I used to get so nervous I couldn't think straight. Over a period of time different before-show habits emerge and these traditions or rituals become important to the emotional preparation for a performance. Terry Clarke reveals some of the idiosyncrasies of the BOSTON COMMON:

We get someplace and we always mess up the plans of the poor guy who wants to be a good host and has the whole day planned for us. Each of us has different sleeping habits, eating habits, even cleansing habits. Larry Tully, for instance, takes a minimum of three showers a day, preferably five. Rich Knapp likes to take a shower as soon as he gets to the motel. We all like to eat. We sing on a full stomach and probably break some rules there, but a full stomach seems to give us our best per-formance. We generally have the same thing: shrimp appetizer, a nice piece of roast beef or steak for entree, and a salad. After we eat, we head for our motel rooms. Larry needs an hour and ten minutes exactly to get ready for a show. That includes time for brushing his teeth and washing his hair. He cuts his hair for every show. It drives us crazy. He's always the first one in the motel and the last one out. He's the last one to get ready

backstage, too. We all have our own habits and we try to ac-
commodate the other guys' habits.

Rich likes to take a shower and then lie on the bed while he
watches television until twenty minutes before it's time to go. I
like to watch TV for a while and then sleep, then get up, put on
makeup, and get into the show outfit before we leave for the
auditorium. The only thing the BOSTON COMMON has in com-
mon is that we love to sing.

We like to find out what time we're expected to sing and then
be at the auditorium just twenty-five minutes beforehand. This
practice must give every show chairman a heart seizure,
because he wants to see us there before the show begins. In
fact, some of our show contracts stipulate that we must arrive
at least a half hour before the show starts. Someday we're go-
ing to get into trouble, but we couldn't get there on time if we
had to. We generally don't even warm up. A couple times we
tried warming up, but there was always a problem. One guy was
always hacking and coughing, and we could never complete a
whole song. That upset the other three, so we said, "The hell
with it. No warm up!"

As performance time draws nigh, emotions intensify. Calm,
reason, and logic may give way to individual emotional reactions.
Many quartets can be swept away with the anticipation and excitement of a show. Experienced quartetters still get butterflies, but they
usually are able to channel the high-adrenalin flow to improve rather
than detract from the performance. Here's Terry Clarke again:

Somewhere along the way, I think on the strength of Lou
Perry's wisdom and advice, we got away from focusing our at-
tention on ourselves or on the audience, and now we're able to
focus exclusively on the song. We feel obliged for every song
we sing to present it as well as we possibly can. I guess what
has happened is that we've learned to instinctively read each
other. It's like osmosis, the way we communicate. I don't know
too many other quartets that have expressed feeling the way
we do. The FOUR RASCALS and the EASTERNAIRES were able
to, I think, and the SUNTONES certainly have that extra sense.
It takes total confidence in each other.

The first thing to do is know that the guy beside you is going
to do the very best he is able. The last thing to do in a quartet is

to remind somebody about a mistake. He knows if he made a mistake. You don't have to rub it in and criticize. He knows he made a mistake and you avoid it; you don't say anything at all.

It comes down to having confidence in each other and singing up to the level of each other's expectations. I don't worry about the lead. I don't worry about the tenor. I don't worry about the baritone. I only have to worry about myself. When we all are thinking with that kind of discipline, we're singing at our best. We're putting our energies and concentration and dedication into the song. Then it doesn't matter how it sounds, because it comes out the best we are capable of producing at that moment.

Speaking of singing discipline, I was interested in a comment Freddie King made. He said a singer should never think about *how* he is doing when he sings. He should think about *what* he is doing. I like that philosophy. If you begin to reflect on specific results, you distract your concentration from the singing, and the song suffers.

The art of quartet or chorus singing demands that each participant develops a keen responsiveness to the other members of the group. Only a unanimous effort is effective, and any deleterious factors at work within the singing unit detract from the desired performed result. After all, singing a four-part song is as much a matter of teamwork as any sport you can name.

Doran McTaggart describes this kind of teamwork in a story he tells about the MERRIMADICS:

Our tenor, Fred Sorrell, had moved away from Windsor, Ontario for a while, but we still stayed together as a quartet. Fred lived in Toronto and was directing a chorus in Oakville, a short distance away. When the chapter chartered, our quartet was invited to sing on their first show.

Fred planned to direct the chorus in an outfit of white trousers and colored suit coat, but the pants material was a little sheer, and you could see a distinct line above his knee where his boxer shorts ended. Every time he moved, it looked bad. It was very distracting. He decided he'd have to correct the problem, so the call went out: Does anybody have a pair of Jockey shorts?

"Yeah, Fred," I said, "I've got some, but you're bigger than I am. Gosh, you don't think you can fit into mine, do you?"

We changed shorts and he was the hit of the evening. I suppose it's one of those sacrifices you have to make when you're in a quartet. Believe me, no greater love hath one singer for another than when he exchanges shorts with him!

Oh, the sacrifices barbershoppers endure in the name of show business; hours of travel, backstage trauma, swapped underwear, just to sing for the folks. Offstage there's a drama no audience sees. It's the transformation that occurs when everyday people from all walks of life undergo the metamorphosis that changes them into performers. There's the process of getting made up, of getting dressed, of warming up voices, of going through the show numbers. And there's the waiting, seemingly endless waiting in the dark shadows of the wings offstage, with curtains, props, and ropes to entangle you. In that unreal world you find singers concentrating on their performances, listening to and watching the show, or getting into trouble. Most notable is the last category. Reedie Wright has an example:

The theme of our Pasadena show one year was "Harmony Rex." The entire production was staged to look like it was under water. A submarine was part of the set, and singers stepped in and out of it for different songs. We also had a mermaid, a beautiful sixteen-year-old girl who was dressed up in a fish suit from her waist down, and she had straps and supports to suspend her by wires above the submarine. The idea was that she would appear to swim gracefully across the stage during one of our numbers. It sounds wild, but was a real success.

She was sitting quietly off stage rigged with her gear, when the MIDSTATES FOUR came down from their dressing room. She was sitting absolutely motionless, without blinking an eye or moving a muscle, and she looked like a lovely mannequin. The daughter of one of our chapter members, she was a gorgeous girl, very well developed for her age.

If you know Forry Haynes of the MIDSTATES FOUR, you know he's a bit nuts to begin with. Forry walked up to where the girl was sitting, reached out with both hands, and said, "Beep, beep, beep, beep, beep, beep, beep!" like he was tuning a shortwave radio. The mermaid was naturally startled and flinched, and poor Forry jumped four feet in the air! It was like he was launched out of a cannon. He swung around and dashed back to his dressing room, embarrassed beyond words. It's hard to imagine Forry Haynes embarrassed about anything, but he was so chagrined he didn't even want to show his face on stage!

Those moments before a performance can be grueling. The waiting and tension can become unbearable. Huck Sinclair has a story about the FOUR HARMONIZERS that emphasizes the point:

> *Years ago we went on the first "Parade of Quartets" show in Detroit. There must have been forty quartets that sang that night, and as champions, we were scheduled last on the program. We were eager to sing, but when it got later and later and later, we began to get edgy. Along about 1:15 in the morning, lead Leo Ives' nerves got the better of him. He got sick and vomited three times. Five and half hours of anticipation and waiting can do that, even to an International Champion!*

Eventually that moment arrives when it's time to do your stuff. You look at the other three guys and sense you've reached the point of no return. The MC starts your introduction. You're on next.

If you're ready, it's thrilling. The excitement builds incredibly. The anticipation wells up like a fever. And the butterflies flap about wildly. If, on the other hand, you're not ready, then there's trouble. Bob Dykstra tells what happened once when the HUT FOUR weren't quite ready:

> *We were in our dressing room making last-minute preparations to go on a show at Carleton College in Northfield, Minnesota, when we heard ourselves being introduced. We made a mad dash for the stage. Fortunately, it wasn't too far from our dressing room.*
>
> *As we came around a corner, though, our tenor, Bob Spong, ran into a wastebasket. He accidently kicked the thing up in the air. It landed in front of him and then he couldn't avoid stepping into it. By this time we were at the edge of the stage and couldn't stop. Out we bounded with our tenor wearing a wastebasket on his foot! What an entrance!*

So there you are in the center of the open stage. The microphone is in front of you, the footlights are at your feet, and if the spotlight isn't too intense, you can see a sea of expectant faces peering up at you. Hopefully, they're smiling faces. Maybe they're not. So sing! On with the show!

Show Time

The house lights dim, a hush falls over the audience, the curtain rises, the show begins. A special ambiance is created. There's an air of anticipation in the auditorium and a backstage bustle of excitement and eagerness. Audience and performers alike feel the magic of the moment. It's barbershop show time!

Though the program may be carefully planned, the script carefully prepared, and the singers carefully rehearsed, nevertheless things can go awry. Some things *will* go awry. There'll be a missed cue, or a missed chord, or a misconnection somewhere along the way, for it's a real, live production. No retakes or second tries allowed. *Que sera sera!*

What will be will be, and it's the moment of truth for the show chairman. His months of planning, weeks of worry, and endless hours of labor all culminate in the evening's performance. What a reward it is for him to witness a spirited, professional, entertaining program emerge from his efforts. Lloyd Steinkamp describes the rewards he reaped when he first assumed the duties of show chairman:

> *I guess one of my greatest barbershop experiences was when I went to Phoenix and joined the barbershop chapter there. Word got out that I had some show-biz background and it wasn't long before I was show chairman.*
>
> *I remember the first Phoenix show I saw before I had anything to do with the production. It was a parade. They had thirty-six quartets, one right after another. The Phoenix Chapter used to contact quartets from all over the Society, and ask if the quartetters would like to spend a weekend in Phoenix in February. We got tremendous responses from Minnesota and Wisconsin, where barbershoppers freeze to death at that time of the year. All they had to do was have four matching uniforms, a couple of songs in their repertoire, and their own transportation. Once here, our chapter members wined them and dined them and housed them and showed them a hospitality second to none.*

That first show I saw didn't have much of a chorus and I wanted to change all that. A group of guys went out onstage in uniform disarray. There were no risers, so they just stood there and bellowed out a version of the "Old Songs," with incorrect words and not too much harmony. Then they sauntered off-stage, some even strolling down into the audience. That was the show opener. That was the chapter chorus! As you can tell, they really didn't have choruses in those days. It was a quartet organization and they didn't have the big, fancy choruses you see today.

As show chairman for the following year's show, I got a group of guys together one night at my house to have a planning session, to rough out a grand and glorious production. Somewhere along the line I lost control of the meeting, because a young man by the name of Jack Murray got us sidetracked. He was a gung-ho barbershopper and wanted to tell us about a super fantastic idea he had.

His wife, as member of the Encanto Park Botanical Society, had the marvelous good fortune to be able to latch onto the stage setting used for the flower show that year. What was it? A showboat! I guess at some time or other every chapter in the Society has thought about putting on an annual show with a showboat theme, with a real paddle-wheeler right onstage, and Captain Andy as MC. Of course all the songs had to be Dixie songs. It was decided then and there!

We didn't leave a stone unturned. Captain Andy was Everett Manning, our chapter's charter president and founder. The Phoenix costume house didn't have too many uniforms, so we took a New York City policeman's outfit and dressed it up to look like a showboat captain's. We put some white mutton-chops on Andy and wrote out a set of palm cards for him so he could introduce the quartets from his notes. With the name cards he could keep track of everything and the audience wouldn't see him carrying a script.

Unfortunately, almost everything imaginable went wrong. For example, we were never able to get word to the stage electrician and he kept shutting off the stage lights, so the only light on the poor captain was a front spot. As a result, when the captain glanced at his cards, they were but a silhouette, so he had to turn his back to the audience, and everybody read the cards together.

At the beginning of the show I welcomed the people to an era of nostalgia. I told them we were going to bring barbershop harmony back from the old days of the showboat. The curtain opened and that was the cue for Bill O'Neil, seated on a bale of cotton, to play "Camptown Races" on his banjo. His last chord was to signal the pitch for the first chorus number. Unfortunately, the front spotlight man never hit Bill with the light. We screamed at Bill to play his stupid banjo and Bill screamed back he couldn't see the frets. We told him to play anyhow and he did, but you can imagine the confusion when the chorus tried to get the pitch.

Our director stood in the wings aboard a wooden case, so the chorus members would be looking up as everyone sang the lyric, "Can you hear the whistle blowin' round the bend; the steamboat is dockin' today." Now, picture if you can, a forty-eight-foot boat which we had made movable with casters. The idea was to have the whole thing offstage and to roll it on as we sang the first song. But there was only forty feet of backstage space there in the theater, so we decided to open the fire doors and let eight feet of the vessel stick outside. At the last minute, though, the fire marshall said the fire doors had to be closed before the show could begin. So, eight feet of showboat stuck out onto the stage instead, for all to see, when the curtain opened.

There we were, all thirty-eight of us, screaming, "Can you hear the whistle blowin' round the bend," with eight feet of the damn ship standing right out in front of everybody's noses! That wasn't enough. Bill O'Neil fainted and had to be carried offstage on a stretcher. We had to pay $17.50 to a stagehand whose only job was to cue up a sound-effect record of the showboat whistle. You can guess what happened with that. First we had the Queen Mary coming through, then a high-speed railroad train came by. We had police whistles and every other conceivable sound, but no showboat whistle. It was a disaster!

Cliff Ford had been in charge of buying casters for the showboat, to allow it to roll in from offstage. He saved us money by going to a baby-crib factory and getting tiny little plastic wheels. They completely disintegrated when they hit the metal stage pockets in the floor. As a result, the good ship Showboat veered off course and leaned heavily toward the audience. It *knocked down phony wood pilings set up as props and scared the wits out of some new members who were dressed as sailors along the pier. The heavy tilt also caused the gangplank to prematurely fall partway open.*

The chorus sang a rousing version of "Let Us Introduce the Captain to You" and that was followed by a series of loud grunts from stagehands who were unable to open the gangplank the remainder of the way. After much cursing and groaning, which the audience enjoyed tremendously, a stagehand managed to dislodge the gangplank, only to follow it with his off-balance body. One of our members yelled, "That's not the captain!" which helped matters tremendously. Captain Andy walked out, stepping on the poor stagehand en route, and began his presentation.

Later in the show, which happened to be on George Washington's Birthday, we had all the lights in the auditorium turned out. Those in the audience with cigarette lighters were asked to ignite them, and everybody sang "Happy Birthday." Onstage, George Jones as first mate and Doc Hughes as second mate were issued candles for this portion of the performance. When the singing was over, the lighters were extinguished and the candles were supposed to be blown out, but Doc's was a trick candle, and it wouldn't stay blown out. At that point Captain Andy ordered the first mate to douse it, and he did so with a bucket of water. We used the old Ice Follies trick. George Jones dashed around after Doc Hughes and completely drenched him with a pailful. Whereupon Doc was to pick up a second bucket of water (but everyone would know it was only confetti), chase after George, aim toward the audience, and toss the funny confetti out into the screaming people in the first ten rows. That was the plan. What happened was that one of our enterprising members thought somebody had forgotten to put water in bucket number two. He obviously hadn't read the script. When it came time to throw the confetti, out came a large, soggy bomb, which splashed down like wallpaper paste on all the people in the high-priced seats. I'm sure they enjoyed it tremendously.

Another interesting turn of events was what happened with our plans for using black light in the finale. The chorus members had to stay onstage for two hours and forty minutes, waiting for the big finale number, "Old Black Joe." But, alas, that, too, was to go awry.

Lou Laurel's quartet, the DESERTAIRS, was on the show that evening to sing, complete with electric guitar. Lou plugged his guitar into an outlet and signaled to the backstage electrician. It seems the same circuit activated both the guitar and the black light together. The audience was treated to not only electric guitar playing, but half black light and half front light on the chorus, which, after hours of scratching and moving about, looked like lepers. "Old Black Joe" took on an entirely different color that evening, to coin a phrase.

All in all, the show was a complete and utter disaster. Yet, at our shows for years thereafter, audiences made fond references to that catastrophe. "Very good program," a comment card would read, "but it will never beat the Showboat!" Most people thought it was an attempt at very dry satire. It wasn't.

I recall having the worst imaginable hangover on Sunday. And on into Monday, too. I tried everything to forget about the experience. Nothing worked. But, you know, everybody ought to have at least one Showboat in his barbershop career!

Although as performers, we'd just as soon do without them, show goofs are often fun for all. While it may take some time for the instigators to enjoy their own calamities, most audiences find goofs a delight. Leon Avakian explains that it's a good gimmick to involve the showgoers in the gags:

Your chapter is truly fortunate if it has somebody who can turn the audience on before the show begins. There were two such fellows in the Asbury Park Chapter, and their names were Jerry O'Reilly and Jim Fleming. Those Irishmen were always up to some tomfoolery that no one else knew about.

On one occasion, just before the curtain opened for our annual show, Jerry and Jim popped out onstage in bare feet and old-fashioned bathing suits. They took along a bucket of Ping-Pong balls and badminton rackets and proceeded to pelt the audience with their little white missiles. Children ran into the aisles to fetch the balls and the showgoers went bananas. The chorus director was completely wiped out. So was the chorus. What a way to begin a show!

On another occasion, the same two decided to climb up on

the scenery during one of our chorus numbers. They thought it would be a good trick to let a few feathers float down over the stage from a pillow they took along. They shook the pillow, but the feathers did not drift out fast enough to suit them, so they tore open an end and dumped the whole load. The chorus members were totally unsuspecting, but the audience saw what was happening and enjoyed every minute of it.

What happened, though, was that the entire pillow emptied and air currents carried the feathers out over the footlights directly into the audience. Gradually, everybody began to gag! Feathers got in people's eyes and mouths, and they coughed and sputtered and gasped for air. It took us a half hour to clear the air, quiet everything down, and get the show back on track.

The MC on a barbershop show plays an important role. He introduces the performing chorus and quartets, of course, but more importantly, he's responsible for maintaining a good pace for the show. He keeps the action and momentum going so the show moves right along. Lou Sisk developed a keen sense for this aspect of the MC's duties:

Early in my MCing career, I was invited on a show about a hundred miles north of where I live. I got there an hour before show time, went backstage, and chatted with some of the chapter members. I put on my tuxedo, got ready, and checked in with the chorus director, president, and a couple of others, including backstage people and the show chairman.

When the chorus began to amble over toward the auditorium to get onstage, I told one of the guys I was going to the john. "Listen," I said, "tell them not to worry. I'll be right back in time to start the show." I checked my makeup and wasn't in there more than a couple of minutes, but when I came waltzing out, I heard singing. The chorus was onstage, the curtain was open, and the show was underway. It was going on without me!

I mumbled softly to myself that they needed Lou Sisk like a hole in the head, and I watched from backstage as the chorus sang five or six numbers. I asked a stagehand if there was a podium set up, and he said there was. I inquired if there was a mike on it. He said there was a mike in the middle of the stage, but I should use a lavaliere mike. He wrapped the cord around my neck and fastened the catch. I had never worked with one of those things before, but it seemed easy enough to use.

When the curtain closed I saw a guy jumping around like he had a hot foot. Then he saw me. "Oh, you're here," he said. "I was told you left. We thought you were sick or something. We had to start the show without you."

"OK," I said, trying to calm him down, "fine and dandy. You want me to go out to the audience now?" Meanwhile, the seconds were ticking by and the stage looked like an intermission. The people in the audience were sitting out there all by themselves waiting for something to happen. The guy dashed out to the center-stage mike and pointed in my direction.

"And here he is," he announced, "our MC for the evening, Lou Sisk!" The audience applauded and I started to prance out onstage. Then, wham! I was stopped dead in my tracks. My neck was jerked back and I thought I was being hanged! The wire from the lavaliere microphone wouldn't let more than half of me onto stage. With a fifty percent appearance, I'm sure the people were wondering just what kind of a jerk the MC was. He had missed the first part of the show and couldn't even get all his body onstage to make an appearance when he was announced.

I yanked at the wire, but it wouldn't budge. I popped back into the wings. "Where's the rest of the wire," I pleaded.

"That's it, man," the guy shouted back at me. "That's all the wire there is!"

"Oh, my God!" I said, and I tried to get unleashed from the mike. I pulled and tugged and got it loose. I made a lunge for the center of the stage and arrived there out of breath, out of patience, and out of words to say to the folks. The applause had ceased long before my arrival. I stood there and looked at everybody. Everybody looked back at me. The only thing I could think of to say was, "A funny thing happened to me on the way to the microphone this evening!" I guess the audience enjoyed the episode more than I did.

MCs, like the other performers, run into their share of onstage dilemmas. Here's another Lou Sisk story:

When the McKeesport, Pennsylvania Chapter asked me to MC a show, I had to attend a Wednesday evening meeting for a rehearsal. I was going to be a barber and introduce the chorus songs and the quartets while I stood by a beautiful, old barber chair at the edge of the stage. The spotlight would hit me, I'd make an introduction, then the light would fade out as the chorus started to sing. Oh, by the way, there was one other detail. Old-time barbershopper George, who hadn't been around much to sing, should be in the show for old times' sake, so he would be my customer. He'd sit in the barber chair, lean back, and be a prop for my introductions. He wouldn't have any lines to say or anything to do. He'd just sit in the chair. I'd be the MC. He'd be my silent partner. OK, fine and dandy.

The night of the show, I started off introducing the first chorus song and old-time barbershopper George sat right up in the chair and said, "Oh, yeah, you don't say!"

"No, no," I whispered to him, "this isn't a vaudeville team act. You keep quiet!" I couldn't keep him quiet. Every time I said something, he interrupted with some foolish and inappropriate comment.

"Where are the girls?" he said. "When are the girls coming out?" His ad-libs had nothing to do with what I said, and I couldn't say a word without his throwing in his two cents' worth. At the fourth interruption I'd had it. I started my lines and he yelled out, "Are the girls coming on next?" When the chorus began to sing, I ducked backstage and found a big towel.

At the next introduction, I seized my opportunity. "Just a minute, George," I said. "I think we need to keep your face nice and warm and comfortable." I wadded up the towel and pressed it down over his face. The audience chuckled. I pushed my hand down on the old-timer's mouth and proceeded with the next introduction in grand style. There were two more introductions after that, and I didn't let my customer make a peep.

At the end of the last chorus song I picked up the towel. "Say, how do you feel under there, now?" I asked. Then I slammed the towel back down again. The audience got a big charge out of my antics and I got a big hand. I suppose it wouldn't have been quite so funny if it had been planned from the start.

That's one of the beauties of a barbershop show; the spontaneity, the reaction to the unexpected. Hugh Ingraham has a story about carrying the unexpected to extremes:

I remember Bob Hafer, former Executive Director of the Society, telling me about a chapter show he and his wife, Ellen, attended. They went into the auditorium, found some good seats, sat down, and looked through the program. The first thing they read was "Master of Ceremonies: Bob Hafer." He knew nothing about it until that moment.

The barbershop show is a marvelously flexible entity. It can be a gigantic theatrical production or a simple song fest. It can be presented in a mighty theater or a small high school auditorium. It can contain all the big-gun quartets in the Society or consist merely of a few local quartets and the chorus. Pleasantly, regardless of format, financial backing, or fame of its performers, almost without exception it's an entertaining and successful presentation. Bud Harvey's chapter's evening of barbershop harmony sounds like a ball:

When our scrawny little twenty-nine man chapter in Stuart, Florida stages its annual "Chicken Chew and Harmony Howl," it's always for a sellout crowd. It's our version of an annual show. We keep planning to have a real production of an annual show, but then back away in fright and substitute a dinner party instead.

The thing is phenomenally successful, and we even make twenty to thirty bucks profit. What it is, in effect, is an afterglow without all the dirty work of staging a show. We bring in a couple of good, entertaining, District quartets and parade our own feeble talents, and everybody goes home happy. We don't get rich, we barely hang solvent, but we maintain intact our record as a fun chapter, and I guess that's what it's all about.

In a barbershop show most jokes and gags are pulled for the express enjoyment of the audience of course. There are times, though, when a quartet plays a trick on another quartet, and the audience may or may not even be aware of what's going on. The MIDSTATES FOUR were notorious jokesters, as Joe Schmitt will tell you:

The SCHMITT BROTHERS sang on many shows with the MIDSTATES FOUR. We were particularly fond of those guys. They used to say we should do the singing and they should do the clowning, but we had to be on our toes, because they were champions themselves and had a real championship sound.

One time Forry Haynes stood behind the shell where we were singing and played his guitar just a half note below our key. It was the same song, same chords, but a half note down. The audience couldn't hear him, I'm sure, but we could, and it was impossible to sing with that discord, so we naturally settled down into the key he was playing. Then he moved the key down another step and we adjusted again. The song must have sounded like a broken record player with all the unexpected key changes we had to make. After our performance we threatened to smash his guitar over his head.

That must have been a favorite trick with Forry, because he pulled it on a number of quartets. Vern Reed tells about the time the BUFFALO BILLS were victims of another MIDSTATES FOUR prank:

One of the most entertaining quartets we ever had the pleasure of knowing was the MIDSTATES FOUR. They won the championship a year before we did, and we often sang on the same show together. One time our two quartets were singing on the Detroit Chapter show at the famous Fox Theater in downtown Detroit. I guess everyone recalls the magic that Forry Haynes could elicit from his guitar and ukulele. Marty Mendro played bass fiddle and was the foil for Forry's jokes and ad-libs. Art Gracey poured out his big, solid bass in abundance and was the butt of many jokes and physical jabs from the other three. Bob Mack was a clown both on and off the stage. Put it all together and it was a great comedy and fine singing act, very typical of the vaudeville barbershop quartets I remember from childhood days.

Anyway, we were well into our second appearance just before the close of the show at the Fox Theater, when something inspired Bob Mack into action, practical joke action. He set off a stink bomb behind the house curtain and shoved it out onstage behind us. A cloud of odors engulfed us smack in the middle of a sentimental ballad. We stopped singing, looked at each other, and Al Shea whispered, "Who did that?" It broke us up!

I made a dash through the center curtain opening, hoping to expose the culprit in the act, the stinker, but I only caught a glimpse of Bob laughing as he disappeared into the backstage shadows.

By then, the odors had drifted out into the audience, and giggles spread along with them. The folks in the first dozen rows or so got a good noseful of the prank. At the afterglow, the MIDSTATES FOUR were introduced as the "Stink Bomb Four!"

It was one hundred percent pure fun, typical of the attitude during that period in barbershop history. Quartets performed to entertain the audience. We were singing popular music, not the classics, so how could we take ourselves seriously? Barbershop music should be presented tongue in cheek, to keep it in the idiom of the vaudeville barbershop quartet which, after all, was the style of singing upon which our Society was founded. I feel that many of today's quartets take themselves too seriously, and are unable to enjoy the frivolous and fun-loving spirit of pranks and practical jokes.

For all their mischief, the MIDSTATES FOUR was bound to find retribution. It came during a barbershop show in Michigan. Forry Haynes tells the story on himself:

As you know, the MIDSTATES FOUR used musical instruments and I played guitar. We were really hot on that Michigan show, but when we got to our final song, "Dinah," something happened. I turned around quickly, just as Art Gracey put his hands up. He hit the end of the guitar and unbeknown to me it cracked. It was a thousand dollar instrument and the neck was fractured right where it joins the body of the guitar, but I wasn't aware of any damage.

As we started into "Dinah," the fracture worsened and the guitar strings gradually slackened. We started the song in B-flat and as I played, the pitch kept dropping. Singing all the way, we slipped from B-flat to A, to A-flat, to G, and we ended in the key of F. It was the funniest doggone thing. The audience thought it was all part of the act. They howled.

We had to get back to Chicago for another show the next night, and because the trains were all snowbound in Canada, we decided to take a taxi and leave immediately following the afterglow. We stopped in Kalamazoo, home of the Gibson Guitar Company, to drop off my guitar, and then drove all the way to Chicago to sing in Parkridge, Illinois.

After paying $200 for guitar repairs, and a taxi bill you

wouldn't believe, we didn't think our "Dinah" bit onstage was quite that funny after all.

Forry reports, however, that he wasn't the only member of the MIDSTATES FOUR to get his comeuppance:

I recall when barbershopping started to get away from the "parade" type of show and shifted more toward "theme" shows. One of the first theme shows we did was in Chicago. It was a two-nighter and we had to work up some special songs and lyrics for a trapeze bit we were asked to prepare. It was a "man on the flying trapeze" skit with a real trapeze that hung down from the loft, and two of us even dressed in ballet costumes.

Marty Mendro is nearsighted and when he takes his glasses off he can't see a foot in front of him, but on the Chicago show he decided to work without glasses because it was a somewhat athletic routine. He had to get back about fifteen feet from the trapeze, make a dive for it, and swing back and forth while we sang the trapeze song.

"Marty," I cautioned, "you know you're pretty nearsighted. You may miss that trapeze entirely." He was unconcerned. The payoff of our act was to be when he got off. He was supposed to tumble offstage out of sight and there would be a great big racket, as though he had smashed through the wall or something.

When we came to that spot in the song, Marty got back fifteen feet, ran up, made a lunging dive for the trapeze, and of course missed. He actually lost his balance and tumbled offstage, down a stairway, and into a heap of theater props. Most of the racket was not sound effects. It's a wonder he didn't kill himself.

Bruised and beat up, he quickly climbed the stairs, came back out onstage, looked at the audience, and said, "Tomorrow night I wear my glasses and I don't care who likes it!" We laughed so hard it hurt.

I think when performers enjoy themselves they give their most entertaining performances, and if so, the MIDSTATES FOUR must have always been at their entertaining best. They always seemed able to turn their performing opportunities into swinging soirees. Here are a couple more examples from Forry Haynes' story collection:

We sang on a show in North Carolina once with the CON-FEDERATES, who, as you'll recall, always appeared in their Confederate uniforms. The producer of the show called us in Chicago and asked us to rent some Yankee uniforms. "You can cause a real riot," he said, "by coming onstage with those Yankee uniforms and breaking up the CONFEDERATES' act!" We thought it was a great idea.

When the CONFEDERATES were onstage, we jumped into our rented uniforms, complete with swords. As the CON-FEDERATES started their second song, the four of us marched out. They looked around and did a double take at our Yankee outfits, but the funny part was they thought they'd go along with the gag, so they pulled their swords. We pulled ours and you've never seen such a blazing battle as the one we waged.

I did my imitation of Errol Flynn, jumping up, over, and around the chorus risers and all about the stage. It was a wonder nobody got hurt. Our swords crashed and banged and swung savagely in the air. The audience thought it was all part of the show. What started as a little gag turned into a rip-roaring, hilarious duel.

Another time, in California, we sang on a beautiful theme show. In the second half of the program the stage was set as a large, formal ballroom with big windows and curtains, and it even had a long stairway in center stage. It was beautiful. Men and women were dressed in formal attire for the performance, and the whole scene was class. They had several lovely dance sequences during the show.

We were working out on the apron of the stage and were nearing the conclusion of our spot. As usual we had all kinds of laughs and gags going, but the curtain was open and all the singers and dancers were in view behind us, standing motionless or sitting on a big davenport. Something happened, I don't recall exactly what, and the other guys in the quartet started to chase me. In a frantic dash around the stage I fell over the davenport. I hit the thing so hard it went over backwards, taking all the occupants with it. In an instant the beautiful, formal setting was knocked topsy-turvy and the place looked like a tornado had hit. People were lying on their backs and general pandemonium reigned.

When I got back on my feet I felt I had to say something, but I couldn't think of anything appropriate, and I blurted out, "Take my horse and head him off at the border!"

It must have appeared absolutely ludicrous, because it brought down the house. The people onstage were supposed to be straight and staid, but they fell all over themselves in laughter. It was amazing how it broke everybody up. What a finale for their show!

Naturally, the name of the game is entertainment, and quartets and choruses go out of their way to please an audience. One frequently-used gimmick is some sort of surprise entrance, to get the performers out onstage. Here's Forry Haynes again to describe some entrances, MIDSTATES FOUR style:

Back in the old days there used to be "morning glow" shows early in the morning. In Grand Rapids, Michigan they were almost as big as the regular evening performances. We appeared on such shows in old flannel nightgowns, with nightcaps and all, and one particular show was in the ballroom of a large hotel. It was packed with people.

We had arranged to use a stretcher to take our tenor, Bob Mack, onstage. The gag was that he was supposed to be sound asleep and we were going to wake him with a pail of water. Audiences love slapstick.

We showed Bob that we had put only an inch of water in the pail. The audience would think it was full to the brim, we told him. When his back was turned, though, just for fun, I filled the bucket halfway to the top.

We carried Bob out onstage and the audience let out a squeal of laughter. We had the nightgowns on and I said, "Folks, as soon as we get Bob awake, we'll start our show, but we've got to get him awake first." Then I picked up the bucket of water and threw it in his face! Bob expected a trickle but got a downpour that doggone nearly drowned him. The people in the audience were beside themselves with laughter.

I like to recall another incident that happened during a morning show in Miami. We arranged with a police officer to escort us from the hotel to the auditorium in a patrol car, and I got an idea about how we could make a surprise entrance on the show. We had to sign a release for the police, stating we wouldn't hold the department responsible for anything that might happen.

At our request the MC periodically asked the audience if anybody had seen the MIDSTATES FOUR. "They're supposed to be here now," he said, "but they haven't arrived yet." Then when it was time to go on, he made another announcement. "Ladies and gentlemen, we've found the MIDSTATES FOUR, but I'm afraid there's a problem. They stopped at a Seminole Indian village and got into trouble, and we had to send the police for them. However, without any further ado, bring on the MIDSTATES FOUR!"

We had old clothes on, all ripped up. We had those fake arrows going through our heads. We had knives in our backs, and catsup all over us. I got on top of the patrol car, behind the red beacon light, and an officer drove the car right onto the stage. The siren blasted away, the red lights flashed, and the audience...I tell you, it was twenty minutes before we got on with the show. Everybody with a camera ran to the stage to take pictures. We were some sight to behold! Marty even carried a great big fish along with him. It was our wildest entrance ever.

Part of the excitement of a barbershop show is when something goes wrong and the performers try to correct the situation without revealing to the audience that anything is amiss. If handled with class, such spontaneity not only solves the problem but gets a good audience reaction, too. When Steve Keiss sang with the GLADESMEN, his quartet was able to snatch victory from the jaws of defeat in just such a situation. Well, almost:

We were attending an International preliminary contest in Cocoa Beach, Florida and at the quartet briefing we were told there was a slight problem with the stage. We could exit stage right behind the curtain; we could exit stage left in front of the curtain, and go down a short flight of stairs into the audience; but we couldn't exit stage left behind the curtain because there wasn't any stage behind the curtain. Construction was incomplete there, leaving nothing but a big, gaping, six-foot hole. Because we were so comfortable with our stage-left exit, we decided to go off to the left and down into the audience. All went well and we won the right to represent the Sunshine District at the International contest in Kansas City.

That evening a lady told us she really thought our exit was fantastic. She said we were like the old SHORT CUTS who were famous for their smooth entrances and exits, and she kept complimenting us until it was almost sickening. It would have been nice if she mentioned how well we sang. She said she was going to bring her husband to the show the next day just to see our fancy walk-ons and walk-offs. Apparently the guy stayed away from barbershop shows whenever he could, but she was going to drag him to the show because our moves on and off the stage were so great.

On the barbershop show the next day, each quartet was to sing on the first half and second half. During our first performance it occurred to me that the audience knew nothing about the stage problem, so we ought to exit stage right. As we finished the tag of our first song and bowed, I whispered to Bob Boemler, "Let's exit right."

"What?" he whispered back.

"Let's exit stage right," I repeated.

"OK," he said.

What I forget to mention was to pass the word to Nick Appolony and Rik Ogden. After our second song and bow, two of us turned to exit right, two turned to exit left. We were all waving at the audience and at the same time trying to crawl over ourselves, and Nick had an "Oh, my God, what's happening" look on his face. Meanwhile, the audience was enjoying the whole affair. Rik wound up in the audience and Bob and I grabbed Nick by the armpits and dragged him offstage.

Nick was livid. The more he thought about it the madder he got. The rest of us thought it was a lark. During the intermission we were still laughing and arguing about it when our lady fan marched over to us. "Thanks a lot, guys," she snarled, with a look that could have stopped a locomotive. "Thanks a hell of a lot! You've probably killed forever the chance of getting my husband interested in barbershopping."

Nick got mad all over again. "See! See what we did!" he snapped.

For our second appearance, all we could do was to enter the stage exactly as we had gone off. Rik came out of the audience,

*and Bob and I dragged Nick back by the armpits, and the au-
dience loved it. We almost got a standing ovation. People told
us it was one of the most beautifully planned comedy bits
they'd ever seen. Of course it wasn't.*

*After it was all over, Bob Boemler turned to us and said,
"Look, if we're going to ad-lib something, let's rehearse it a
couple of times beforehand!"*

Talk about spontaneity! Just wait until someone has a memory
lapse, or transposes a couple of words in a song, or finds himself doing the right thing but at the wrong time. That's the time for spontaneity. Pete Donatelli of the FREE LANCERS reports, however, that
the call for spontaneity is not always well answered:

*Vernon Leonard was just as funny offstage as on, but he
used to rattle Nelson Lawhon with brief memory lapses during a
performance. Although he could recite the Gettysburg Address
without a flaw, he would at times forget the most simple of song
passages.*

*One of our routines was a George M. Cohan medley that in-
cluded "Yankee Doodle." Once when Vernon came to his bass
solo, "Yankee Doodle went to London, just to ride a pony," his
mind went blank, and in his strongest voice he improvised, "Da
da da da da da da da da da da da da da." Nelson said if he
didn't love Vern so much he'd hate him.*

Sometimes a missed line, or word, or cue is only noticed by the
singers. The effect can be just as damaging, nevertheless, as Dick
Johnson relates:

*When I joined the Society, the ESCAPADES were the Illinois
District champions. The quartet was rather popular and had
quite a few shows lined up, but the lead singer had to leave the
group. I tried out for the part, got it, and then embarked on a
crash program to learn the quartet's show tunes and material.*

*I didn't have much trouble with the music, but the lyrics oc-
casionally threw me for a loop. I found, even rehearsing, that I
had to constantly think ahead. My mind would be racing just to
figure out what words were coming up next.*

*In our first public appearance our opening song was "Men-
tion My Name in Sheboygan." Some of the lyrics, you'll recall,*

*go like this: "Just tell them all you're an old friend of mine, and
every door in town will have a big welcome sign." I was doing
very nicely until we got to the middle of that line. Then I drew a
total blank. I tried desperately to think ahead and remember the
words, and I finally decided they had to be "...and every home
in town will have a big welcome sign." Unfortunately, the correct word was "door," but then it was too late, because I had
already started to sing "home." In a split second I realized my
error and quickly switched to the word "door," so what I sang,
regrettably, was "...and every whore in town will have a big
welcome sign."*

*I'm certain the audience didn't catch this minor, passing slip,
but to this day I'm sure they're wondering why baritone Gil
Stammer and bass Jim Bond collapsed on the stage in
hysterics. As a matter of fact, tenor Don Marth and I had no
idea what had happened until after the show when we were
able to figure out precisely what I had done. If only that line
didn't make so much sense the way I sang it!*

Even the best-known quartets occasionally have their problems.
Reedie Wright tells one on the BUFFALO BILLS:

*The most embarrassed I've ever seen a quartet was right
after the BUFFALO BILLS left "The Music Man" on Broadway.
It was only a few weeks before the Pasadena show, so I asked if
they would appear on our show. They agreed.*

*Their biggest request was for "Lida Rose," but do you know,
those guys stood there on stage for what seemed like five
minutes trying to figure out the key to "Lida Rose." I suppose
they always received the pitch from the orchestra when they
sang it for "The Music Man." I've never seen a quartet so embarrassed. They finally got the starting note and sang a very
crowd-pleasing performance of the song, but even at the
afterglow, those guys were still absolutely mortified!*

It's strange how the familiar can become totally unfamiliar without
a moment's notice. It's like forgetting your own name. There is absolutely no reason it should happen, but it does. Tom Masengale:

*My quartet, the CHORD BUSTERS, had a wonderful arrange-
ment of "Home on the Range," and we sang it one night on a*

show with Gene Autry in Tulsa, Oklahoma. We got to the middle of the song where our lead, Bob Holbrook, was supposed to pick up the solo, and he stood there with a big smile on his face. We all smiled. We all smiled for a long time, then took a bow and walked offstage. "Who the heck was supposed to come in there?" he demanded. He was shocked to find he was the one who messed up.

"Bye, Bye Blues" was another number we sang a lot. I had a small solo part in that one. We were doing it a couple of times each night at a gay nineties show at one of the local Tulsa theaters and suddenly I couldn't remember the words. Just before we went onstage to sing, I went completely blank. I hastily scribbled the words on the palm of my hand and had to read them to get through the number! All week long I had to read them off my hand. We knew that song forwards and backwards.

We did the same thing with "Kathleen" in Wichita one night at an afterglow. We tried to start it and couldn't. Three times we tried and three times we failed. It was a number we had sung hundreds of times. Back at our table we figured out what went wrong. We had always started the song on a unison note and then moved to the tonic chord. That night we tried to start on the chord and got completely confused. Those memory lapses are nasty little devils!

The act of forgetfulness is not by any means restricted to a singer's words or music. It also occasionally makes an appearance in other aspects of his performance. Jiggs Ward of the PITTSBURGHERS tells a story that Tom O'Malley would probably prefer was left untold:

Our lead, Tom O'Malley, recognized as one of the best community-sing leaders of all time, was asked to handle the job before the second half of a show in Boston. Tom decided to wear a sport outfit for the community sing and then make a quick change into his tuxedo for our quartet performance. He did an excellent job as usual. The audience sounded like a barbershop version of the Tabernacle Choir!

With a little help from the rest of us Tom made the costume change with a few seconds to spare. We got a big hand when we walked out onstage and we opened up with a fast-moving version of "Somebody Stole My Gal." The song had a real fireman's finish and for extra showmanship, Tom dropped down on one knee, ala Al Jolson, and threw his arms wide apart. The crowd went wild. They applauded like mad and they laughed and hollered, too.

We had never received a reaction quite as enthusiastic before, and we couldn't understand why all the fuss. Then we noticed that in his haste, Tom had neglected to attend to the zipper on his trousers! I must say we were rather disappointed to find it wasn't our song that turned the place upside down.

The MIDSTATES FOUR also fell victim to the same oversight, as Marty Mendro reveals:

We had a regular unofficial fan club of Chicago-area enthusiasts who followed us all over the Midwest and among them was Frank Vechiola. I don't know how he did it, but Frank always managed to get a front row center seat to watch our act. He knew every song we sang, every gag we pulled, every move we made onstage, but he'd be at one show after another. We'd just walk out onstage and he'd break up. Tears would tumble down his cheeks and he'd almost roll in the aisles with laughter. We could never understand why he didn't tire of our antics.

In one of our acts we used to make a couple of quick changes. We started out onstage wearing horrible-looking zoot suits with bright red-and-white jackets and overpadded shoulders, with bright green, tight-waisted pants, and with huge, oversized hats. Underneath that we wore two other costumes, one of which was a grass hula skirt and a light plaid Hawaiian shirt.

On a show in Menomonee, Wisconsin, in our haste to get ready, Bob Mack forgot to zip up. Since there were two costumes on underneath, this was a perfectly harmless mistake, but it didn't look too good from the audience's point of view. There he was agape, with a husky clump of straw from his hula skirt protruding like a hay bale from the open zipper.

As soon as we got out onstage the audience cracked up. Frank Vechiola was in the front row. We'd seen him laugh at us before, we'd seen him applaud, and we'd seen him enjoy our foolishness, but we'd never seen him fly into such hysterics. Poor Frank was having a fit!

In those days there was a barbershop ethics committee which reviewed quartet acts to assure they contained nothing but good, clean fun. Ours was always classified as strictly "G-rated," but there, also in the front row, was the national chairman of the ethics committee. He seemed anything but pleased with our appearance. Mind you, we weren't even aware that Bob's zipper was wide open. We figured we had ourselves a real rip-roaring audience.

Halfway through the first number Forry Haynes or Art Gracey spotted it and with sign language signaled for me to look over and down at Bob. I was standing next to him. He was on the end of the line of us. When I saw his problem, I took the string bass and put it in front of him to give him a chance to cover up, but he had no idea that something was amiss.

We went all the way through to the end of our number and when Bob bowed, his straw bale bulged like a stuffed silo. The audience howled! He finally figured out what was wrong, but instead of going to the wings to zip, he merely turned his back on the audience to perform the operation. He squatted down, zipped, and turned around, and the audience broke up again.

We were worried about the chairman of the ethics committee, but he must have realized the incident was strictly an accident. It definitely wasn't written into the act. We'd never do it intentionally.

Marty has another story about missing an important duty. This one concerns timing, vital and critical in the entertainment business:

In one of our gags we used a big, eighteen-inch-long, hand-sewn rat that was dragged across the stage on a fishline by someone unseen in the wings. Forry Haynes would notice the rat when it was halfway across stage and would shoot at it with a .38-caliber light pistol. However, the rat would keep right on crawling across the stage.

Then Forry would take off his shoe and hold it in front of the rat, and of course the rat would die instantly. But the real punch line of the gag came when Forry would sniff at the shoe himself. One sniff and he'd fall over backwards in a dead faint. As he executed a stiff-backed prat fall, I was supposed to get behind him and catch him just before he hit the stage.

During a show in South Bend, Indiana, however, something

went wrong. I couldn't get over behind Forry in time and he went over like a maple tree, landing smack-dab on his southern exposure. There was a loud thud, a cloud of dust, and the audience came apart.

When the laughing subsided somewhat, Forry looked up at me with the most mournful expression I've ever seen, and in a loud and plaintive voice said, "You missed your cue!" That broke everybody up all over again.

The amazing results of a purely coincidental set of circumstances made a SALT FLATS show even more zany than usual. Carl Hancuff recreates the action:

I was introducing the members of the quartet during a show in Idaho Falls, Idaho, when I heard the crowd start to snicker. I assumed Dale Taylor behind me was clowning around, so I turned to see what he was up to, but he was just looking off toward stage right. I looked and there was a pure white cat walking out onstage as sure of itself and in charge as could be. The audience thought that was funny, so I kept an eye on the cat.

We use a gun in our act and it makes one heck of a loud noise, and when the cat got near us, Milt Christensen shot at it. BANG! You've seen cartoons where an animal jumps up in the air and its feet go a hundred miles an hour, but the creature doesn't go anywhere. That's what happened to the cat. When the poor, frightened beast finally landed it didn't have any traction. Its feet were still going a hundred miles an hour, but it looked like the animal was on a sheet of ice. Finally it got a hold and tore off the stage at the speed of light. Milt stepped up to the microphone and blew at the end of the gun. "Nobody messes with our act!" he said confidently.

A cat may be manageable, but some performing obstacles are almost too much to cope with. However, until the show-must-go-on law is repealed, barbershoppers will keep the faith. Bill Conway has a good example of real performer stick-to-itiveness:

A long time ago when the Pittsburgh Chapter had a barbershop show in the 4000-seat Syria Mosque, the power company ran into a strike. With only limited power in the entire Pittsburgh area, we rented some gas-powered electrical generators for standby use, just in case they were needed.

The LAMPLIGHTERS from Cleveland were onstage singing the "Whiffenpoof Song," when the lights went out. The power was gone, the lights were gone, the sound system was gone, and the whole Mosque was plunged into darkness and quiet, but the LAMPLIGHTERS sang on. Through two more numbers they sang in the blackness, giving enough time for the electricians to switch over to the emergency generators.

Even the most important of life's events may be postponed, or at least interrupted, if there's a show commitment. For Bob Dykstra's quartet, a show commitment was a sacred vow:

The HUT FOUR was a busy quartet and every Saturday we were booked on a barbershop show. When Lou Ann Conselman and I decided to get married, we had a problem. All the weekends were reserved for the quartet. When could we have the wedding?

We were married early in the afternoon, Saturday, October sixth, in Shell Lake, Wisconsin. After the ceremony we attended the reception for a while and then slipped away from the guests. With the rest of the quartet we drove two hundred fifty miles to Fairmont, Minnesota for a barbershop show that night. It may be a little unorthodox for the start of a honeymoon, but when you commit to do a show, you don't let a marriage get in the way!

To the best of my knowledge, nobody in my family or Lou's knew about our show job that night.

There are times, though, when it's impossible for the show to go on. Frank Lanza of the FOUR STATESMEN tells of one experience that was a near show-stopper, and then another that was indeed an honest-to-goodness bring-down-the-curtain show-stopper:

Shortly after we won the International Championship, we were singing on a show in Montreal. In those days we took along the big Society Championship trophy to our engagements. We were proud of that trophy, and while we performed, the trophy was onstage in front of us so the audience could see our prize.

*The auditorium in Montreal has a large stage with a main cur-
tain that rises rather than parts in the middle. Prior to our appearance in the second half, we placed the trophy out front. I
was first onstage when the MC announced us and I couldn't
believe what I saw. As the curtain went up it got tangled on the
trophy, and the trophy was dangling thirty feet in the air! All I
could imagine was witnessing that big, beautiful prize plunging
to the stage and.smashing into a million bits. The audience
gasped.*

*The curtain was lowered cautiously and everybody heaved a
sigh of relief when the trophy was safely recovered. Then they
burst into applause.*

*Another time, in Montclair, New Jersey before we went on to
sing in the second half of the show, I heard a commotion in the
audience. The MC said there was a celebrity in the audience,
and he introduced Buzz Aldrin, the second man to walk on the
moon and a native of the Montclair area. I've never seen such a
response from people. They jumped up and shouted. They applauded. They screamed. They carried Buzz Aldrin on their
shoulders. Everybody marched up on the stage and down
again. It was a solid half-hour standing ovation.*

*That was the end of the show. There was nothing else to do
but close the curtain and go home. It was an incredible outpouring of pride and feeling, the most phenomenal audience reaction I've ever come across.*

Strangely, when the obstacles are greatest, when a performance
appears unquestionably doomed, it is then that the barbershop
showmen frequently make their grandest efforts and produce their
greatest shows. Carl Hancuff was confronted with an impossible
situation:

*It was a Wednesday night show at the University of Utah
Homecoming celebration, and I guess I was really in the
groove. I surprised myself I was so hot. My timing was flawless.
One-liners were flowing out of me like honey. When it was over
the other guys told me they'd never before seen me so funny.*

*We were scheduled to appear on a show the followng Satur-
day, but I said we'd have to cancel. "You see," I explained,
"just before the show tonight, my brother called and told me my*

mother passed away in Washington. I have to attend the funeral.''

The other guys couldn't understand how I could be so funny, let alone do the show, but it was simple. I guess it was my way of drowning my sorrow, or working out my anger, or channeling my emotions. I just decided to do the show. It wasn't tough at all; it was easy. It gave me a way to release the feelings that were bubbling up inside me.

One of the greatest fears singers have is that they'll run into voice problems. It's a terrible feeling to catch a bad cold a day before a big show. Naturally, it happens. The ADVENTURERS' lead, Ronnie Menard, describes what it's like:

The Burlington, Vermont Chapter hired us for their annual show, but when I woke up the morning of the big day, I couldn't sing. I couldn't talk, either. I could hardly breathe. We were concerned about our commitment and decided to make the four-hour drive to Burlington anyway, in hopes I'd find my voice along the way. Joe Kopka, Ed Chacos, and Jim Ringland wouldn't let me say a word during the whole trip, to make sure my voice got as much rest as possible. Unfortunately, when we reached Burlington, I still wasn't singing or making a sound. I had an acute case of laryngitis.

The FOUR RASCALS were on the same program and we asked them for advice. Our concern was for the show and the Burlington Chapter. We wondered if we should jump in the car and drive back home. How could we get off the hook? Don Dobson told us the chapter needed our quartet on the program. He said it was too late to get a substitute. We should give it our best try.

When we were introduced we walked out onstage beaming with confidence. I hope that's what we beamed, because I was terribly apprehensive. Remember, I was supposed to sing lead and without me there would be no melody part in any of our songs!

That night I worked hard on stage presence. I had nothing else to do. We put on our usual package of songs with one exception. The other three guys did all the singing; I did all the acting. I mouthed every word and went through every gesture and we put on a bang-up performance. At least three of us did.

I must have done some convincing pantomime job, because we got lots of applause. Joe Kopka sang the lead pickups, where I normally would have come in alone, and the other three guys sang marvelously. We were careful to choose well-known songs with melody lines so familiar to the audience they could be "heard" even though they weren't sung.

Then we had our chance to sing at the afterglow. We were called to sing right after we ate and I decided at the last minute to take along a pocketful of sandwiches. While the other three sang, I stepped back, took out a sandwich, and took a nibble. Some people in the audience started to chuckle and then laugh out loud. The rest of the quartet thought they were laughing at our poor singing job. Our final song was "Roll Out of Bed with a Smile," and in the middle there's a spot where we clap our hands together in unison. Most of the audience was familiar with the song and they waited to see what would happen to my sandwich when I clapped. I threw it in the air, clapped, caught it on the way down, and everyone laughed.

When the rest of the quartet realized I was spoofing behind them, they broke up, too. That eased the tension and from then on we had a thoroughly enjoyable time, though I still couldn't utter a sound. The Burlington Chapter hired us back the following year to hear all four of us sing. Come to think of it, after they heard me, they never invited us back again!

Ernie Winter tells how his quartet was able to solve the problem when his voice gave out:

When the DESERTAIRS received an invitation to sing on the Colorado Springs show, we decided to take our wives along. The evening before the show we drove from El Paso, Texas and it was snowing and cold when we got to our destination. We went out to dinner and ate, sang, and were merry. We woodshedded long into the night.

The next morning I woke up speechless. Literally. I couldn't make a squeak. I panicked. I'd never before had laryngitis. Tenors and leads sometimes have trouble with their voices, but a bass never does. I called a doctor and made an appointment. I also tried everybody's home remedies: hot showers, exercises, strange concoctions. Of course I did what the doctor prescribed, too, but when it got close to show time, I still couldn't sing a note. We put on our quartet costumes never-theless, hoping for a miracle. If at the last minute I still couldn't sing, we'd just have to make our apologies to the audience.

Morris Rector, bass of the International Champion GAY NOTES, happened to be at the show that night and when he heard of my trouble he offered to fill in for me. He knew several songs in our repertoire so the show went on as scheduled, while I stood off in the wings and ate my heart out listening to Morris sing my part. He probably sang it better than I ever could.

The "miracle" solution wasn't exactly as I wished, but at least the show wasn't spoiled in any way.

Losing your voice may offer one set of problems, but losing your consciousness is another matter entirely. That presented an interesting challenge for the Louisville Thoroughbred Chorus some years ago. Ken Hatton tells what happened:

One of the chorus members sang a solo in "Aura Lee" on a show and did a fine job with it. The excitement may have been a little too much for him though, because during the next chorus song he got dizzy. He leaned to the right against one chorus member, then to the left against another, and they steadied him, but he passed out anyway.

Bill Benner was directing the chorus at the time. He motioned for the curtain to be closed, and sent Tim Stivers out to entertain for a few minutes. As you know, Tim is our chapter comedian, and he has a Society-wide reputation for his ad-libbing and MCing talents.

It was an unusually small stage and there wasn't room to move the unconscious singer off to the wings, so the chorus members passed him up over their heads and dumped him off the back of the risers. The curtain opened and we completed the show!

Contrary to what you may think from all these tales of hilarity, a barbershop show is not merely one big barrel of laughs. There are many fine moments of beautiful barbershop harmony. There is indeed much mighty music in addition to the merrymaking.

Have you seen the OSMOND BROTHERS on TV? Not too many years ago they were wooing barbershop audiences with their quartetting. One of their early performances is described by Val Hicks:

The Osmonds were in Southern California for the weekend of the Pasadena Chapter show. I had been coaching the boys and had made arrangements for them to sing during the cast party after the show Friday night. Art Baker, the perpetual MC of the Pasadena show, heard the boys and was impressed. He and Reedie Wright had a proposal for me. "Val," Art said, "we want to put the boys on the show tomorrow, so if you can have them out in the auditorium, I'll call them up to sing."

The only seats we could find Saturday night were in the back of the large Pasadena Civic Auditorium. In the middle of the show Art Baker interrupted the proceedings. "Ladies and gentlemen," he announced, "there are some boys in the audience tonight I'd like you to meet. Is there someone out there by the name of Allen?"

From the rear of the auditorium a small boy's voice answered, "Here."

"Is there someone named Wayne, someone named Merrill, someone named Jay?" At that time Jay was only about six years old. One by one the boys answered and one by one they made their way down the aisle and up onstage. They were in their quartet outfits and were instructed to sing only one song. But the audience was charmed and the kids couldn't get offstage without singing two or three. Everybody was thoroughly enchanted by the sweet, young voices of the OSMOND BROTHERS. Everybody, except perhaps the quartet that performed immediately thereafter!

The OSMOND BROTHERS were signed up for a full performance on the Pasadena show the following year. So was a slapstick, comedy quartet called the DESERT KNIGHTS. One of the DESERT KNIGHTS, Sam Aramian, tells what happened behind the scenes:

We were to follow the OSMOND BROTHERS on the first half of the show, and were waiting backstage while the Osmonds sang. Waiting in the wings with us was Dick Mack, the producer-director of the show. Dick had been involved in show business professionally on Broadway before he retired and settled in Pasadena.

The five of us watched the Osmonds in sheer fascination. They were great. The audience was eating out of their hands. Dick turned to us, nodded at the performers, and in his thick Brooklynese said, "You know, fellas, one of the toughest things in show business is to follow a kid act or a dog act." He paused, looked back at the Osmonds, then continued, "And this is the first time that one is following the other!"

There are gripping, touching moments too, in barbershop shows. Reedie Wright tells about such a time in another Pasadena show:

Art Baker was quite a notable character here on the West Coast; in a lot of movies, MC of the television show "You Asked for It," and a very prominent figure in radio. He was a member of the Pasadena Chapter and MCed our shows for over twenty years before he passed away. Art used to close every show with "God Bless America." After the finale and after all the quartets were brought back onstage for a final bow, he walked to center stage and asked the audience to rise. He asked for the lights to be put out and led everyone in "God Bless America." It was most inspiring. With his striking silver-gray hair and his flair for directing, it was always a powerfully moving moment. The spotlight focused into an intense, narrow beam aimed right at Art's head. All you could see was that gray hair and the white cuffs of his shirt as he directed. Then the curtain closed. It became a high point of our show each year.

The year after Art died, we didn't know how to handle the finale. Art had quite a following. Many people attended our show as much to see Art Baker as to see the quartets, I'm sure. Many knew he was gone, but perhaps many did not.

At his last show we had made a recording of the chorus and audience singing "God Bless America" under his direction, so we decided to use it. I went to the center of the stage, just as Art would have done, and asked the audience to please stand. I asked for the lights to be dimmed in memory of the late Art Baker. I said there might be some in the audience who never had the privilege of singing under the direction of Art Baker. "I'm going to ask you now, probably for the last time, to join with Art leading us in 'God Bless America.'"

The tape was put on and we started to sing. I backed away from the microphone into the chorus and the spot focused down to a narrow, brilliant shaft of light that played on the silver microphone in center stage where Art would have been.

You talk about drama. Wow! The curtain closed and the audience stood there motionless. No one moved. There wasn't a dry eye in the house. It was as dramatic as could be and seemed a fitting tribute to the great Art Baker.

The show is concluded, the auditorium is empty, the stage is again bare. With cold, dark stares the once bright and colorful lights look down upon a lifeless theater. The energy and sparkle of the evening's performance have been transformed into memories. Another barbershop show is over.

Afterglows and Such

Two to three hours of harmony during a barbershop show are hardly sufficient for many barbershop enthusiasts, so when the show concludes, all such fanatics head for the afterglow and another chance for singing and good times. Whether it takes the form of a massive convocation or an intimate cast party, whether it features a fabulous food feast or only light refreshments, whether it's held in a grand ballroom or an ancient lodge hall, the afterglow offers yet another stage from which to issue forth the barbershop sound. It also offers barbershoppers who appeared on the show or worked backstage a chance to relax and enjoy the other show performers.

Afterglows are generally rather informal affairs, so they give quartets a chance to try out new material. The BLUEGRASS STUDENT UNION used such an opportunity for the first performance of a new number. Ken Hatton tells the story:

We had learned a song called "I Found My Sweetheart Sally," but were having trouble with it. We were concerned that we weren't selling it properly, that it wasn't getting across, that it just wasn't working, but we decided to try it out anyway at the afterglow following a show in Charlotte, North Carolina. We had even talked about dropping the song from our repertoire. We thought we'd give it a first and last chance at the afterglow.

In the front row of the audience was a red-haired girl, pretty, probably twenty-three years old, and as we sang the lyrics, she broke down and cried, right in the middle of the song.

Something in the words or music or delivery or the moment set off her emotions, and to get such a strong response, we concluded we must be doing something right, so we kept the song.

We continued to work on it some more and three years later took it to Cincinnati for the International contest. We won. Now it's one of our big numbers. We like to think that a red-haired girl named Sally at an afterglow in Charlotte helped us win the Championship.

Acceptance, appreciation, applause. Those are important ingredients, I think, that keep a quartet or chorus going. It's the enthusiastic audience reaction during a show and the kind words thereafter that keep a group together, when other factors may tend to tear it apart.

I remember singing with the UNLIKELY HOODS on a show in Baltimore, Maryland. The show wasn't one of our best performances, to be sure, but the afterglow went reasonably well. At its conclusion we lingered awhile, hungry for those encouraging words.

I looked about and saw a lovely, middle-aged lady walking toward me. Her eyes twinkled and her smile was as warm as the Florida sun. "Oh," she said, "I so enjoyed your performance." Pride, deserved or not, welled up inside me. I started to reply but she didn't give me a chance. "You know, I was watching you all evening," she said, "just you." I beamed as I awaited her praise, compliments, and admiring comments. "And I must tell you," she went on, "that you remind me of one of my children."

Well, in view of the encouraging buildup, I thought the punch line was disappointing, but there were apparently no other well-wishers in attendance, so I figured she held the only ticket for my evening's ego trip. "Isn't that nice," I said, trying not to sound disappointed. "Thanks very much."

"Yes," she continued, "I don't know what it is, but your expression, or maybe it's your eyes, well, whatever it is, there's just an amazing resemblance to...my daughter!"

I noticed that my ego trip had come to a rather abrupt halt. I had expected a plum but was hit with a pickle instead! She was a dear, friendly person, though, and I'm sure she had no idea that she not only dashed my hopes of accolades but also thoroughly punctured my praise-hungry ego! Win a few, lose a few!

It's strange how the desire for kudos colors a quartet's reaction to strangers. If someone comes up to you with a big smile after a performance you're proud of, deep down inside you know what he or she is going to say. "Hi," you say confidently.

The stranger speaks. "Do you have the time?"

"Well, thanks very much," you say in humble modesty. "Glad you liked it!"

Surely a group like the SUNTONES, with their years of popularity and success have grown a little jaded when it comes to "common-folk" recognition and praise. According to Harlan Wilson, not at all:

At the conclusion of a forty-minute VIP tour of the White House, we spotted a lady studying us from a distance. As she walked toward us she slapped her hand on her forehead. "I don't believe it!" she said excitedly. The four of us were dressed alike, so we weren't too difficult to recognize. She stared at us and repeated herself. "I don't believe it. I just don't believe it!"

We felt pleased and proud to be recognized, and I suppose we each began to formulate in our minds the modest words we'd utter in return for the sweeping praise we expected from her. We had big smiles all around. "I just don't believe it!" she exclaimed for the fourth time. "It's, why it's the DEALER'S CHOICE!"

Our egos were punctured and our smiles must have deflated accordingly, but we weren't nearly as embarrassed as our would-be admirer. And once we got past the surprise, we thought the whole incident was hilarious.

Another time when we were walking along a long corridor at the Atlanta airport, we were stopped by a man wearing a Society membership lapel button. "Aren't you guys a barbershop quartet!" he inquired. Gene Cokeroft spoke up to answer him.

"We sure are," he replied expectantly.

"What's your name?"

"We're the SUNTONES," Gene announced, a little disappointed at not being recognized.

"Oh, yeah?" the guy said. "Never heard of you!"

Put-down experiences can be laughed at after a brief period of ego recuperation, because there are compensating moments when sincere encouragement and compliments are offered up to a performing chorus or quartet. If you believe you've done your best and sung your best, then such moments warm your heart. I'd say it's the best pay a performer can receive. It doesn't have to be a lengthy or lavish testimonial; just a simple statement, if sincere, is sufficient. Dick Johnson tells of his most treasured words of praise:

What makes it all worthwhile for me is knowing that my quartet's performance is appreciated. After a show there are lots of people who gather around. They congratulate us and say nice things, but we never really know if the compliments are just so many words or if they're really sincere.

Some time ago at the conclusion of a VARIETIES show, we were in the midst of the after-show throng and I caught a glimpse of an old man standing on the outskirts of all the activity. He was standing with his head bowed, patiently waiting. When the crowd dispersed, I got a good look at him. His hat was in his hand and he was wringing it in front of him. His hair was silver, his face a brilliant red, but his forehead was white. He probably wore the hat while working out in the fields every day. He had on a Hawaiian sport shirt with a string tie fastened by a little arrowhead clasp. He wore a blue sport coat, brown slacks, white socks, and work shoes, and he was as timid as it's possible to be. He seemed to be wrestling with himself to get up the courage to speak to us. He had waited a long time before he stepped forward, cautiously. He didn't even look into my eyes. Rather, he gazed somewhere in the vicinity of my collar button, and in a bashful voice said, "Youse vas de best vons." Then he turned quickly and walked away.

Around these parts, if you want to pay the ultimate compliment to a quartet or chorus, all you have to say is, "Youse vas de best vons." I wonder if the old gentleman knows what an impression he made on us that night. It was simple, short, sincere, and was the best compliment we ever received!

Afterglows are like big family get-togethers. They let the quartetters relate closely with their audience, barbershopper to barbershopper. The casual character of an afterglow allows teasing and banter that would be improper in the more formal show setting. It also provides opportunities for making special song dedications, such as that described by Jim Sherman:

One of the greatest experiences for the SAN FRANCISCO

STORM DOOR AND WHALE OIL COMPANY quartet took place at a cast party after a Friday night show in Los Angeles. When we learned that a barbershopper and his fiancee were there, we dedicated a song to them. It was "My Cup Runneth Over With Love" one of our favorite ballads, featuring a tenor solo by Wayne Mansfield. We sang it expressly for them and I don't think we ever put more into that song; I doubt that we've ever sung it better. We saw tears in her eyes and it was a touching, tender moment for us.

Later that evening we got a shock when we were told the girl was deaf. But she had read our lips and understood every word we sang. She said she loved our song. We'll never forget that performance for we learned there's more to singing a song than making a pretty sound. We sang with love and she had heard it, though she listened in silence.

Such moments are magnificent. It must be the ultimate satisfaction for a barbershopper to transmit to another person a joy so rich and real that it evokes a sincere, tearful reaction.

The joy transmitted by song is the subject of another story about the STORM DOORS, this one told by Jim Sherman's wife, Jane:

When I accompanied the quartet to Calgary, Alberta, Canada for a barbershop show, it was a blustery, stormy night only fit for staying home! Nevertheless, thousands packed the Jubilee Auditorium and the warm feeling bestowed on the quartet elicited one of their finest performances, one that exhilarated me and filled me with pride. A few hundred of the faithful followed to the afterglow. There, an elderly lady stopped me to say she had been a fan of barbershopping for many years, but had never before attended an afterglow. "This is my first," she said, "because I've never heard such a lovely blend of voices as the STORM DOORS."

When the afterglow ended at 2:30 a.m., I found her in the crowd and thanked her again for her earlier, kind comment. I asked if she was going to join us at the after-afterglow that was to follow at the hotel. "Oh, no," she told me emphatically. "I must go home to bed now, so I can get up in time for church in the morning."

It must have been close to 4:00 a.m. when the after-afterglow began to wind down. The people had intently listened to everything in the quartet's repertoire and then some. I scanned the faces in the enthusiastic group and saw the same lady sitting in a chair in the corner of the room. I moved to her side. "How nice to see you again," I said. "What changed your mind about coming?"

"You know, I've never missed church before," she explained, "but maybe the Lord will forgive me this week. I'll never again get the opportunity to hear such beautiful singing!"

Such is the stuff that drags quartetters away from their families so many weekends a year. Such is the stuff that turns barbershop singing into an exchange of love. Along with notes and words in a song are love and feeling which the performer wishes to convey to the listener. It's a step beyond the music and chords and when it's turned on, it warms the coldest of blizzards and melts the iciest of dispositions.

Barbershopping is a people-to-people activity of the finest order and it's hard to call an end to such a consanguinity. Sometimes no one does and the merriment continues indefinitely, as Jack Macgregor describes:

One of the friendliest chapters we ever visited was in St. Johns, Newfoundland. It's a long way from Connecticut to Newfoundland and the SOUNDSMEN had to leave on Friday to be there in time for a show Saturday night. The hospitality chairman was director of a senior citizen's rest home and had made arrangements for us to stay in an unoccupied, fully-furnished, four-room house on the rest-home property. Talk about comfort! We were given the red-carpet treatment throughout our stay.

Following the show and afterglow, some diehards decided to have an after-afterglow. Our genial host escorted us to our temporary home away from home and most of the chapter members, their wives, and friends tagged along. Fortunately, we're the kind of bunch that has to be dragged off bodily to bed anyway, so we were glad to continue with the singing and merriment. There were at least thirty people at the party and we stayed up all night.

When the sun made an appearance the next morning, everybody helped us pack and then formed a long convoy for our trip to the airport. In the waiting room the chapter members

*and quartetters alternately sang songs to the pop-eyed au-
dience of early travelers until our departure. What a trip!*

A barbershop show can be a real trip, with both meanings of the
word. It's an experience of giving and receiving. A quartet gives its
best on stage and barbershop fans give their best in appreciation. It's
a formula where the participants receive more than they give in spite
of their efforts to reverse that balance.

Going Home

Then comes the proverbial morning after, when four weary singers
must get their act together to become four weary travelers and catch
planes or trains or taxis or whatever for the trip back to the real
world. Only then is there any question about the wisdom of the long
night before.

You wake up with your eyelids feeling like sandpaper, your mouth
tasting like a turnip patch, your head feeling as if it was squeezed into
an hourglass, and with the realization you're about an hour behind
schedule. The motel room looks like a tornado spent the night there
because that's exactly the way you left it when you fell into bed the
night before. Make that two and a half hours before.

With a little luck you'll get to the airport in time to make your plane
and you'll be able to catch a few winks during the flight. Without a little luck you'll have to drive, or you'll miss your plane, or you'll be hi-
jacked to Cuba. Well, that's show biz!

Quartets that really travel in style fly by charter or private plane
and they leave the piloting to somebody else! No worries, no
problems, no schedules to contend with, no lines of travelers. One
time my quartet took a private plane for a singing engagement in
Halifax, Nova Scotia. For the return trip Sunday, we got to the airport
fairly early. It was rainy and windy and the pilot decided to delay
departure a few hours. We waited and waited and finally left him
there and took a commercial flight back late that night. The weather
was so bad the pilot didn't get the plane out until the middle of Monday. I guess the private planes are no panacea. Even with clear skies
and a tuned-up aircraft, there can still be problems. Here's one of
many Carl Hancuff experienced:

For a long time we flew to and from our shows with Hugh

Lyman, a friend of ours from Salt Lake City. He was a fine pilot, had a terrific aircraft, a twin Cessna 310, and he was certified in everything you can be certified in, so we felt most comfortable with him. But we never let him know that. We used to refer to his landings as controlled crashes.

Flying back from Canada early one Sunday, we found that the first international flight to land at any commercial airport on Sunday had to pay a tax, to the tune of about three hundred dollars. The commercial airlines generally pay the tax, but the first commercial flight wasn't due where we wanted to land until two hours later. We didn't have enough fuel to sit up in the sky that long, so we were in a dilemma. Then with a couple of radio calls, we learned there was a loophole in the law. If you land at a border town where there is no international airport, you can get by without paying.

A place called Sweetgrass, Montana (honest) is such a border town and it had a landing field. That's exactly what it was, a field. There were cows grazing all over the place, happily munching the grass. We had to buzz the field twice to scare the dumb animals out of the way so we could land, and the landing was one of the most harrowing I've ever experienced. They must plow the field daily to get it so bumpy.

The highway patrolman there doubled as customs agent. He took a peek at our luggage, we sang him a song, and were on our way again in no time.

Frank Lanza and the other FOUR STATESMEN almost had a worse flight:

We chartered a plane to sing on a show somewhere in Pennsylvania. The flight out Saturday afternoon was fine. We asked the pilot if he wanted to see the show, but he declined, preferring instead to take it easy and rest up for our early departure Sunday morning.

Up at about eight on Sunday, I called the desk to get the pilot's room number. "He's doing just fine," the desk clerk told me. I didn't understand. "The operation was a complete success," the clerk said. "Oh, didn't you hear? The pilot had appendicitis and was taken to the hospital, but he's just fine now."

We wondered what would have happened if his attack had hit a few hours earlier or a few hours later. We insisted on a co-

pilot for subsequent flights.

Of course most flights home are routine; totally, mercifully uneventful. On the other hand, a chance meeting with a celebrity may splash a little pleasant conversation into an otherwise humdrum excursion. Jack Macgregor tells of a trip the SOUNDSMEN took when the quartet encountered a pair of well-known personalities:

We always sing on airplanes or anywhere else we go for that matter. We dress alike on our trips and one thing leads to another and before you know it we're singing a few songs. After singing on a flight to Pittsburgh, we spotted familiar faces across the aisle. They belonged to the late Ted Mack and the late Bishop Fulton Sheen. The quartet had been on the Ted Mack Show, and when we reminded him we hadn't won, he laughed. "Don't feel bad," he said. "When Ann-Margret was on the show, she took second place to a guy who played 'My Gal Sal' on a banana leaf!"

From Pittsburgh to Altoona we rode a twin-engine, twelve-passenger plane, and Bishop Sheen was on that flight, too. We joked together and the quartet sang some more. He was traveling to participate in a ceremony at an Altoona cathedral. We used one of the jokes he told us on our show that evening.

Waiting for our plane on the trip back home Sunday morning, we saw Bishop Sheen again. He asked if our show was a success. We said it was. We asked if his "show" was a success, and he smiled. "It was most impressive," he remarked, "but I would have gotten more laughs if you fellows were along."

Years back it was just the same. Maybe the mode of transportation was different, but the spirit was the same. Huck Sinclair describes the train ride home after a show in Decatur, Illinois more than three decades ago:

The FOUR HARMONIZERS and MISFITS were seated in the lounge car of the Wabash, on our return trip to Chicago, when Art Bielan, lead of the MISFITS, noticed Charlie Grimm, manager of the Chicago Cubs, engaged in conversation at the other end of the car. Out of a clear blue sky Art commented in a loud voice, "I see the damned old Cubs lost again today!" Now, mind you, this was in the middle of winter! Charlie Grimm looked up, startled.

He saw the eight of us chuckling over the foolishness and from then on we had a regular party. Both quartets sang and Charlie played his mandolin. We had such a good time, Charlie hired the FOUR HARMONIZERS to sing for the upcoming mid-winter banquet of national league managers, and he signed up the MISFITS for the following year.

There are many stories of pleasant chance meetings and stories of fearsome adventures on trips back home from barbershop shows, but, to be sure, most such trips are no more than tedious, tiring travel. There's much valuable lost sleep to catch up on and often there's not much of a storehouse of energy remaining to engage in fun-making even if opportunities presented themselves. At such times singers have but a single purpose, to get home, and attempts at levity are usually not well received. One of Buzz Haeger's experiences emphasizes the point:

When the FOUR RENEGADES sang shows and afterglows, I used to tell a World War II story about Seaman Mitzel, who was up in the crow's nest of a destroyer looking through his binoculars to spot enemy planes and boats. When he spied a German submarine, he called to the captain, "Submarine's coming!"

He waited for the torpedo to be fired, but nothing happened. The sub came closer and closer, and Mitzel got frantic. "Mitzel to the captain," he shouted into the horn with his strong Jewish accent. "Mitzel to the captain, the submarine's comin' close at a thousand yards. Please fire that torpedo!"

Still no action.

"Mitzel to the captain," he pleaded. "Mitzel to Captain. For God's sake, fire that torpedo! I'll pay for it!"

One time after a show we were flying back from New York in my airplane. As usual, the other three were sleeping and I was piloting the craft. They always bought newspapers for the flight, not to read, but to put over their heads to keep the sun out of their eyes. For fun I thought I'd wake them up and give them a little scare. I could run one of the gas tanks dry, and when the fuel pressure dropped, I could switch over to the other tank, but that would cause the engine to cough and sputter, and I thought in their half-asleep state, the guys might get a kick out of the idea we were out of gas.

Jim Foley was sleeping in the front seat next to me; Tom Felgen and Ben Williams were in the back. As schemed, the fuel ran down and the engine choked, coughed, and died. Out of a sound sleep Jim sat up straight In his seat, yanked the newspaper off his head, and shouted out loud and clear, "I'll pay for it!"

Those long trips home are hard. My quartet travels by car to many of our shows, and coming back late at night, perhaps four or five in the morning or after only a few hours' sleep, is an ordeal. If I'm driving, it's a fight to stay alert and keep my reflexes sharp. If I'm not driving, I can sleep, but then I worry terribly about whoever is driving. I know how groggy he must feel and that's not very comforting!

It's with this perspective that I appreciate the story Bob Dykstra tells of a HUT FOUR automobile trip home:

Anybody who has sung in quartets and done a lot of shows around the country must have a thousand travel stories. We were driving back from a show to Minneapolis early one Sunday morning. Dan Howard was driving, John Hansen was in the front seat with him, and Bob Spong and I were in the back. All of us except Dan were sawing wood pretty seriously. Suddenly John screamed out, "Dan, Dan, Dan!" in a voice of clear panic. Bob and I woke with a start and Dan swerved on the highway at the outburst.

When the commotion settled, John explained what had happened. In his sleep John's hat had fallen down over his eyes. When he awoke drowsily, he found himself in total darkness. He thought the car had run off the highway and we were all dead!

You are finally home again, and in your mind the weekend's experiences merge into a montage of singing moments mixed with a crazy quilt of travel, show, and afterglow incidents. It all swirls together to make a pleasant barbershop memento.

But there are other matters to think about. Home chores have been postponed, family needs have been neglected, and by the way, you have to be at work first thing Monday morning, so the snap back to reality is a particularly abrupt one. However, reentry into the real world is paved with a fresh new supply of barbershop recollections plus the realization that the weekend's rewards were most liberal.

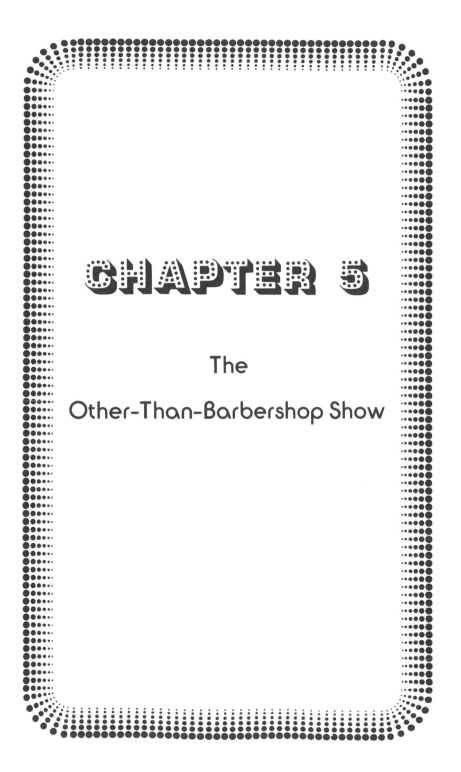

CHAPTER 5

The

Other-Than-Barbershop Show

The Other-Than-Barbershop Show

For it's always fair weather
When good fellows get together
With a stein on the table
*   and a good song ringing clear.*

Richard Hovey

ven though the barbershop show is the most popular arena for performing quartets and choruses, there are nevertheless countless other opportunities for songsters to perform. From weddings to wakes, hospitals to night-clubs, PTAs to Lions, Elks, and Moose meetings, barbershop harmony is in demand, and tales of such "extracurricular" performances abound.

Shows to Remember

When you've sung in shows for, let's say, a dozen, or a few dozen years, the memories sift together into a broad reservoir of pleasant recollections. As you think back, the golden moments can be re-

157

trieved and enjoyed again in your mind, as favorite old possessions stored away in the attic can be dusted off and enjoyed once more.

While nearly all shows are memorable, there are a select few that seem to leap to the forefront of a barbershopper's memory bank. Such is the story Jiggs Ward of the PITTSBURGHERS recalls:

During our year as champs, Jim Duff, then Governor of the State of Pennsylvania, organized what was known as the "Pennsylvania Train," a publicity train that traveled throughout the state and was a popular and successful political gimmick. Of course the governor and other top state officials were on board, and there were also representatives from the entertainment and sports worlds including actor Jimmy Stewart, who came from Indiana, Pennsylvania; Ham Fisher, who created the comic strip character Joe Palooka and hailed from Scranton; Hollywood gossip columnist Hedda Hopper; and Ezra Stone, star of the then top-rated radio program, "Henry Aldrich." The quartet was invited along, too.

The stage was a flatcar decorated in red, white, and blue stripes, and when the train stopped, the celebrities spoke, or in our case, sang. The crowd at some cities numbered three to four thousand people! We generally opened with "I've Been Workin' on the Railroad," and when we got to the last verse, our tenor, Chummy Conte, stepped back and Jimmy Stewart took over in his place. He sang a darn good tenor, too, and we assured him he could always sing in a barbershop quartet if things ever got tough in Hollywood!

Two days before the train was to depart, Chummy had a new set of dentures installed, and while we were concerned about his ability to adjust quickly to his new mouth geometry, he was confident he'd have no trouble.

Our first tour stop was in Lancaster. After the train pulled onto the railroad siding, we all assembled on the platform where the program began with a welcome speech delivered by the Lancaster mayor. During the speech, Chummy had a violent sneezing spell, and at one roaring "ah-choo," I thought I noticed something fly by. Yes, it was a brand-new set of upper dentures.

Fortunately, they were durable and did not break on impact. Chummy was very cool. When his teeth stopped bouncing around on the platform, he calmly reached down, picked them up, brushed them off, and returned them to their rightful niche as though nothing had happened. Needless to say, the mayor never quite made it to the conclusion of his welcoming address!

Such an incident can make a show memorable, as can the thrill of performing for a special audience or the excitement of performing with a symphony orchestra. Buck Dominy tells of his two most memorable performances:

Since the wife of one of the members of the Washington, D.C. Chapter was closely associated with Mamie Eisenhower, we thought our chorus, the Singing Capital Chorus, might be able to entertain at the White House. President Eisenhower's heart attack had kept him confined to the White House for quite some time, but arrangements were eventually made for us to sing at a Presidential dinner, the first following his illness. The chorus was permitted to send forty singers to entertain in the East Room.

It took a great deal of discussion and negotiation to decide on the program. Every one of the selections we wanted for the concert had to be submitted to government officials for review and approval. We were told that under no circumstances could we sing an encore, only the reviewed and approved songs. The program was timed to the minute and we were not allowed to exceed our time allotment.

On the night of the performance, each chorus member was carefully screened before being permitted into the White House, but each of us was allowed to bring a guest. The program was engraved with the gold Presidential Seal and was titled, "An Evening of Musical Americana, presented by the District of Columbia Chapter of the Society for the Preservation and Encouragement of Barber Shop Quartet Singing in America, Incorporated." All of our songs were listed: "Keep America Singing," "Down by the Old Mill Stream," "Rocked in the Cradle of the Deep," "Steal Away," "Sweet Adeline," "Minnie the Mermaid," "Back Home in Indiana," "You'll Never Know the Good Fellow I've Been," "Waiting for the Robert E. Lee," "Carolina in the Morning," and as the final song, one we felt was particularly appropriate, "May the Good Lord Bless and Keep You." The audience consisted of about a hundred twenty-five people, including Vice-President Nixon and his wife, senators, representatives, and other top federal officials.

We were really "up" for the performance and we really did a super job! At that time the Singing Capital Chorus was one of the best in the Society, having won the International Chorus Championship just a few years before. As we sang, I glanced over at Mamie Eisenhower a couple of times and saw that she was thoroughly enjoying the show. With a bright smile she watched the President and seemed to delight in his enjoyment of our songs. The next day's newspapers reported that below her long dress Mamie's toe could be seen tapping to the rhythm of the music.

When we finished our final number there was enthusiastic applause; not just a polite, courteous response, really spirited applause! We had been carefully instructed in protocol for the conclusion of our performance. No one in the room was to make a move until the President of the United States moved first. We were told that when the President stood up, the program was over, but until then, not a soul was to move a muscle. Well, when our singing was over and the applause diminished, the President remained seated. All eyes were fixed on him. We had received no instruction on contingency plans, should the President not rise, so we waited. The room became quiet, but the stalemate continued.

Then President Eisenhower raised his hand with one finger extended, signaling he wanted another song. So in spite of previous prohibitions about an encore, we had to sing another song for the President of the United States. The only trouble was that we were somewhat unprepared to sing another song for anybody. Our director, Major H. H. Copeland, made a quick decision and we sang "Coney Island Babe." Would you believe it, "Coney Island Babe" was the final number for our White House performance, much to the President's pleasure.

After that, the President got up, and with Mamie, went to the side of the room where all his guests, including members of the chorus and their wives, were formally presented to him. I never realized what a thrill it would be to shake hands with the President of the United States and speak briefly with him. It was a grand experience and a great honor. In the excitement, I squeezed Mamie's hand harder than I should have. When I later spoke with other chorus members, they said they had similar feelings of honor and awe. The President and First Lady were very gracious, and they had a kind word for each of us. It was an incredible ending to a great barbershop evening!

Another memorable barbershop experience was singing with the National Symphony under the direction of the famous Howard Mitchell. Mr. Mitchell himself came to our chorus rehearsal to direct us and work with us.

It was interesting to rehearse with such a famous musician, and it was amusing to find that he had some difficulty getting used to our methods. Of course we had a good deal of trouble adjusting to his. Barbershoppers generally pay little attention to strict musical time since it isn't essential for barbershop singing, but as Howard Mitchell explained, we had to sing absolutely with the beat because orchestra people are totally dependent on it. The man with the cymbals, he said, might be counting sixty-four beats, and when he gets to sixty-four he's going to crash them together and it had better be right!

Our rehearsal with the symphony was a delight. Mr. Mitchell scolded some of the musicians for playing too loudly while the chorus was singing. "We're trying to hear the singers," he shouted to the orchestra. I guess it must have been an unusual experience for them, also.

When the great evening came, we sang a beautiful medley of songs with the symphony, and there's no doubt about it, that performance was a once-in-a-lifetime experience!

One of Dick Johnson's "shows to remember" was also with an orchestra:

As chorus director I find it difficult to convince the chorus members how really good they are. I think barbershoppers don't appreciate the professionalism they display and the fine singing they're capable of. I am reminded of this when I recall the time my quartet, the VARIETIES, was invited to sing with Chicago's Grant Park Symphony Chorus and Orchestra. Their concerts were rather prestigious events and we were greatly pleased to be asked to participate in a performance which included excerpts from "The Music Man" and "The Most Happy Fella." It meant a lot of rehearsals with the group and a lot of time learning new music, but we didn't mind that at all.

One song we sang from "The Most Happy Fella" was "Abondanza," a striking piece of music, with a momentum that drove and grew in intensity all the way to the end, but the tag was disappointing because it led to a big, fat, unison note; no chord at all. As barbershoppers will, we toyed around with it and finally put together a tag so strong it would scrape the paint off the ceiling! The lead singer ended up singing a high B-flat, and our tenor was on a D. Singing baritone, I had to cope with a high G. It was fantastic! We also learned the dull, unison ending, just the way the music came to us, and we went down to Grant Park for a couple of rehearsals.

There we met Louis Lane, the conductor, who was surprisingly young but impressively capable. The orchestra and chorus, too, were clearly outstanding. We were among highbrow musicians, classically trained and thoroughly professional, but we weren't intimidated. We were there to sing barbershop and we had done our homework carefully.

We sang "Abondanza," and even with the unison tag, we tore the place apart. The musicians loved it. We began to feel our oats. We proceeded to sing some of our other numbers, "How Can There Be Any Sin in Sincere," and "Lida Rose," and as each song was so well received, I gradually got up the courage to approach Louis Lane. Naturally I was apprehensive, but I asked if he would mind if we expanded the last note of "Abondanza" into a four-part chord. I expected lightning and thunder from heaven to strike down around me, but instead, he smiled. "Sure," he said, "give it a try. Why not?"

We did. We sang with the chorus and orchestra in that rehearsal and plowed through the tag, and when we ripped into the last chord, we shook the rafters. The whole place shivered with the ring of our sound. From those professionals, those high-brow, high-class musicians came thunderous applause. And along with the applause came a couple of words I'm sure we won't often, if ever, hear again. "Bravo! Bravissimo!" they cheered. When you get that kind of a reaction from members of the orchestra and chorus, and from Louis Lane himself, you have to be convinced that our music is not only popular, but very professional, too!

I'll never forget the night of the performance. There were a hundred orchestral instruments and close to a hundred twenty-five magnificent singers whipping up some powerful sounds together in "The Wells Fargo Wagon Is A-Coming Down the Street," and it was driving and moving and building tremendously. Then at one particular point in the song, our quartet stepped to the microphone and, all alone, a cappella, negotiated a key change for the entire mass of musicians. Maybe it doesn't sound like much, but boy, I want to tell you, it raises the hair on the back of my neck just thinking about it!

Apparently a show can be memorable for no other reason than where it's performed or who's in attendance. Russ Seely had a couple of dillies in that category:

A downtown Detroit bistro isn't exactly a typical setting for a barbershop quartet performance, but it was "Honky-Tonk Night" there and they were raffling off an old-time piano, so we thought it might be fun. Besides, that particular bistro was frequented by members of Detroit's courts of law—city attorneys and judges—and it had a good reputation for being the watering hole for all the legal eagles in the area, including His Honor, the Mayor. In any event it was successful and my quartet, the FOUR FITS, was well received.

When the place was about ready to close, a black man wearing a tuxedo came in and sat down at a front table. The owner of the establishment went over and spoke with him and then came over to us. "You guys have been real great about donating your services this evening," he said. "I wonder if you'd care to go to a kind of afterglow?" It sounded like a good idea, so we agreed. It was then 1:30 or thereabouts, but the owner said we should hang around until the place was closed and cleaned up, because we'd need special identification to be admitted at the party. It wasn't much of an inconvenience, so we waited around as requested. We were told the black man was going to play piano at the party.

A short time later the owner, piano player, and four of us piled into a car and traveled just a few blocks to an inner-city residential area that was in terrible shape. There were dilapidated houses and beat-up tenements and it was a rather wretched section of Detroit to say the least. We turned onto a street with no lights and stopped in front of an old, two-story frame house that looked like it was ready to go with the wind at any moment.

"We're here," the bar owner said.

We got out of the car and looked around. "We're where?" we asked each other. The black man led the way to the front porch and knocked on the door. We heard a number of locks being opened on the other side. The face of an attractive black woman appeared through a barred peephole. The piano player identified himself and the rest of us. The woman was skeptical, but after some discussion loosened the final chain and opened the door.

We walked in and were we shocked! Talk about a Shangri-la! What had been a slum of a house on the outside was a palace on the inside. It was decorated beyond belief with plush carpeting, marble tables, candelabra, rich, lavish furnishings. The living room and dining room had been converted into a single large sitting room with a baby grand piano at one end, and in the room beyond was a bar. Behind the bar was an attractive young lady, and as we looked around we saw a number of young ladies, all attractive, both white and black. Then to our amazement and amusement, we noticed a number of city officials, attorneys, lawyers, and a couple of men from the city council.

We found ourselves in the middle of a high-class brothel, and we were four very unusual guests there. Since it was close to 2:30 in the morning by then, the clientele was in a rather festive mood. A few had seen us sing in the bistro earlier, and one quickly piped up, "Hell, you guys gotta sing for us."

So we sang and we sang for probably two hours or more. That's all we did, mind you, just sing. I think we may be one of only a few quartets, if not the only quartet, that went to an afterglow only to find it was a house of ill repute, and then sang for an audience which I'm sure had gone there for an entirely different kind of entertainment!

The amazing part was that the men and women sitting on the floor around us were probably the most gracious and receptive audience we've ever sung for. Each time we tried to stop, they begged to hear more. That night we really wowed them, the FOUR FITS did, from bistro to brothel!

Another interesting performance for the FOUR FITS was the result of a call we received from a local booking agent. The agent handled many of our bookings in Detroit and wanted to know if we would be available to sing on a given date. He said he couldn't give us any more details about the engagement, couldn't even tell us the location. Our calendar was open, so we said we were available. The agent was reputable and assured us there was nothing illegal or questionable about the job. He said the reasons for all the mystery would be understood the night of the performance.

Even in the early afternoon of the day of the show we didn't know where we were going to sing. The other guys needled me about getting them into such a hokey situation. Two hours before we were scheduled to sing, we got a call from an Investigator O'Brian. I wanted to know investigator for what, and he told me the Federal Government!

It turned out to be a party for FBI agents. When they have a gathering they obviously can't publicize where or when it will be. All the arrangements are made surreptitiously. They had selected a casino on Belle Isle, an island in the Detroit River, and they converged on that spot from all parts of the country. It was eerie to see so many cabs and police cars arrive at the casino and discharge passengers. There were about a hundred twenty agents, and they were the greatest audience in the world. They looked like a crazy cross section of the American public, from junkies to businessmen, but they were all FBI agents. The printed program described us as "Killer Wearing" and "Wife-Beater Seely," and the evening was wall-to-wall laughter from beginning to end, a most pleasant job for us.

When it was over, the agents left as clandestinely as they had come. In true cloak-and-dagger style they scattered in every direction. After a half hour you'd never guess the meeting had ever taken place.

Some of those shows sponsored by other than barbershoppers can be just as interesting, rewarding, and memorable as the traditional barbershop show. Sometimes perhaps more so.

Shows to Forget

Into every life a little rain must fall, and into every barbershopper's life a little show disaster must fall. I wish I could forget a performance my quartet, the UNLIKELY HOODS, made in my early barbershopping days. We sang at the Masonic Temple in Poughkeep-sie, New York for a Demolay ceremony of some sort and when we were called into the room to sing, we knew we had a challenge. The audience consisted of about forty people, half of whom were dressed in impressive robes and ceremonial garb and were seated in what looked like royal thrones spaced along three sides of the room, while the other half stood stiffly behind us along the fourth side of the room. It was like singing to a tapestry. Our jokes and jolly songs were about as well received as a hijack announcement on a plane trip to Disney World.

It wasn't that we sang poorly. It wasn't that we sang well, either, I have to admit; it was just that the audience wasn't in any frame of mind to be entertained. At least that's what I like to think was the problem. Joe Schmitt says the SCHMITT BROTHERS had a similar disaster:

> *Over the years we've had a chance to sing in over 2500 per-formances, and among all the flowers and sweet fruit, we've encountered our share of thorns. Once we sang for a recogni-tion ceremony conducted for employees who had been with the company for twenty-five years. That year there were only five such employees plus seven company officers at the meeting.*
>
> *We started off our singing with an exciting, up-tempo opener and when we finished we stepped apart and bowed. No one ap-plauded. They just sat there, each apparently unwilling to be the first to start the hand clapping. If you want a real experience, be a quartet spokesman when you don't get any applause. Your first comment is usually "Thank you very much," but when no one claps, you can't say that. I stood there and looked at the dozen of them for a moment and then said, "You know, in my whole career, this is the first time we've ever sung a song and nobody applauded. I really don't know what to say. I do hope you enjoyed the song because we enjoyed singing it." We im-mediately went on to our next number and, pleasantly, they clapped for that one!*

The same thing happened to Tom Schlinkert and the ROARING 20's:

> *The first quartet performance we did outside of our high school variety show was at a community center in Cincinnati*

where teenagers were having a dance. For some reason the social director thought our barbershop quartet would be just the thing for those kids. At the time we were teenagers, too.

When we went out on stage to sing, they didn't even turn off the dance music. Some kids in the back kept right on dancing. Only a few watched us perform. We sang "Minnie the Mermaid," and "Riding Down a Canyon," and when we finished, the social director came over to thank us. "Gee, thanks for coming by," he said.

"Well, Leon," I said, "you're welcome, but is there any reason why they didn't applaud for us?"

"Oh, don't worry about that," he said casually. "Even if you were good, they wouldn't applaud!"

When a performance goes poorly as a direct result of your own doing, then it's not only unpleasant, it's also unforgettable. Keith Clark recalls a show he'd prefer to forget:

Once my quartet, the MIDTOWN AIRES, sang for a group of speech teachers at Genesee State Teachers College and at the time we were using a funny story about a guy with a stutter. How perfect, we thought, for the show.

We began our performance with a big-sound song and got a rousing ovation. Our second song went well, too, and then it was time for my stutter joke. I thought I told it well, and was consequently surprised and disappointed at its poor reception, but I noticed a kid in the wings hooting and hollering and jumping around, so I figured at least somebody got a kick out of the gag. For our remaining numbers, though, the audience was noticeably cool and unresponsive.

When we were finished and offstage, the kid explained that in the audience were not only teachers of students who stuttered and had speech problems, but also many of the students themselves! After a performance is clearly not the best time to learn of such important details. The damage was done, however, and we all paid dearly in embarrassment and chagrin. It sure makes a person uncomfortable to have to shoulder the responsibility for such a monumental faux pas!

I never again told that story onstage nor any other that might offend someone in the audience!

Here's Tim Stivers' "show to forget":

I recall very well the day and date of the fiasco: Friday the thirteenth. My quartet, the CLUB HOUSE FOUR, had an engagement to sing at a sales meeting in New Orleans for the Coleman Company. I had to work the following day, so I thought I'd fly us down and back Friday evening in my plane. However, a friend of mine offered to let me use his DC-3. He said I'd have to hire a crew, since I'm not qualified to pilot a DC-3, and I'd have to pay for the fuel, but he'd let me use the craft for nothing. What a bargain! So it was settled.

I hired a crew and then got to thinking. Since there were twenty-one seats on board, we could take along some friends and have ourselves a party! We could fly down, sing for the Coleman people, go out to dinner afterwards, and it would be a ball!

There must have been eighteen of us who finally gathered at the Louisville Airport and piled onto that airplane. By the time we took off, we were a half hour behind schedule. Head winds held us up another half hour, and when we got to New Orleans, we couldn't get the cabs we needed for another forty minutes or so. Arriving at the hotel, we were fearful our tardiness might delay the program. It didn't. Nobody was there! A couple of guys were cleaning up but everybody else had gone home. We had completely missed the whole doggone meeting! By then I was in a fuming rage. I had to jump into a telephone booth and have a short attitude talk with myself.

We went out to dinner anyway and tried to make the best of our bad situation, but as I recall, I wasn't in the best of spirits for our gala party. Back at the airport we pumped in four hundred twenty gallons of fuel and five quarts of oil and took off for home. At Louisville I had to fill it up again, so including the cost of the crew, the fuel, the dinner, and other incidentals, that little jaunt to entertain our friends and go to dinner in New Orleans cost us about seven hundred dollars!

An almost mirror-image version of that story is the tale Lou Perry tells about an unnamed quartet:

The quartet was invited to sing at a Christmas party in Nashua, New Hampshire for a fee, and the quartetters arrived at the designated location at the appointed time. It was quite evident that everybody there had finished dinner and had made a good deal of headway into an evening of drinking. The singers searched for the man who had hired them, but he couldn't be found. They mingled with the guests, inquired about their performance, but could learn nothing. After an hour they still didn't know when they were to perform, or exactly where, or for how long.

Finally the man who had hired them spotted the quartet, rushed up, and shook their hands warmly, trying at the same time not to spill his drink. "Boys," he said after a sip, "you were great! That was the best barbershop performance I've ever heard! Here's your check. Thanks very much. Maybe we can have you again next year!"

The quartetters looked at each other in bewilderment as the man rushed off into the crowd. After a brief conference they decided not to rock the boat, so they pocketed the check, walked out the door, and called it a day!

Come to think of it, maybe I've got that story in the wrong department; it might better belong in the "Shows to Remember" section instead. I know I've got Ken Beard's story in the right category:

As contact man, I had been pestered for many months to have my quartet, the SCARBOROUGH FAIR, audition for an agency. We were told the agent's many contacts in the showbiz world would prove invaluable to us. Unconvinced, we nonetheless agreed to appear on one of his shows, a variety program on Friday night in Peterborough, Ontario, for the benefit of Extendicare.

We pulled into the parking lot of the Peterborough Auditorium at 7:40 p.m., later than we would have preferred. Something was wrong. At twenty minutes to show time, ours was only the ninth car in the lot. Undaunted, we grabbed our costume bags and made a dash for the dressing rooms where we quickly changed. We were ready to go at five minutes before eight. Milling about backstage with an odd assortment of other acts, we tried to find out what was going to happen next. I peeked through the curtain and saw a grand total of twenty-eight people in the audience. Without our wives, there would have been only twenty-four.

Then we found our agent, meeting him in person for the first time. He wore a faded, printed-pattern beige jacket; an open-necked, printed-pattern shirt; and printed-pattern, powder-blue pants. He looked like a giant, three-dimensional road map. "There has been a problem," he announced to no surprise from the four of us. "The good folks of Peterborough apparently don't seem to care much about Extendicare."

We inquired if there had been much advertising and promotion for the show. "Advertising?" he asked. We thought his response was a rather crummy answer to a fairly significant question. "Ah, but the show must go on," he proclaimed optimistically.

"Why must the show go on?" we inquired.

"Because," he explained, "I won't get any more jobs if it doesn't go on!"

Our quartet was the headliner, but the agent asked us to open the show so the program would begin with as much vigor as possible. The curtain parted and out we ran to the warmest reception that the audience, which by then had swelled to thirty-two, could offer. For your information, such a reception isn't very warm at all. The silence was deafening! What with our wives' laughter and our own whispered mutterings, "What are we doing here?" and "Let's get the heck out of here," our performance was, I'm sure, somewhat less than our best.

If our opening was a bad dream, the remainder of the show was a nightmare, absolutely the worst piece of production imaginable. There were eleven unbearably long acts, some of which, most of which should have been "gonged." I think the magician must have bought a six-in-one magic kit the day before he performed. The program was so terrible, it was hilarious. We kept shaking our heads in disbelief.

Great yawning gaps in the show were commonplace. "And now, ladies and gentlemen," the MC announced, "miming Frank Sinatra's greatest hits, here's Marcel Schwartz!" There were a few disinterested handclaps and then there was a minute and a half of dead silence before Marcel made an appearance. The first half of the show concluded at five minutes to eleven!

Having withstood such punishment long enough, we asked our good friend the agent if we could open the second half rather than close it. We explained that we had to travel back to

Toronto, and mercifully he agreed.

We started the second half at twenty minutes past eleven. Out we went to hoots from our wives, and meager applause from those few who remained. We did our best to give an inspired performance, then packed up, and left the parking lot at fifteen minutes past midnight. The show was still going strong. No, I should say the show was still plodding clumsily along.

If that wasn't enough to make it a show to forget, we had another constant reminder of this scintillating experience. Our fee payment check bounced faithfully for weeks!

While it may be rather rare to have so thorough a show disaster, it's rather commonplace to have some sort of catastrophe, large or small, accompany each show. Dick Floersheimer has a story about such a catastrophe. He says it's true, but I'd say it's a little hard to swallow:

During the six years I sang bass with the MAIN STREET FOUR, we lived through many pungent, funny, bittersweet, and stimulating incidents, like most show quartets, I suppose. One warm night we appeared before an attentive and receptive crowd at the Philadelphia Academy of Music. We were singing onstage in the intense glare of a strong spotlight. One of the local moths found the spotlight rays attractive and spiraled lazily in and out of the bright light's path, each time flying closer and closer to the four of us. We were singing an all-out "gut buster" and my enthusiasm for the song lessened and my concern grew as the moth circled ever nearer.

The inevitable happened. As we reached the tag, I stood with my arms widespread and my mouth wide open and the moth, in a death dive worthy of Baron von Richthofen, plunged into the opening with a savage attack on my left tonsil! Right down the old epiglottis it flew, I kid you not.

Now, moth does not taste good at any time, especially not onstage while singing a show!

It's difficult for a singer to give his best performance when he's worried or sad or depressed, and when the whole quartet feels that way, it's next to impossible to put on a good show. Imagine the difficulty of performing under such circumstances when the entire audience is also at an emotional low. Such was the handicap the SALT

FLATS faced for one of their shows, as Carl Hancuff recalls:

> *The hardest time for us to be funny and put on a good show*
> *was the day President John F. Kennedy was assassinated. That*
> *night we were scheduled to sing on a show. About two hours*
> *beforehand I was asked if I thought we should go ahead with*
> *the program. All sorts of events were being cancelled. I said we*
> *should. Everyone was so depressed by the tragic news, I*
> *thought some laughter and song might help raise people's*
> *spirits.*
>
> *To say it was a subdued crowd is putting it mildly. I suppose*
> *we probably weren't working as hard at being funny as we*
> *should have, either. It was by no means one of our best per-*
> *formances, but if we were asked to do it again, I'd say we*
> *should. Performers have a responsibility to their audience and*
> *it's important to honor that responsibility. Personal feelings and*
> *individual emotions should be secondary to the duty and honor*
> *of entertaining showgoers.*

A Slice of Show Biz

Irving Berlin wrote a song about it, "There's No Business Like
Show Business," and barbershoppers get a pleasant taste of its
allure whenever they sing for an audience. The show business allure
is part of barbershopping's appeal.

Some barbershoppers get more than a taste. They perform in
popular quartets, have a full schedule of show engagements,
perhaps one or more shows every weekend of the year, and get the
opportunity to sample and savor the record-making, radio, TV, and
theater end of show business as well.

The SCHMITT BROTHERS have enjoyed more than a quarter-
century of quartet singing and in that time have been involved in
many different phases of show business action. Joe Schmitt
discovered early that each performing medium has its own unique
demands and challenges:

> *It was a great thrill for us when Decca asked us to make a*
> *record. We went to the Universal Studios in Chicago for the*
> *recording session. We had practiced, rehearsed for hours. We*
> *were ready. We thought. We sang our first song and only then*

discovered what record making is all about. We had sung that first song so many times over the years it was part of us, like our arms and legs, yet we recorded it seventeen times before we were satisfied with the result.

I don't know if it was the song, or the fear, or getting ready, or the unfamiliar recording-studio discipline and surroundings. In a few takes we heard a distracting squeak and it took some time to discover it came from someone's shoe. Now when we record we sing barefoot so if somebody wants to move, he can, without a squeak.

It's an interesting experience, attempting to do something as perfectly as possible. Perfection is not a readily attainable goal, particularly in a quartet, and making records demands unfamiliar disciplines. As show-performing barbershoppers we react to the audience. Audience applause and appreciation inspire us to give a better performance. But when we're singing to a guy with a headset in a glass-window control room, we find he's not much of an inspiring audience. So in a recording session we spend a lot of time trying to inspire each other. We have to smile at each other and encourage and congratulate. We find ourselves standing in a circle when we record so we're better able to share feelings and emotions and it helps our sound.

For me, record making is the single toughest performing challenge I've ever experienced. It demands total dedication and is both mentally and physically exhausting.

Val Hicks reports that some professionals are able to devise schemes which lessen those physical and emotional demands:

Some time ago the Society Music Education and Services Director, Bob Johnson, was invited to Hollywood to supervise the recording of a Fred Waring's "Pennsylvanians" barbershop album. Actually, they weren't Pennsylvanians at all, just a group of Hollywood studio singers contracted to sing for the record. Bob Johnson invited me along to act as music consultant for the session.

I expected to see Fred Waring diligently rehearsing the chorus, but he had turned everything over to Johnson. "You handle the recording session, Bob," he said. "My name will go on the album, but you're more of a barbershop expert than I am, so you direct the chorus." Waring took off for a day of golf!

Television is another exciting show business medium with its own peculiar demands on the performers. When the FOUR STATESMEN appeared on Canadian TV, they caused quite a stir, at least in one household, as Frank Lanza explains:

Jim Gillespie from the Montreal Chapter was one of the first men to actively encourage barbershopping in and around New Brunswick, Nova Scotia, and Prince Edward Island. He had been a railroad man with the Canadian Pacific and I presume he had a free pass to travel all over that part of the country. On one trip he asked us to go along to see if we could stir up some interest. At the time there was one chapter in Kentville, Nova Scotia.

We went to Nova Scotia and managed to sing on a half-hour show presented by the Canadian Broadcasting Company television station in Halifax. As far as I know it was the first televised appearance of a barbershop quartet in Canada. We were anxious to see the taped program when it was broadcast but were traveling between towns at the time, and there were no restaurants or other public places where we could watch a TV set. We started looking for homes with TV antennas.

Spotting one, we stopped and dispatched Don Beinema, the biggest guy in the quartet, to knock on the door. One of the wives who accompanied us also went along so the family living there wouldn't be too apprehensive. I'm sure the family was leery when Don asked if we could watch a TV program, but they agreed, and all ten of us stormed in and made ourselves comfortable. There were quartet members, wives, Jim Gillespie, and friends.

The family was flabbergasted to see us on their TV screen and they treated us like celebrities. They gawked at us and chattered about us like we were visiting royalty. From all appearances, the family really enjoyed their uninvited guests. I know the guests had a good time!

Frank Lanza also tells an interesting tale about a quartet interview on radio:

We were scheduled to participate in an interview on a local radio station prior to a Hartford, Connecticut show. I was in New York City on business during the day and planned to drive to Hartford for the seven o'clock taping session, but just my luck, we were hit with the worst rainstorm in years. The traffic and driving conditions in downtown Manhattan were impossible. It soon became apparent I'd miss the interview.

I got to a telephone booth and called the other guys at the radio station. Good fortune had not abandoned us, for Vinnie Zito, an avid, experienced, and longtime bass-singing barbershopper, was with them and we quickly decided he could take my place for the broadcast. We figured nobody would ever know we made a last-minute substitution.

Listening to the radio program in my car, I heard the interviewer ask Vinnie how it was, if he was the quartet tenor, that his speaking voice was so deep and basslike. I sensed that our deception was doomed to failure and I wondered how in the world my surrogate would ever be able to gracefully wiggle out of his entrapment. Vinnie replied without hesitation. "Well," he said matter-of-factly, "I always sing falsetto." I thought his answer was a stroke of genius, but if you've ever heard Vinnie's voice, you'd have to say it was nevertheless a little preposterous.

Barbershop music is beautiful, special, and unique, but its appeal is not universal. Some people prefer jazz, or rock, or classical, or something else entirely, and of course no one should attempt to force his own particular music preference on another. Now this brief lesson in courtesy is intended to lead us into a story told by Steve Keiss about an experience he had singing with the KINGS MEN:

After seven weeks of stringent rehearsals, we went to Nashville, Tennessee to compete in a Dixie District quartet contest, and we won. Saturday night at the afterglow we met Jack Irvin, who was in charge of special events for the convention. He told us we were scheduled to appear on the "Grand Ole Opry" in the Wyman Auditorium, three blocks away. The "Grand Ole Opry" was broadcast nationwide on radio and as quartet contest winners we were to sing on the show.

Backstage we felt uncomfortably out of place. The other performers traipsed about in their sequin suits with their fancy electric guitars; everything there was strictly one hundred percent country music. We eyed each other nervously in our out-of-place, formal tuxedos. Then we were introduced.

We sang "That Old Soft Shoe," but I'd say the audience reaction would have been more enthusiastic if our act was tying our shoelaces. The people were courteous enough to applaud mildly. We finished our song and hustled offstage and as we did, the people came back to life again. Electric guitars were plugged back in and the place started to jump. The music came on strong and loud; the people came on likewise.

We left quickly by a stage door which led out into an alley. In the dim light I saw somebody approaching us. My mind began to race. He's probably a typical country-music fan, I thought. His pickup truck is parked on a side street somewhere and there are probably a couple of rifles on a gun rack in the back window. The man was huge and he stopped in front of us, blocking our way. "Are you-all the fellas that just sang up there on the stage?" he inquired with a drawl. I figured we were in for a lot of trouble and I tried to maneuver unnoticed to the back of the group. He reached out and clamped his hand on my shoulder. "I asked a question, sonny," he said.

"Yes, sir," I said bravely. "As a matter of fact, we are indeed the quartet that just sang on stage." All the time I was thinking that if he took a swing at me, hopefully I'd be able to duck, and maybe he'd hit Jack Irvin or one of the other guys in the quartet. He was obviously rather upset that we had interrupted his country music.

He stuck out a huge fist that gobbled up my hand and said, "I just want to tell you that's the finest thing I've heard in years! I sure do 'preciate it!"

We all breathed a sigh of relief and thanked him from the bottom of our hearts. I don't know whether we were pleased with his praise or just thankful to be alive. Probably both.

I wonder how many thousands of barbershoppers have appeared in local productions of "The Music Man." I was a member of that school-board quartet during a County Players' production of the play in Poughkeepsie, New York. What a time we had. What a marvelous musical it is, with great songs, great dialogue, and a warm, satisfying story line.

Almost everybody knows the BUFFALO BILLS appeared on Broadway and in the movie version of "The Music Man." Vern Reed reminisces about the early days of that show, before it was a smash hit, when the idea for the story was just emerging, and when the production was just starting to take form:

> *After winning the International in 1950, we made some records for Decca. Shortly thereafter, Meredith Willson and Tallulah Bankhead, who starred together in "The Big Show" on NBC radio, used a couple of our recordings on the air, so I wrote Meredith to thank him. Several years later, he and his wife Renee stopped in Buffalo, New York on a lecture series and were interviewed on "Luncheon Club," a radio program that originated from Buffalo's local NBC affiliate station. By coincidence, the interviewer was the announcer for our weekly BUFFALO BILLS radio show, and he thought it would be great if we sang a couple of songs on the "Luncheon Club" and met the Willsons.*
>
> *Afterwards at lunch together, we first heard about "The Music Man." Meredith said it was a musical inspired by the memory of his boyhood days in Mason City, Iowa. Much of the story was to center around the town's pretty, young piano teacher and a con artist's attempts to sell uniforms and instruments so he could organize a boy's band. He recalled a barbershop quartet, the RUSTY HINGE FOUR, that performed at every civic event, and he said he wanted us to audition for the quartet parts in "The Music Man." It was a truly tantalizing possibility, but we quickly filed the idea in the wastebasket, where we had deposited so many other grand hopes, wishes, and promises that never came to pass.*
>
> *Then came our big year, 1957. In February we appeared on the Arthur Godfrey Talent Scouts show on CBS-TV. The program originated from Lake Placid, New York, where Arthur was appearing as guest of honor at the Annual Winter Carnival. We were one of three acts selected for the TV show and were fortunate enough to win. As a prize, we appeared on Godfrey's morning TV show from Lake Placid every day for a week.*
>
> *A month later I got a call at my office from Kermit Bloomgarden, who said he was producer of a new Broadway musical entitled "The Music Man." He wanted us to try out. I thought it was too good to be true. Soon we were in New York City onstage at the Majestic Theatre on Broadway, singing songs and going through the ritual of a musical comedy audition. I was surprised that the audition people seemed more interested in our acting than our singing abilities. I suppose our singing*

talents were known while our acting skills were not. Director "Tec" DaCosta was there, as were choreographer Oona White, musical director Herb Greene, the head wardrobe mistress, and of course Kermit Bloomgarden and Meredith and Renee Willson.

After an hour's workout in front of that small committee in the large theater lit only by one onstage work light, we received the inevitable report: "Don't call us. We'll call you."

Surprisingly, three weeks later they did call, with a request to go back to New York for another audition on the following Saturday. There was another hour of intense auditioning and another convening of the jury. Then Meredith came onstage with a big smile and outstretched hands to welcome us into the cast.

Suddenly we had a part in a real Broadway musical! We had actually made it! The BUFFALO BILLS were in "The Music Man." Broadway was something we had always thought about, dreamed of, but then the realities began to set in. We wondered what it would mean for our kids, our wives, and our former quartet way of life.

Suddenly we realized we'd also be carrying the responsibility of the entire Society into show business. How would the audience accept us? How would the Society react? Would "The Music Man" make it or fall flat before ever opening, like so many Broadway productions? If the musical did make it, would it provide the showcase to propel us into TV, concerts, nightclubs, fairs, recordings, and other facets of show business we'd need to be able to perpetuate the quartet? These were but a few of the questions that began to pile up and puzzle us.

To that point in the BUFFALO BILLS career, we had the excitement of barbershop shows, occasional appearances on national TV, our own local radio and TV shows, some recordings on major labels, our regular jobs, and of course we had our homes and families. You could say we had our cake and could eat it, too! We wondered how much peril a show-business life would pose, but how oh how could we turn down such an opportunity, such a chance to fulfill a lifelong dream?

On October 21, 1957, we gathered with the rest of the cast at a rehearsal hall on the lower East Side of New York. It was a new world. No tinsel and glamor there, just an old, sparsely decorated building with an atmosphere of long hours of work by dedicated professionals who had it all on the line. Meredith and Renee presented a two-person synopsis of the show. The two-inch thick script was absolutely frightening. We were advised we were to open in Philadelphia for our "out of town tryouts" in less than a month! In that short time the entire production would have to be created from scratch, with a cast of sixty-five. It seemed impossible!

We worked seven days a week, twelve to fourteen hours a day. The number of changes in the script was incredible. Forty-five minutes were completely cut from the original version of the musical. We'd just get some lines memorized or a song learned, and it would be altered, revised, or tossed out altogether. The lines, songs, stage blocking, and choreography were in a constant state of flux. What was learned one day had to be unlearned the next.

Finally, it was opening night in Philadelphia and along with the excitement and anticipation came the jitters, fueled mainly by the uncertainty and insecurity resulting from so many changes. People were already filling up the theater when the entire cast was called onstage. Tec DaCosta gave a brief pep talk which he concluded with the admonition, "When you look out into that audience, make believe they're all sitting on toilets!" A big laugh went up from the cast and as if that were a cue, the orchestra began the overture. The cast took their places and "The Music Man" was on the boards and rolling. The opening scene played great, the audience responded, nerves calmed, and the pace of the show slipped into high gear.

After the curtain came down on the last act, we all gathered at a local restaurant to sweat out the critics' reviews. Meredith read aloud each newspaper review as it came in. They were all very favorable, and a big, happy cheer rocked the room when the last review was heard. Strain and tension from three trying weeks of rehearsals were released in one tremendous cheer.

But Meredith's perfectionist nature wasn't satisfied. Bright and early the next morning the full cast was back in rehearsal. A major weakness in the script was a means of smoothly introducing the four of us into our stage role as a quartet. You'll remember that at the beginning of the musical, four school-board members are the mayor's henchmen, and they're supposed to confront Harold Hill and bring him into line. In those roles, we were constantly arguing, bickering, and fighting with one another. There was no smooth way to transform us from a foursome of bellicose board members into harmony-loving barbershop singers.

Frank Loesser, who wrote several great musicals, including "The Most Happy Fella," came to Philly to help iron out a few of the rough spots. He suggested use of some vocal principle to make the transition, and several implementations of his idea were put into the script and tried out onstage, but nothing seemed to work. The days slipped by and that one portion of the dialogue remained the weakest. Then with just eight more performances left in Philadelphia, Meredith called me in my hotel room at four o'clock in the morning. "Vern, I've got it!" he shouted in my ear. "Come to my room right away." I still have the envelope on which he had scribbled the key phrase for the transition: "You see, singing is just sustained talking."

"Hey, what's this I'm hearing?" Robert Preston said to us when we demanded to see his identification papers. He turned to Bill Spangenberg and blew a pitch pipe.

"Look, I don't sing, if that's what you mean," Bill said to him.

"Well, you see, singing is just sustained talking," Preston would say. "Here, say 'ice cream.'" Bill sang it in his deep bass voice. "Now you, sir," Preston would say as he turned to Scotty Ward, "sing this note." I had the final note on top of the chord. And that's how we began "Sincere," and turned the fighting school board members into a friendly barbershop quartet.

Audience reaction was great and the song added another high spot to the show. It seemed to be the missing link that solved the last remaining problem in the script. The changes and refinements were finally locked in with only three performances left before our closing night in Philadelphia.

When the last curtain fell, we dashed for the train to New York City. The cast had run-throughs all day Sunday to firmly establish the new lines in our minds and to familiarize ourselves with the theater. By Sunday night all the sets had been hung and we went through two full performances with costumes and scenery. So we wouldn't lose momentum, rehearsals continued all day Monday, Tuesday, and Wednesday, with "benefit" performances in the evenings.

At last, Thursday, December 19, and our premiere opening on Broadway! Backstage spirits were high and when the curtain went up, the cast brought that stage alive with the sound and excitement of "The Music Man," and kept it that way right through to the final curtain. The audience stood and clapped wildly in rhythm to "76 Trombones," while the cast took so many curtain calls, we lost count. All the reviews were "rave notices." What an experience! We made a total of 1320 performances before leaving the Broadway stage to make the "The Music Man" movie, and I wouldn't trade any one of them!

I bet most barbershoppers would give their right vocal cord to be able to trade places with Vern Reed and have his barbershop singing experiences. Surely, he had some of the best.

In show business, though, for every success there may be a dozen failures, maybe a dozen dozen failures. But for some strange twist of fate, so many golden opportunities and hoped-for dreams are missed. Buzz Haeger tells about one of them:

Our good friend Walter Latzko, who was coach and arranger for the CHORDETTES and the BUFFALO BILLS, became involved in "Bub," a new musical written by a marvelous fellow, George Church. Walter recommended my quartet, the FOUR RENEGADES, for the show and he asked if we would go to New York for an audition.

The play was based on a true story about someone with the nickname "Bub," who enlisted in George Washington's Revolutionary Army, became a scout, and developed an uncanny talent for moving undetected in and out of enemy lines. After a number of phenomenally successful scouting missions, Bub was promoted to sergeant, later wounded, and only then was discovered to be a girl. Her name was Deborah Sampson. She was every bit as famous in her day as Barbara Frietchie or Betsy Ross. Walter Latzko sent us all the music and we spent two frantic weeks of concentrated rehearsals in preparation for our tryouts.

When we sang for the people who auditioned us, we really fractured them. As an organized quartet we had a tremendous advantage over other auditioning groups because most foursomes had never sung together before. Their quartets consisted of four excellent singers, each of whom had little or no quartetting experience. We particularly impressed George Church and it was decided then and there that the FOUR RENEGADES would be four soldiers in the show.

Westinghouse agreed to underwrite the entire quarter-million-dollar expense of producing the show and putting it on the road and it looked like "Bub" was destined to follow along the same path to fame and fortune that was blazed by "The Music Man." But then fate stepped in with two strange turns of events.

The first was musical. "Bub" was to be performed entirely a cappella, without any instrumental accompaniment whatsoever. One of the reasons Westinghouse agreed to finance the show was to test and develop a new wireless sound system. A wireless throat microphone and transmitter made by Westinghouse were to be worn by each member of the cast, and all transmitted signals were to be fed to a large Westinghouse console, amplified, and projected throughout the theater. This offered no vocal, technical, or sound problems, but it did run afoul of labor problems. When the musicians' union learned about our all a cappella musical, they said that would be just fine. However, they went on to say there would be a minimum of fifteen musicians in the orchestra pit for each and every performance, whether or not they opened their instrument cases, and each musician would be handsomely paid! That created an unexpected and significant cost roadblock.

The second roadblock was encountered on the streets of New York City. About the time the musicians' bomb exploded, Doreen Church, the author's wife and a wonderful lady, was mugged for the second time. It was the last straw for George. He called us all together and announced he had reached his limit. He took his script and marvelous music and moved to Naples, Florida where he has been ever since, as far as I know, and that was the end of "Bub."

Yet, though the show never saw the light of an opening night, it was quite an exciting experience as long as it lasted. It would have been a fabulous show!

That's the story of show business; the smell of the greasepaint, the roar of the crowd, the bright, blinking marquee lights, success, fame, fortune. By the way, there is also the disappointment, the big chance missed, the heartbreak, the sorrow. Like the song title says, "There's No Business Like Show Business!"

The Gift of Music

Barbershoppers often receive requests to donate their singing talents to worthy causes and they respond eagerly to such requests. As a matter of fact it's not at all unusual for quartets and choruses to solicit singouts at hospitals, children's homes, senior citizens' homes, and other such organizations and institutions. Such singouts offer barbershoppers additional opportunities to perform, with an extra reward—the satisfaction of giving. Tom Masengale of the CHORD BUSTERS describes it well:

The most satisfaction I ever got out of barbershopping was singing at St. John's Catholic Hospital in Tulsa, Oklahoma. We became pretty well known there. We'd sing for almost any occasion and we'd walk up and down the halls and sing at the nurses' station so patients in nearby rooms could hear us. We sang one night at a dinner for doctors, and later the nurses took us to an operating room suite. All the nuns came from their dorm next to the hospital and we sang for them for an hour or more. We had a captive audience, so we really took advantage of it.

Another night we went to the hospital to sing for a friend and wound up singing for all the ambulatory patients on the floor. Most of the nurses were there, too, and many of the nuns. When the Mother Superior asked if we'd sing for one particular patient, we told her we'd love to. We would sing for anybody, anywhere, any time. She returned pushing a wheelchair with a gentleman in it. He looked very tense. His muscles were rigid, his expression was a grimace, and he didn't move. He was one of the local Baptist preachers, a prominent man in Tulsa, involved in civic affairs, always busy with activities for the benefit of the community. None of us knew he was in the hospital.

We started to sing, "I'll take you home again, Kathleen," very softly, and as we did, we noticed the lines in his face soften. We sang directly to him and saw his muscles relax, slowly at first, then more and more as we sang softer and softer. At the last chord of the song he slumped over in his wheelchair, limp as a blanket. The Mother Superior quickly wheeled him out of the room. We continued our impromptu concert for the other patients and nursing staff there.

The Mother Superior was in the lobby waiting for us as we left

*the hospital. She wanted to thank us for singing "Kathleen."
She said the minister had been in the hospital for more than a
week with an extremely severe nervous breakdown and the
hospital staff had been working unsuccessfully all that time trying to break his tension. What the doctors had been unable to
do, she told us, we had done by singing "Kathleen." With the
tension broken, treatment could begin for his recovery to get
him back on his feet and back into public life again.*

*As we walked out of the hospital we felt ten feet tall. We
stood on the steps for a moment and then shook hands and
congratulated each other. All we had ever given to barbershopping was more than repaid that one beautiful evening. We had
truly helped someone!*

When a barbershopper himself is confined to a hospital bed, he's
likely to be visited by his compassionate compatriots. Such was the
case with a SALT FLATS hospital visit, as related by Carl Hancuff:

*One of our chapter members had a massive heart attack and
was in the hospital, so the quartet decided to pay him a visit. He
wanted us to sing a song and we thought that was a good idea.
"Let's sing our new one," I said eagerly, but I couldn't think of
the title. The other guys didn't want to. "Come on," I begged,
"it's such a pretty song."*

*They talked me out of it and we sang something else. I still
wanted to sing our new number but got nowhere with the idea.
After we left, they told me the name of the song I was so
anxious to sing. It was "There Goes My Heart."*

It seems there is no human experience or ceremony that cannot
be enhanced by the application of barbershop harmony. Here's an
example in a story from Bud Harvey:

*Joe Wolfe worked for the Wilson Sporting Goods Company,
was well known in the world of professional golf, and loved
barbershop singing. Though his golfing travels kept him on the
move, he still enjoyed cracking an occasional chord, and
whenever I encountered Joe at the PGA Championship, or the
Masters, or the Open, we would give those "Sweet Roses of
Morn" one dickens of a going over with just two parts, lead and
tenor. On his winter jaunts to Florida, he frequently attended*

the Palm Beach County Chapter meetings with me.

When Joe died after a dreadfully long siege of leukemia, his widow called and asked if I could get a quartet together to sing at his funeral. He had expressly asked her to do that. Now you don't casually throw together a pickup quartet to perform for anything as touchy as a funeral, but what could I say? I told Grace I'd try my darnedest.

I called Wally Speir, a real jack-of-all-parts; Dr. Steve Aliopoulios, fine bass and even finer dentist; and Carlos Capp, home-builder and lead. We had a quick rehearsal at Wally's house, mastered a couple of lugubrious hymns, and went off in haste to the funeral. We went off very well, indeed, thank you. In the packed funeral parlor it actually sounded lovely! Even the minister was pleasantly surprised.

"When I told him I was having a barbershop quartet, he nearly panicked," Grace said after the service. "He thought you were going to sing 'Coney Island Baby' and 'Sweet Adeline.'" Then she thought a moment and added, "To tell the truth, I think Joe would have preferred 'Coney Island Baby' to 'Just a Closer Walk With Thee.' "

Maybe the audience of golf pros and other people in the sports world would have, too, but they seemed suitably impressed with our spur-of-the-moment performance. Several told me later they'd never heard a barbershop quartet at a wake and thought it was super!

The old-time barbershop songs work a grand therapy on people. They shove aside immediate cares and concerns and let the listeners ruminate in the harmony. Lou Sisk tells of a time when the magic was particularly potent:

On one occasion we were scheduled to sing for a group of senior citizens, a mixed crowd, mostly women, numbering a couple of hundred. It was a cold winter night, the weather around Pittsburgh was lousy, I didn't feel well, and I didn't want to go. I knew I could call somebody else to take over the directing of the chorus for me, but then I thought again. No, it was a responsibility, so I decided to go, and by the time I drove the twenty miles to get there, I was feeling pretty good anticipating the show. It was something worthwhile. We were going to sing for some nice people, give them an entertaining night. That was pleasant to contemplate.

As part of our performance I always made a habit of talking to the audience. I'd get a dialogue going with them and we'd yell and shout at each other and have a good time. I'd get everybody joining in a sing-along and make a real party out of it. Anyway, at one point in our show I yelled out, "Is there anybody here named Nellie?" Of course it's pretty rare to find a Nellie in a crowd, but some lady in the back of the room yelled back something to me. She was about sixty-five years of age, very tall, a nice-looking lady, with bright red hair. A few people around her tittered, but I didn't hear what she said. "Is your name Nellie?" I yelled.

"No," she shouted, "my name's not Nellie. My name's Martha!"

"All right, Martha," I told her, "we're going to sing this next song just for you, in your honor." It was all a setup for a song gimmick that we used. The chorus sang "Wait 'Til the Sun Shines, Martha," and when we sang "Martha," we all pointed at her. It's a never-fail crowd-pleaser.

When we sang the song Martha started yapping at me even before we reached the tag. So back and forth we went. It was a real craziness we had going on, with spontaneous comments flying about like snowballs. "How did you like that, Red," I hollered.

"Listen here, little fella..." she hooted right back. We were insulting each other left and right.

When the show concluded, Martha came over to me, patted me on the back, and we exchanged still more jabs and barbs. Then cookies and coffee were served and everybody lined up for the food. A lot of people said nice things about our performance and it was pleasant to bask in the compliments and kind words. As I munched on a cupcake, the recreation director came over to talk to me.

"I want to tell you something that might be of interest," she began in a serious voice. "That woman has been here for well over a year and hasn't spoken a word to anyone for the last eight months. She tried suicide twice and we were terribly worried about her. Her reaction here tonight is the first communication we've heard from her for such a long time, and I want to thank you on behalf of all the people here, particularly for Martha and her family. You got something out of her tonight

that was beautiful and we're seeing Martha the way she used to be!"

"Oh, my God," I said aloud. "I guess that's why I'm here." I told the director that I hadn't felt like coming. I guess I had come for Martha, and it made my heart glow like a blast furnace. There was indeed good reason to have that kind of fun and be there that night. It was good old "Red," good old Martha! After our show she was high and I was high, too, on something called laughter and love.

I guess there are performing times when we touch people without even knowing it, when the harmony and mirth of the moment really make a difference in someone's life. It's quite a thrill to have a part of that kind of action!

Dick Hadfield's quartet had an experience that closely paralleled Lou Sisk's singout:

I entered the ministry and the Reading, Pennsylvania barbershop chapter in the same year. Actually, I joined the chapter as a member of an already-formed and performing barbershop quartet called the FIRESIDE FOUR. With financial support, encouragement, and humor from my dad, Homer, who also sang with us, our quartet enjoyed many years of satisfying barbershopping.

As natives of Phoenixville, Pennsylvania, we were asked by the Soroptomist Club to sing at Christmastime for the County Home as part of their annual gift-giving visit. We willingly obliged. We were one of but a few groups allowed to tour and entertain in some of the "sensitive" wards, where there were elderly folks in diapers, patients clutching dolls, men and women staring blankly at nothingness, neither willing nor able to communicate. The quartet vowed to make the trip every year as long as it was geographically possible for us to do so. We have now made our fourteenth annual appearance at the home even though the quartet disbanded long ago.

One Christmas was especially memorable. Singing our way through the wards, we were led by the nurse to a room set apart. Peering closely we saw the form of a woman whose large, dark eyes gazed out suspiciously at us from under the sheets. We were told she had been a patient for ten months and had not once spoken during her stay, nor had she spoken for several years prior to her admission to the institution. Her gnarled body was resigned to bed and her existence seemed little more than a countdown to her demise. We began to sing "The Lost Chord," and as we did we saw the woman's lips quiver. As we sang through those majestic chords, a strange and wonderful thing happened. The woman actually began to sing along with us, each word distinct and on pitch. The nurses stared and listened in amazement, then hurriedly called others to the room to witness the happening. When we reached the song's conclusion, her voice sang out loud and strong with "the sound of the great Amen." Word spread through the home quickly: A woman unable or unwilling to speak had actually sung with a barbershop quartet.

The Soroptomists and the FIRESIDE FOUR had participated in a moving and inspiring moment and had felt a sensation very much in tune with the spirit of the Christmas season!

Barbershoppers have a long and admirable record of charity work. I'd say it's part of the Society member's character; the desire to perform and please and entertain an audience, the wish to help others, the need to share the joy of singing and song. And barbershop charity is not restricted to vocal performances. Singers are just as likely to pitch in with time, muscle, and money for worthy causes. It was this attitude, this yearning to contribute for the benefit of others, that led to the adoption of a Society-wide service project. Reedie Wright tells how it got started:

The Institute of Logopedics project was first introduced in the early 1950's by Ed Fahnestock who lived in Wichita, Kansas, but it was sidetracked at the time, although there had been talk for years about supporting a charity on an international scale. Then in 1964 President Dan Waselchuck appointed a committee to study the possibility of having an international charity project. On the committee were Rupert Hall, Lou Laurel, Al Smith, and myself.

We made inquiries of a number of organizations such as the Heart Fund and the Tuberculosis Fund and got enthusiastic responses from them all. The Institute of Logopedics was again suggested and the institute's executive director, Dr. Palmer, invited us for a visit to look over the facilities. We accepted the invitation and were thrilled with what we saw. Most impressive to us was the use of music to break through the barrier of silence that many of the children there experienced. We saw a therapy session with a little boy who had never spoken a word before. Conventional methods of communicating with him had failed, but music had not been tried. We watched as the boy gradually sensed the rhythm of music played for him on a piano. He gazed about the room aimlessly for awhile, then started beating out the rhythm on the floor with a stick. It was remarkable to witness.

The trip made it crystal clear for us. It was so beautifully appropriate that we as a musical organization should support such important work where music plays such an important role. And that's how the Society came to accept the Institute of Logopedics as our national charity. Their slogan at the time was "That they shall speak." We thought for our use it would be fitting to add as preface "We sing." It has been the motto of our charity work ever since.

The Society has now raised millions of dollars to help the children and adults at the Institute with their awesome communication handicaps. As chairman of the International Logopedics Service Committee, I've dedicated much of the rest of my life to this project. It's a great privilege to be able to give time and energies to this committee and to the Society's efforts with this project. It is the third cornerstone of our Society. We have administration, musical ability, and we have charity. In time our Society will be as well known for its charitable work as it is for its singing.

Such is the spirit of these fun-loving creatures they call barbershoppers. Each is a singer with a song in his heart. Each is a singer with a heart in his song!

Entertaining the Troops

Many barbershop quartets sang for United States servicemen overseas during military actions in Korea and Vietnam and for troops stationed in post-war Europe. Barbershop singing tours were first conducted in conjunction with a program initiated by Dean Snyder of Alexandria, Virginia, who held many official positions in the early Society years. He reports:

The Society's Armed Forces Collaboration Program began with me. In 1947, as secretary of a Presidential Commission, I was sent from Washington, D.C. to Fort Knox, Kentucky to help prepare a report on the advisability of extending the wartime draft into peacetime. One of the many problems of such a proposal concerned the kinds of recreational activities that would be available for peacetime soldiers who had no military combat mission. While at Fort Knox I met Captain H.H. Copeland, who was directing some experimental unison and glee-club singing programs for young draftees. I didn't know him well, but I said, "Captain, that's not the kind of music you want for these men. And besides, I wonder how many barracks have pianos! Have you ever heard barbershop singing?"

"I've heard of it, but don't know much about it," he confessed. I told him I'd have some barbershop arrangements sent to him, and I telephoned Carroll Adams, at that time the Society's Executive Secretary, who sent a whole bundle of materials.

The next year Copeland was assigned to Army Special Services Headquarters in Washington and I got a phone call from him one day. "Remember our discussions in Fort Knox?" he began. "Colonel Bishop and I want to come over and see you right away." In my office they told me they were ready to propose that the military adopt a program of barbershop quartet singing and they asked if I'd help. Of course I would.

At the next Society Board of Directors' meeting, Bishop and Copeland presented their proposal to the Board's hearty endorsement. From that beginning we developed a barbershop program that included training manuals and special quartet arrangements for the homefront camps, and almost immediately we began planning overseas tours. I was the first International Chairman of Armed Forces Collaboration, and it has been gratifying over the years to see my early efforts produce so many successful barbershop singing tours for the Army, Air Force, Navy, and the Marines, both at home and overseas.

Those tours turned out to be memorable for servicemen and singers alike. Here are Jack Macgregor's reactions;

During the Vietnam War it was the custom of the USO to invite barbershop quartets to sing and bring some laughter to the wounded recuperating in hospitals throughout the Far East.

With great pride the SOUNDSMEN accepted the invitation, and through the cooperation of our understanding wives and employers, we embarked on a twenty-day tour which will remain in our memories as the greatest experience of our barbershopping careers.

Our singing began in Tokyo at three large hospitals. Each performing day was four to five hours long, with appearances in about five wards at each hospital we visited. That was the scheduled portion of our trip. Unscheduled, we also made numerous appearances at officers' clubs, NCO's and enlisted men's clubs, and almost anywhere else we got a chance. The throat spray and lozenge portion of our carried-along medical supplies got a lot of use.

Volumes could be written about the spirit and courage of those tens of thousands of young men in the Far East, but the emotions of four middle-aged men singing around big lumps in their throats can never be satisfactorily described. When we left for home we had nearly lost our voices, but we found the warmest imaginable glow in our hearts.

We were sent overseas to amuse and inspire those men, but they turned the tables on us. They inspired us with a renewed faith in American youth. There were no turned-off teenagers, just a bunch of beautiful kids doing a dirty job that had to be done. They laughed at our antics, applauded our acts, and talked—my how they talked—about everything from how they got where they were, to what they planned to do when they got back to the United States.

Those young men liked barbershop singing. Maybe it was because the songs were a bit of "back home" to them. They thanked us for taking time to go over there and entertain. Imagine that. They thanked us for doing what we love most to do.

There's no feeling greater than the satisfaction you receive when you are able to stir up some happiness for those in need. This was especially true for the SOUNDSMEN. So many of those GI's were young enough to be our own sons. Our singing tour is now many years behind us, yet it left us with an impression that remains as potent and poignant as if it happened yesterday!

The BUFFALO BILLS went over on a couple of early tours, one to

Europe, another to Korea, and Phil Embury went along as MC:

> *I consider myself most fortunate to have accompanied the quartet on those overseas tours. I want to tell you their performances before those soldier audiences were electrifying. From the expressions on their faces it was clear the GI's were thoroughly entertained. I asked a Special Services officer how the quartet compared with other entertainers and he said the BUFFALO BILLS were one of the two or three best performing groups ever.*
>
> *The year after our European tour, we went to Japan and Korea. That was another heartrending experience. I have a picture of a soldier audience behind the Thirty-Eighth Parallel and that picture is worth ten thousand words. It's priceless. The war was on when we were in Korea and we went into the MASH hospitals behind the lines to put on shows for paraplegics and so many young kids chewed up by the war. I got right down and lay on my back to talk to one of them who was strapped in a harness, face downward. It would make you cry to see those boys. I felt such sorrow for them.*

Here are some of Vern Reed's reactions to those BUFFALO BILLS' tours:

> *I wish I could adequately describe the impact we felt as a result of some of our experiences. The trip to Europe in 1951 was trying, with the ravages of World War II still so apparent. Many buildings remained in a state of rubble, and the people, too, continued in a state of shock. But despite the language barrier, our performances reached the people. The German people particularly impressed me with the way they responded to our songs and the spirit of our vaudeville barbershop quartet type of presentation.*
>
> *In Korea we spent a week with the Fighting 999th right on the front lines. We were with the MASH people as they picked up the wounded and we sang for those same GI's later at their hospital centers. Some of the sights are painfully recalled. I can clearly see the sixth floor of the Tokyo hospital where there were five or six dozen Stryker frames in a single large open room. Each frame supported a soldier who was suffering some degree of paralysis, but the men seemed to enjoy our singing*

efforts. We were not always able to get our vocal cords to function the way we wished while observing such a shocking scene.

I climbed Mt. Mansfield a few months ago, all alone, and when I reached the peak and looked out over the great expanse of the Champlain Valley below, I immediately recalled a scene from twenty-eight years before, when the BUFFALO BILLS were in Germany. We had gone to the top of the Zugspitze, highest mountain in the Bavarian Alps, and at the summit the four of us couldn't help but throw our heads back and sing, ''I'm Sitting on Top of the World.'' On Mt. Mansfield I closed my eyes and recreated that image in detail from long ago. Such quartet events are constantly and easily and vividly recalled, for they made an immeasurable impact on us. To this day they influence our thinking, reasoning, and actions, in all facets of our lives.

When the MIDNIGHT OILERS went on tour to South Vietnam, Bob Johnson went along. Tom Hine describes some experiences:

We flew directly from Travis Air Force Base to Tan San Nhut in Saigon by way of Anchorage, Alaska and Yakota, Japan on board a Pan American Clipper with a hundred sixty GI's and civilians. After a day in Saigon taping a TV show and doing a couple of live performances, we were flown to the Seventh Fleet which was operating in the Gulf of Tonkin off the coast of North Vietnam. Our first big thrill came when we were ''hooked'' aboard the flight deck as our plane landed on the Bennington. What a jolt!

We performed on the aircraft carriers Bennington, Ticonderoga, and Enterprise, singing on hangar decks, in mess halls and staterooms, on closed-circuit TV, in sick bays, and we even rang a few chords in the head. On the Enterprise twenty-five officers and enlisted men were trying to charter the first sea-going Society chapter.

We flew to Vung Tau and performed for an ammo group there but the show did not go well. The audience of fifty-five men was almost hostile. We had been billed as a rock 'n' roll group, but that disappointment wasn't all that turned them off. The sound system didn't work and on top of that, although the show was outdoors at night, there weren't any lights! It was disappointing for all, but it was the only unsuccessful show of the tour.

The next day our transportation failed so we hitch-hiked by air to Saigon aboard a C-123 carrying seven dead bodies. We had to come face to face with the cold hard facts of war. From Saigon we went north by armed convoy to a group of the 199th Infantry for an afternoon show. We continued by convoy to Long Binh and performed that night for the 90th Replacement Headquarters. Several days later we were taken to Hill 35 as guests of the 5th Marines for a show before one of the most enthusiastic audiences of our trip.

When we contacted the 362nd Army Signal Compound in Da Lat in the Central Highlands, they asked if we would be willing to go to an outpost on top of Long Bian Mountain. We agreed, and an armed convoy was arranged. The camp was on top of a mountain 8500 feet high, site of the second largest communication base in South Vietnam. After the show we had to leave immediately so the armed convoy could get us down and get themselves back up again before dark. We were armed for the trip and had air protection both ways. It was the dustiest ride of the tour.

Once we were about to touch down on a runway somewhere in the Mekong Delta when all hell broke loose. Mortar fire turned the runway into Swiss cheese. Our pilot pulled back on the stick and we all pulled our C-130 back into the clouds. We skipped that performance and flew directly to Soc Trang.

We didn't get more than a few hours' sleep that night when we were awakened by earth-shaking blasts that sounded like the world was coming to an end. Our quarters were in front of the big guns that pounded the surrounding hills and the cannon fire was ear splitting. Poor Bob Johnson. The light bulb next to his bunk vibrated out of its socket, hit the concrete floor, and exploded with the sound of a hand grenade. Bob shot out of his bunk like the planes that catapulted us off the Bennington! Our itinerary was changed twice because of heavy fighting in areas where we were scheduled to perform, and we were constantly, awesomely aware of the sights and sounds of the war.

When it was time to play, the GI's had an insatiable capacity for fun and song, but in the split second it took to sound an alert, that jovial, easy-going attitude changed to the business of warfare, and the young, smiling faces were quickly etched with lines of concern and determination. We saw the transformation occur several times, but never once did we hear a murmur of despair.

The most amazing recollection I have of the trip was standing atop the Caravelle Hotel in downtown Saigon at about 8:30 in the evening before our departure. I still cannot fully comprehend it. We looked out beyond the city and saw the flashes of howitzers and heard the thunder of man-made devices working their destruction. It was hard to rationalize the fun and joy of barbershop singing with the sorrow and pain of war.

Here are a few of Marty Mendro's recollections of the MIDSTATES FOUR tour of Korea:

We were scheduled for a Sunday afternoon show and I guess the GI's were pretty skeptical about spending an afternoon listening to a barbershop quartet. We started out with about twenty-five guys in the audience. By the time we finished our first number, though, we had maybe a hundred twenty-five. The outside speakers were hooked up and by the time we finished our first set, the tent was jammed with GI's. When we finished the second half of our show, I think the whole compound of 1500 kids had packed in there. We had to do twenty minutes of encores.

Of course the kids weren't allowed in the area with loaded sidearms or rifles; all weapons were supposed to be left out in the compound. But some of the GI's had their rifles with them anyway at the shows. We used a lot of corny gags and one-liners in our performance, and whenever we did, the kids would slide the bolts of their rifles as if they were loading ammunition.

"Run into the roundhouse, Nellie; they can't corner you there!" was one of a million one-liners we used. "Roy Rogers tore his pants and at last we found his hide out!" Sometimes the clicking sounds were deafening.

On one of the first shows we did, in Taegu, I was struck with the appearance of a youngster in the front row. He looked no older than sixteen, was a handsome kid, sweet face, and he ate up our performance. He thought our whole show was great. Two weeks later we were back in Taegu for a hospital show and there he was again in the front row. This time half his face was bandaged and one arm was in a sling. Even though it was a hospital show, he had somehow managed to get hold of his rifle and at every corny line he clicked the bolt. It was near the end of our tour and we were going home again, soon. The kid was, too. For him the war was over.

While the singing tours must have been tremendously grueling, with heavy show schedules and tedious travel arrangements, there were still times for sightseeing and even shopping. Carl Hancuff recalls a couple of stories from a SALT FLATS Far East tour:

> *In Japan we went into Tokyo to do some shopping. I don't know how it happened, but on the return trip we got on the wrong train. It was seven o'clock at night, we were loaded down with packages, and we must have been thirty miles from where we wanted to go.*
>
> *Those Japanese trains really move. A hundred miles an hour is nothing for them. We were chatting and laughing and having a good time when I realized something was wrong, and when we figured out what had happened, we panicked. I went up and down the aisle looking for help. None was to be found. The train was filled with elderly Japanese people; not one could speak English.*
>
> *About then my good old American ingenuity told me the first thing we had to do was get ourselves off the train. We did at the next stop, but we still didn't know where we were. In a minute the train was gone and we were standing almost alone, lost in a dark, remote, little village of Japan.*
>
> *We decided that the most logical thing for an American barbershop quartet to do when lost is sing a song. We huddled together and sang a song.*
>
> *A small crowd of people gathered around us as we sang. A few had a "Yankee go home" expression on their faces and most gave us frowns and looks of suspicion, but at the end of our song I asked if anybody spoke English. A sweetheart of a thirteen-year-old girl stepped forward. She took us to the right train, got us on board, and headed us back to our proper destination. It was an experience I'll never forget.*
>
> *Another rather touching experience on our Far East tour involved a gentleman named Ramon, our driver in the Philippines when we were singing there. Thieves thrive in Manila, so wherever we went, Ramon had to stay with the car. It was summertime, a hundred ten degrees, and Ramon had to sit out in that sweltering heat all day while we enjoyed ourselves in*

pleasant, air-conditioned buildings. It seemed unfair.

Ramon and I quickly struck up a friendship and we had long talks together. I learned he was married, had some kids, and our conversations got me homesick for my own children. At the end of our stay we wanted to give Ramon a tip. We chipped in and gave him twenty dollars. He didn't want to accept it, fought like a tiger, but we explained we wanted him to buy something nice for his kids.

The next day, our final day, when he picked us up, he had bought a gift, but for us! When it was time to leave, we felt a deep, warm relationship with Ramon. As we parted we shook hands and he held the back of my hand against his forehead for a brief moment. I didn't understand the gesture, but it seemed special.

In Tokyo, we found a Filipino houseboy who understood its meaning. "Oh, that's very nice," he said. "It simply means 'I love you.' " It was a touching moment for us.

Of course the SALT FLATS also had their share of *shows* in Japan, Okinawa, and the Philippines. Carl Hancuff describes some particularly impressive experiences:

In the hospitals we visited, many men were bedridden and couldn't get to the show, so we sang and did our stuff from ward to ward. After two or three songs we always tried to strike up a conversation with the guys and find out where they were from. We had sung in so many cities around the United States, we could usually describe something familiar about their home towns and that seemed to help.

Once we sang for a ward of four guys and one wouldn't even look at us. I assumed he was shell-shocked or just freaked out by the war. Anyway, when it was over, Dale Taylor tried to talk to him. The boy didn't say anything at first, but then reluctantly muttered an answer. Dale talked with him for a couple of minutes. When we left the ward we found out Dale was the first person the GI had spoken to in more than a half year. He had simply refused to talk or even acknowledge anybody, but as performers we got through to him and that was pretty gratifying.

Another time we were about ready to go into a ward where there were broken limbs, shattered legs, guys all strung up with their arms and feet in the air, like those cartoons you see, when a nurse came out. Teary-eyed, she asked if we'd come back later. She said the most popular guy in the ward had a sudden blood clot or other complication and had died. He had been tremendously well liked. His father was en route from the United States to visit him. Everybody in the ward was terribly shaken up. We were asked to delay our performance so the body could be removed.

We returned an hour later. The nurse reiterated that it was a close-knit ward of patients, a simply terrific bunch of guys. "Give it the best shot you've got!" she admonished us as we started in.

We went in there and put on a full thirty-minute show. It was one of those situations where there were no holds barred and we did stuff we had never done before, just to entertain. The beauty of it was that after a while we got them going. We had them laughing and we had them applauding.

We did a song called "Old Joe," during which I take out my teeth. The FLATS have done the bit for a hundred years. I portrayed a drunk and the act just hit them right. Everybody was enjoying it and we were working harder than ever to put it across. I don't think we ever tried so hard to entertain, with so much hurt in our hearts for the people in our audience.

It was so unbelievably tragic over there to see those eighteen-, nineteen-, and twenty-year-old kids. They were on the threshold of life, had beautiful, strong bodies, but half of their bodies were missing or mutilated. It was tough to see, tough to accept, and tough to perform to.

Those sights and feelings must have been tremendously difficult to contend with for touring barbershop quartets. Yet, as hard as it was, I'm sure a great satisfaction must have accompanied the ordeal. Here are some of Buzz Haeger's recollections from the FOUR RENEGADES' trip:

We were privileged to do a USO tour of the Far East just prior to Christmastime. We spent seventeen days in Japan, Okinawa, and the Philippines, and then came back through Guam and Hawaii to Travis Air Force Base in San Francisco before returning home. In Tokyo our performance preceeded the Bob Hope Show, and we were able to meet Bob Hope and his son Toby.

We met Les Brown and Roosevelt Greer, a marvelous fellow, and Pamela Plummer, who was Miss World, and Ann-Margret.

We also sang in a number of hospital wards, where we were told none of the other entertainers had the guts to go. We were in our 1890 show outfits and they put smocks over us and surgical masks on us so we could go into the burn ward. It was grim facing those hideous realities. You have to have a strong stomach. But you can't imagine how appreciative those guys were. When we came out of the burn ward all four of us had tears in our eyes. We couldn't help it.

We sang in a hospital in the Philippines at Clark Air Force Base and one of the fellows there was a triple amputee. He only had one arm left. He enjoyed our performance, wanted to applaud, but the only way he could show his appreciation was to slap his bare stomach!

Like a number of other barbershop singing ambassadors, the FOUR STATESMEN went on tour at Christmastime. Frank Lanza has some thoughts about the trip:

Bob Hope was on tour at the same time and of course was doing all the big shows while we were performing in the hospitals, singing for as few as one or two patients or in most cases a wardful of wounded GI's.

We gave up our Christmas at home for the tour because we thought our music and presence might be most appreciated then. We spent Christmas Eve on Guam, and with a group of about twelve other Americans decided to go carolling at midnight. We thought we had run the gamut of emotional feelings with our hospital performances, but our midnight singing wrung out yet another from us. In Guam's heat in the strange surroundings and without our families, the carolling left us melancholy and maudlin. We realized how much we missed being home for Christmas and how very much those young GI's must miss Christmas at home, too!

Listening to barbershop music may not be the all-time favorite GI pastime, but witnessing the affection, fondness, and feeling of four sincere singers is an experience of another dimension!

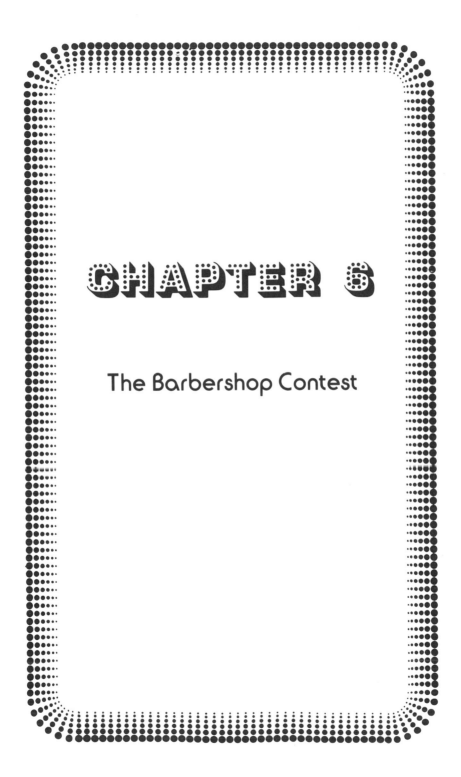

CHAPTER 6

The Barbershop Contest

The Barbershop Contest

Sing, riding's a joy!
For me I ride.

Robert Browning

year after winning the Championship, the Dapper Dans Chorus from Livingston, New Jersey returned to the International stage for a performance as outgoing champs. From the show they put on, I'd say they were also trying to prove they could have won it all over again if rules permitted. The lyrics of one of their songs contained a line with a message: "It's neat to compete!" It sure is. In International competition, at the District level, or even in a chapter contest, competing is a special kind of barbershop singing with its own challenges and rewards.

When a quartet or chorus sings on a show, it is measured by audience reaction. In a contest it is measured by a panel of experienced judges who evaluate the group's sound and stage presence and the song's arrangement and interpretation. Numerical scores

203

are given by each category for a two-song, four-to-six minute performance and the sum, minus time and other penalties if incurred, determines each group's rank. Compared to a show, competing is a whole new ball game.

Competitions are a basic and essential ingredient of contemporary barbershopping. They provide motivation for quartets and choruses to improve and a mechanism whereby the style of barbershop music can be safeguarded. As judges evaluate barbershop performances, their scoring encourages singers to strive for a perceived ideal barbershop music form. Thus, barbershop music is preserved. Yet it may still evolve as the judges' consensus of the ideal shifts over time.

All of the great emotions of a World Series swirl around a barbershop competition, and the competitors ride along on the crest of the excitement. Talk about excitement! It used to hit me so hard I was an absolute mess before a contest. I was so anxious to perform well that I'd enter panic mode the Tuesday or Wednesday prior to a Friday night competition, and it would build from there! By the time I was backstage I wasn't sure I'd remember my own name, let alone the words and notes of our songs.

Maybe that's part of the reward, just living through those contests! Over the years, though, experience has mellowed me. My panic has now given way to mild terror.

Seriously, it has been a point of some pride with me that I no longer plunge into a catatonic state when my quartet name is announced. I haven't exactly rocketed to the heights in quartet competitions, but I've found a number of other satisfactions. I've found a number of disappointments, too, I'd have to say. Disappointments? Heck, that's an understatement. Some contests were absolutely devastating! How could those judges...

Well, the judges called them as they saw them and heard them and I have no cause for complaint. I wish we had done better. I usually wish that. But then I wish I were a millionaire, too. I think what hurts most is facing fellow barbershoppers after a stunning defeat. I've never found anything cleverly witty or richly philosophic to say under such circumstances but neither has anyone I've talked to. Only time soothes and heals the wounds.

Lest I sound as if I'm contradicting my own premise, let me quickly add that in spite of the sting of a disappointment, I'd still rather compete than not compete. For me the best of barbershopping is the singing, not the listening. Indeed, it's neat to compete. Clearly Bud

Harvey shares my sentiments:

> In the Washington, D.C. Chapter I sang baritone with the
> TRUMPETONES, one of the worst and certainly loudest but en-
> tirely lovable quartets that ever graced or disgraced the contest
> stage. We traveled to Philly for the International Convention and
> while the SUNTONES may have won the golden lyre, the
> TRUMPETONES won the freestyle street-corner and barroom
> championship in a walk. I doubt if there's a joint in the City of
> Brotherly Love that isn't still sweeping out fragments of frac-
> tured chords left behind by our visit.
>
> Leo Fitzpatrick, our tenor and another novice barbershopper,
> had only recently tumbled to the exciting tenor resolve at the
> end of a tag, when the tenor takes the elevator to the pent-
> house, then rolls in an Immelmann turn and floats back to the
> tonic note. Leo and I were rooming together, but, as befits the
> elder statesman of the group, I retired early. It was not to sleep,
> however, because my room was next to the hotel air shaft and
> until 4:30 a.m. I could track Fitzpatrick from floor to floor by his
> screaming tenor voice resolving tag endings.
>
> Needless to say, the TRUMPETONES fared poorly in com-
> petition. That was not a matter of great concern to us. Our forte
> was simply singing for fun, a way of barbershopping life to
> which I'm still firmly committed.

> When I was the baritone in an inept but enjoyable quartet in
> Miami called the COCONOTES, we always competed and
> always finished nowhere. The maddest experience of all was
> the year we competed at Lehigh Acres in west Florida. Tenor
> Tom Davey was smitten with laryngitis on the eve of the con-
> test, but we were determined to go to Lehigh Acres anyway. We
> hoped for the best. For the entire trip across the Everglades we
> alternately dosed Tom with bourbon and tried singing. His tenor
> croaked encouragingly a few times and we were buoyed by the
> belief he might be coming around.
>
> By evening he was speechless, absolutely soundless. We
> went on anyway and sang as a trio with Davey mouthing the
> words and occasionally emitting a wounded screech. We fin-
> ished unmentionably, of course. The next morning at the
> quartet critique a sound judge studied his notes in disbelief,
> then looked up at us. "To tell you the truth," he said, "I couldn't

hear the tenor at all.'' We explained why, and he shook his head. ''Then, for heaven's sake, why did you compete?'' he asked.

We thought our answer was logical and irrefutable: ''Why not?''

Although barbershop quartet and chorus singoffs are conducted with the utmost of good-sportsmanlike conduct, and there is even friendly cooperation between contenders, there is also good-natured teasing, bragging, and other forms of precontest verbal skirmishes. The competition sometimes just naturally extends to mild forms of psychological warfare. For example, once when the Poughkeepsie Chapter competed, we left some sheet music in the final warm-up room where choruses assemble before they go onstage. Our toughest competition sang immediately after we did so we knew our rivals would receive our message minutes before their performance. We wanted them to know what we thought of their chances for winning. The sheet music was ''The Impossible Dream.''

As director of the Poughkeepsie New Yorkers Chorus, Bill James was expert in the art of such gamesmanship:

I remember when the New Yorkers came into their own in a category I call ''snookers.'' It was the first time we were aware of our prowess in that department. We were onstage for a ten-minute rehearsal session three or four hours before the actual contest. All choruses have an opportunity for such a brief, on-stage practice. We felt confident about our songs but really didn't expect to win the contest. As we lined up on the risers we saw the New Bedford Chapter chorus entering the auditorium. They were heir apparent to the championship and their ten-minute rehearsal on stage followed ours.

That year we had a gangbusters of an opening in one of our songs, ''Roll Out of Bed with a Smile.'' We were able to sing the whole song pretty well, but with the opening strain we could really lay out a sudden and impressive surge of sound and power. I wasn't particularly interested in having all of us stand there and get nervous with the New Bedford Chorus watching and listening, but I sure didn't want to turn tail and run, so I decided to go ahead with the practice.

We started out with the first few words of the song, and it was so loud and so full and so startling, I stopped the chorus right there. I wanted to congratulate everybody on the really super introduction, but, having stopped the singing, it seemed more appropriate to say, "Okay, guys, that's it." The chorus looked at me kind of dumbfounded and walked offstage. We probably used two minutes of our ten-minute warm-up period.

The New Bedford Chapter members sat there with their mouths agape. They must have thought that if we could sing the whole song the way we started it, nobody could beat us. We strolled back to our dressing room feeling confident we had done everything we could to demoralize the opposition. But we left a spy, Steve Plumb, to see if our spontaneous scheme had its desired effect.

Sure enough, Steve burst into our dressing room a few minutes later with a report. New Bedford's director had spotted him in the auditorium. He didn't want anybody from Poughkeepsie watching, so he closed the curtain. We felt like maybe we were going to win the contest after all. And we did! When the director closed the curtain for his rehearsal, he effectively told us he thought we could outsing his chorus. More importantly, he also unwittingly gave the same message to every one of his own chorus members. Their chorus was defeated before a single contest note was sung. It was the first District championship for Poughkeepsie and was, as I say, the first time we became aware of the powerful game called "snookers."

It's interesting to note that there's just as much mental conditioning going on *inside* a chorus or quartet as there is between groups. It's critical that singers reach an optimum mental state before competing. It's essential for a peak performance. For me such a state is reached by building an increasing momentum of optimism and encouragement and by focusing all my mental energies toward the single objective of singing and performing well. Often other techniques are employed, as Freddie King explains;

To show how psychology really worked on our lead singer, Jim Grant, let me relate what I did to him the year the ORIOLE FOUR won the International Championship. I concluded that he didn't do his best unless he was a little angry, so I nearly drove him insane. We felt the SUNDOWNERS had the best chance of beating us and as it turned out they came in second. They had a tremendous sound and were an extremely talented bunch of guys. Just the thought of competing with them made us quake.

When we packed our bags to get ready to go over to the hall for the quarter-final competition, I wrote a little note and put it in Jim's suitcase. It read, "Some people say Larry Wright is the best lead in the world. You have two songs to change their mind."

"What the hell is this?" he mumbled when he saw it. My plan was working.

For the second session I had written another note and placed it where Jim couldn't help but find it: "Some people are beginning to doubt that Larry Wright is the greatest lead in the world. You have two songs to add to their confusion." He was really getting hot.

Then came the finals. I wrote, "Some people say that Jim Grant is the greatest lead in the world. Prove it!" He went out on the contest stage and did just that!

You'd never believe all the imagination and effort that choruses and quartets exert in preparation for barbershop competition. Careful planning, hard work, much time and money are invested, but only occasionally are the investments rewarded with victory. Often the outcome is catastrophic disaster. For example, according to Bob Morris, the Thoroughbred Chorus from Louisville, Kentucky rehearsed the clapping portion of their song routine for three straight days. Then for the contest they put on their gloves, and the sound and feel were so foreign, their whole performance came apart.

When the Westfield, New Jersey Chapter ordered new uniforms for the chorus, everyone was afraid they might not be delivered in time for the District contest in Atlantic City. Russell Malony explains that timing wasn't the problem:

All our fears were allayed when the new outfits arrived a full week before the competition. However, every jacket was cut to the trouser size! Consequently, a man who ordered a size forty jacket and size thirty-three pants, for example, found himself trying to squeeze into a size thirty-three jacket instead. The uniforms were useless, except for a chorus of dwarfs!

Then in a District contest in Washington, D.C., Westfield wore navy blue blazers, gray slacks, white shoes, and bright red ties. While the chorus warmed up outside Constitution Hall, the bright sun somehow reacted with the fabric of the ties and changed their color. Some turned gray, others turned black, but since our singing bombed during the contest anyway, we didn't even bother explaining to the judges why we had different colored neckties.

Trying a different approach in another District contest, one of the Westfield Chapter members brought his priest to the pre-contest rehearsal session to bless the chorus performance. Somebody piped, "Now we'll know who to blame if we don't win." That seemed but a meager consolation when the chorus placed fourteenth out of fifteen.

Lindy Levitt tells a story about the Mt. Rushmore Chapter's first contest at a District convention in Wichita, Kansas:

The chorus sang a Society arrangement of "'Til There Was You," and we sang it letter-perfect. The River City Chorus had sung the identical arrangement two years before us and had scored well, so we knew nothing could go wrong. After our performance we all had the taste of victory. Then we got the news: We were disqualified! It seems in that two-year period the arrangement category had changed and our song no longer met the barbershop arrangement criteria! Judge Jack Baird explained that the music had at least three "contrived chords," but as far as we were concerned, the judge's explanation seemed contrived!

Ah yes, it's neat to compete, even though there are moments when such a contention is very much in dispute. The best of efforts and intentions ofttimes meet with far less than hoped-for results. Tom Cogan learned that bitter lesson in his first contest with a new chapter:

Contests have always amazed me. I'll never forget when I was a member of the Ravena-Coeymans-Selkirk-Glenmont-and-Cedar Hill, New York Chapter. As a matter of fact, we received our chapter charter during the convention, and twenty-seven gallant men went up in barber outfits to do their best for the contest judges.

Of course most of our members had never even seen a barbershop contest before and were scared to death. Unfortunately, I was directing. It was an abysmal performance. Dur-

ing the critique afterwards one of the judges commented, "Your chorus looked like twenty-six pallbearers plus an inept director. Except for one fellow in the center of the back row, everybody looked deadly! Only that one man sold the song and showed some good stage presence. He alone sang with his heart and soul in the music. If everyone else performed the way he did, the chorus would have scored very well."

The gentleman referred to was Ben Kirby, a splendid individual who brought several new members into the chapter. But Ben was a hokum comedian and couldn't carry a tune in a bushel basket. For two songs Ben didn't miss a single word or note, because he didn't sing a single word or note! I didn't have the heart to tell the judges. If everyone in the chorus had sung like Ben Kirby as recommended, the audience would have been treated to five minutes of dead silence!

The poor judges. They take the blame when singers score poorly but get none of the credit when singers score well. They really take a beating. Sometimes literally. When Russ Seely directed the Lake Shore Chorus from Grosse Pointe, Michigan in a contest, it became clear that judging can be hazardous to your health:

We had a baseball game in one of our contest performances and it really ended up on a sorry note, because we discovered our batter was a little too expert with a bat. He connected with a plastic ball and hit a line-drive bullet that smacked a judge right on the top of the head! Fortunately, there isn't any point penalty for injuring a judge, but I have a feeling it might have affected our score anyway.

Judges make every effort to be fair and impartial and to assure that each competing group performs under identical conditions. When the sound system or lights aren't quite right, the chairman of judges must take action to correct the problem. This all led to a little embarrassment during a contest MC'd by Leon Avakian at the Asbury Park, New Jersey Convention Hall:

During the contest, after the first few quartets had sung, Ray Glynn, Chairman of the Judges, jumped up and stopped the proceedings. "Stop all that infernal noise backstage," he demanded. I told Ray I was sorry, but it would be impossible, because the sound wasn't backstage at all. The convention hall had been built to jut out over the ocean, and as a result, huge waves rolled in underneath the structure, pounded against the pilings, and created the deep, rumbling noise he objected to. Ray got a chuckle out of that but must have felt a whit silly, too. With tail between his legs, he went back to the judges' table, and the contest resumed.

The following year when Ray was again chairman of the judges and the contest was again in the same hall, he laughingly reminded me of his impossible demand. I told him that no demand is impossible and took him outside to the promenade. Lo and behold, the ocean was no longer there! It was held back by a huge stone breakwater, constructed at a cost of more than $700,000.

Later in the weekend when Ray got a chance to address the convention, he remarked that the people of Asbury Park seemed willing to do almost anything to improve the facilities for barbershop contests. Maybe I should mention that as City Engineer for Asbury Park, I had been involved in the planning stages of the breakwater for years. I suppose I ought to add that the breakwater had nothing to do with barbershopping, but rather was constructed to save the building!

Occasionally a judge has a chance to "get even." He can't tamper with the scores but can enjoy a moment of mental retribution. Val Hicks had one of those rare experiences:

At a convention in Kansas City I heard a quartet singing in a deserted ballroom and stopped to listen. They were singing a song I had arranged and I wondered if they were indeed using my arrangement. They were. That was strange, since they couldn't have obtained it from me, so I stepped inside to see who it was. I won't mention the group's name, but it was a prominent medalist quartet. They didn't know me from Adam.

My presence must have disturbed them because they stopped singing. One of them spoke to me rather brusquely and curtly. "Can we help you?" he said. It was more a request to leave than an offer of assistance.

"Well," I said, "I was just curious to see who was singing that song."

"Now you know," he said abruptly. At such a rebuff I left the *room.*

That night I was sitting in the judges' pit when the same quartet marched out onstage to compete. Like many experienc-ed quartetters, they scanned the faces in the audience and judges' panel as they sang. When the rude singer's gaze met mine, he registered an instant look of panic. Of course I didn't penalize them for their rudeness or bad manners, but they didn't know that. A performance by a bunch of guilty barber-shoppers always suffers!

As if judges don't have enough trouble with sore losers, long hours, and poor pay (judges contribute their services; they receive no pay), they also have to contend with difficult travel arrangements. It's not unusual for a judge to travel hundreds, even thousands of miles to a contest, often farther than the competitors. Dick Ellenberger's trip to a Division contest in Kentville, Nova Scotia is a good example:

One Friday afternoon in the middle of March I left my office in Schenectady, New York at three o'clock and drove to Beverly, Massachusetts where I met the gang from the Beverly Chapter plus a number of other Northeastern District barbershoppers who were going to take part in the contest. After a quick bite in a diner, we boarded a chartered bus at seven and started off for Nova Scotia.

Time passed quickly with all the singing and laughter, but the farther north we got the more snow we encountered. As we headed up a hill in northern Maine on a small country road which was supposed to be a shortcut, the bus lost traction in the snow and slid off the road into a ditch. It was 2:00 a.m.

We pushed and shoved and rocked, but the bus wouldn't budge. Finally two hours later, with help from the state road maintenance people, a sander truck, a bulldozer, and the sheriff, we were on our way again. We stopped at Calais, Maine for breakfast, and when we arrived in St. Stephen, New Brunswick, we were five hours behind schedule. The bus driver spent sixteen hours with us until his replacement took over at St. John.

When our weary busload reached Kentville, it was late Satur-day afternoon, almost time for the contest to begin. I checked in at a hotel, took a quick shower, and dashed over to the school auditorium. It was a fine contest and there was a great show afterward. The afterglow that followed lasted far into the night.

Not much more than an hour after everybody turned in, it was time to load back onto the bus for a drive to the Kentville Curling Club, where we received a fine breakfast and saw a curling demonstration. We said our good-byes and started off for the trip home.

Late Sunday night we approached the city limits of Beverly. I still had a two-hundred-mile drive ahead of me to Schenectady. When I got home Monday morning it was too late to go to bed, so I ate a leisurely breakfast and went directly to work, arriving there at eight o'clock. This kind of trip illustrates that you don't have to be nuts to be a barbershopper, but it helps!

If you're willing to endure that kind of ordeal, you're either a dedicated barbershopper, a nut as Dick suggests (or both), or you're a masochist. It's neat to compete, but isn't it a smidgen far to travel just to sing two songs in a Division contest? Maybe not. Barbershoppers around the country resort to such marathon bus rides to get them to contests. Lloyd Steinkamp went along on a great Phoenix Chapter expedition:

For one contest we took almost the entire chapter of forty-four men on a bus to Alameda, California, a distance of eight to nine hundred miles from Phoenix, and the bus smelled like a gymnasium when we got there. (It was even worse when we got back, by the way.) We had a couple of quartets when we started off, but when we got to Alameda we had eleven. Obviously we didn't have eleven tenors, so we switched people around to sing different parts and we entered all eleven quartets in the contest. We wanted everybody to participate.

That eleventh quartet really lacked something, though. Why, we couldn't even get them to take pitch properly. We paid their five-dollar registration fee anyway and entered them as the FOUR WALKERS.

When contest time came, they were introduced to groans from the audience. "Not another Phoenix quartet!" The men walked out onstage beaming with confidence. They stepped to the microphone, took a fine, deep bow, stood up straight, and promptly exited! The FOUR WALKERS were true to their name.

Their sound score wasn't bad, but the judges gave them a

three-hundred-sixty point time penalty.

Because of strict contest rules and regulations, a barbershop contest may not be quite as entertaining for an audience as a barbershop show. Apparently that wasn't the case, however, when Dick Hadfield and his father went to their first contest:

> *We went to a fall Mid-Atlantic District Convention in Washington, D.C., just bursting with enthusiasm for our then newfound hobby of barbershop singing. We had no chapter affiliation, although we had established friendships in several chapters in southeastern Pennsylvania. We sat in the balcony reveling in the four-part harmony as the quartets and choruses competed.*
>
> *Dad was seated next to a quiet and intent fellow, and Dad proceeded to tell him everything he knew about barbershopping—the kind of music it was, the swell members, everything. Dad was new to barbershopping, but what he lacked in barbershop experience and knowledge, he more than made up in enthusiasm. He was a regular evangelist. All the while the man smiled politely and nodded acknowledgement. He left shortly before the intermission. I was worried that Dad's exuberance scared him off.*
>
> *After the intermission a community sing was announced and the fellow who came out to lead it was the man who had been sitting next to Dad. He was Bob Johnson, Director of Musical Activities for the Society!*

While the uninitiated may suppose that a barbershop contest is exclusively a singing competition, experienced competitors know better, for there's far more to it than merely making barbershop sounds. For example, in a quartet contest each foursome must walk on and off the stage, and it can actually win or lose points in the process. As a result, entrances and exits are rehearsed and refined along with the singing portion of a contest performance. Bob Seay explains the potential pitfalls:

> *One Mid-Atlantic District Convention was in Philadelphia at the Bellevue Stratford, and the quartet contest was held in a small theater at the hotel. My quartet, the B STREET FOUR, had brand-new outfits consisting of lemon-yellow slacks and*

*maroon jackets, and we were looking forward to the competi-
tion. Our singing was mediocre at best, but we had a neat
stage-presence routine, a new "peel-on, peel-off" entrance and
exit routine.*

*It wasn't complicated but it had a lot of pizzazz. Instead of
walking onstage as a unit, all four of us turning together at the
microphone, we peeled off one by one when we got to center
stage. Exiting was in the same manner but in reverse. We practiced the maneuver from both sides of the stage so there
couldn't possibly be any trouble. We had it mastered.*

*At the quartet briefing we learned that the quartets had to
enter from stage left and exit to stage left, because of an
obstacle in the stage right wings. No problem. After all, practice makes perfect. We went through the motions a couple of
times more to make sure we were comfortable with the procedure.*

*For some reason the easy becomes difficult under pressure
and the well-rehearsed can disintegrate into mind-boggling
chaos. Our entrance was beautiful. Our singing was barely ade-
quate, but we expected that. Then after our final grand bow it
was exit time, and much to my horror I found Vern Leonard
walking in front of me off to stage right! I had no choice but to
follow him, as did the lead and tenor in turn. It was a splendid
exit, if I do say so myself, except that we wound up in a little cul-
de-sac in the wings. It was barely big enough to hold any one of
us, let alone all four. We were pinned in there against stacked
chairs, props, and a dusty old grand piano, with nowhere to go
but back onstage. However, we were all certain that such a
reappearance would not in any way enhance our stage-
presence score, so we were trapped. The next question was
"Where do we go from here?"*

*The audience buzzed with surprise, but the MC and other of-
ficials were apparently unaware of what had happened. Before
we could come up with a graceful solution to our dilemma,
another quartet was onstage singing. The auditorium quieted
down and we had to stop shouting at Vern how dumb he was.*

*We couldn't imagine remaining motionless indefinitely in
those cramped circumstances, but what was the alternative?
We felt like sardines in a can. There were still four more
quartets to go before intermission. Then we spotted a tiny door
down behind the piano in the back wall of the stage. It was out*

of sight of the audience and our only hope.

With brand-new lemon-yellow slacks and maroon jacket, I carefully crawled over, around, and through the stacked-up furniture. After breaking a few fingernails I pried open the small door. I stuck my head through the opening, but instead of reaching freedom, I found myself looking into the hotel's grand ballroom, over the shoulder of what I guessed was the treasurer of AT&T making his report to an annual meeting of stockholders. With all due haste I withdrew, closing the little door as quickly but as quietly as I was able.

We had to stay in that hot, dusty corner until intermission time. Then to our embarrassment the MC introduced us once again as we tried to make our escape. The only pleasant part of the experience was that we got a bigger hand for our second entrance than we did for our first. For all I know we got additional points, too, but we still wound up twenty-ninth out of thirty-three.

Quartet and chorus contests are generally pretty serious affairs. The contestants try their hardest and the competition is often intense. However, every now and then a group comes along with more interest in having a good time than in getting a good score. Such moments make for a good time for all and are frequently more memorable than many of the more serious performances. Here's a favorite of Bob Royce's:

A quartet called the C-NOTES was a "biggie" quartet in the Livingston, New Jersey Chapter when I joined. The group wasn't an outstanding singing quartet, but they were exceedingly entertaining, and I remember the first time they made the cut at an International preliminary contest. In the finals they came out dressed as a cop, a bartender, a gay blade, and a guy with goggles and gloves who looked like he had just jumped out of his roadster. It was a great set of costumes, strictly early 1900's garb, and the first song they sang was "To See My Anna from Indiana."

In the middle of the song the lead stepped forward and sang the lyric in a real sassy, egocentric way. The baritone in the bartender outfit looked disgusted with all the puffery, grabbed a custard pie from the tray he was holding, and really lambasted the lead smack in the face, right in the middle of the quartet finals! It was so startling and funny, it tore the place apart.

The C-NOTES didn't win any prizes in that contest, but they sure made a place in history and won a place in my heart.

If you want to win a contest, if you're serious about coming in tops, then you know it's a numbers game and you do whatever you can to maximize your points in each of the various judging categories. But there's the rub. You are trying to second-guess what the judges consider to be a good performance. You're also making trade-offs. To improve your score it might be necessary to concentrate more on stage presence and less on sound, or vice versa. You have to keep tinkering with each of the variables in the formula until you find the right combination. Then of course you still may not win, but at least you'll score as well as possible.

There is, however, one exception to that general rule: human error. By that I mean judge error. When everything else fails, maybe human error will come to the rescue. It did for Steve Keiss and his quartet, the REBEL ROUSERS:

In our best effort the REBEL ROUSERS were mediocre. We rang chords occasionally, but it was so rare, we'd stop and celebrate when it happened. It didn't really matter though, because we enjoyed ourselves.

We competed with ten or eleven quartets in a Dixie District contest once in Knoxville, Tennessee and as miracle would have it, we made the cut. I never did figure out how, but I assume either the judges were sick or there were an awful lot of bad quartets in the contest. I really didn't think we deserved to make the cut, but we did.

So we sang in the finals Saturday night and did one of our usual mediocre performances. Maybe it was even less than mediocre. Anyway, we were backstage when they announced the top three quartets. The third-place quartet was the SHORELINERS from Pensacola, Florida. They went out on-stage, got their trophies, sang a song, and exited. Then I heard the MC ask for quiet. "In second place," he said slowly, "from Atlanta," and at that moment I wondered which quartet was from Atlanta, and the MC said, "the REBEL ROUSERS!" Of course, I thought, it's the REBEL ROUSERS. The REBEL ROUSERS! The instant I realized it was our quartet, our lead, Will Fussell ran past me like a madman, jumped over a guy sit-

ting on a chair backstage, and just barely caught our tenor, Warren Capenos, as he ran onto the stage.

Ron Glover, our bass, strolled over to me and said, "What did he say?"

"I can't understand it," I said. "The MC said we're in second place!"

"Oh, my gosh," he said. "I don't believe it."

Ron and I sauntered onto the stage and found the audience rumbling and mumbling. There was a smattering of applause, but it was mostly a disbelieving crowd out there. I looked at Will. "Shut up and accept the trophy," he whispered.

I forget who presented the trophies to us, but he had the same puzzled look of skepticism on his face. We fumbled our way through an acceptance song and retreated with haste. There was polite—that's the only way I can describe it—reaction from the people in the audience. "Will," I said, "this is ridiculous. We don't deserve to be second."

"Well," he replied, "obviously everybody else did a worse job than we did, so don't worry about it." The MC announced the CHORD CRACKERS as contest winners and District champs.

It was about 12:30 a.m. Sunday when the score sheets were distributed. By then Warren Capenos had already left the convention for home in Atlanta. I was standing in the Atlanta Peachtree Chapter hospitality room trying to apologize for our second place ranking, when Will Fussel walked over and put his hand on my shoulder. "Hey, buddy," he said, "have I got news for you. Take a look at this score sheet."

I looked. I grimaced. The secretary of the judges had made a hundred point error. The REBEL ROUSERS were not second; we were fifth. The CHORD CRACKERS were the winners, but the SHORELINERS should have been second and the BRIGADEERS should have been third.

At the quartet critique late Sunday morning, everybody was trying to apologize about the whole thing. They asked us to give back the trophies and of course we did. At least three of us did. Warren had taken his home with him and to this day I don't know if he gave his back. We told the BRIGADEERS we were sorry. They were miffed, not mad at us, but pretty ticked off at the secretary of the judges.

An hour later I was standing in line at the motel checkout

desk. Standing behind me was Jess Teater, tenor of the BRIGADEERS. He is probably six feet four inches tall, weighs about two twenty-five, and is head-to-toe muscle. He has shoulders the span of three ax handles and he looked like he could toss anybody he wanted through a wall. He was still mad, not merely upset—mad!

Ron Glover strolled over to where I was standing. "Hi, guy," he said. "Guess what happened to me this morning."

"Ron," I said, "cool it."

"I got up this morning," he continued, "and all the engraving had disappeared from my trophy."

"Ron, for heaven's sake, shut up," I begged. "That's Jess Teater behind us."

"Hey," he said casually, "I understand this thing isn't over yet. You'd better stick around because we're going to have a best-two-out-of-three singoff for second place."

"Ron," I pleaded, "will you shut up! That's Godzilla standing there!"

Teater was mad, but he must have got a chuckle out of our dialogue.

The following Monday night when the quartet went to chapter meeting, we felt rather sheepish and embarrassed about the contest. It wasn't our fault, but we were nevertheless the principals in the whole mix-up. We were looking for some sympathy and a fellow named Jack Hale stopped us to make a pronouncement for all the chapter to hear. "Listen, guys," he said, "we know how you feel, but we just want you to know that the entire Peachtree Chapter is behind you one hundred percent. In our hearts you'll always be fifth!"

The following year when I switched from baritone to lead and sang in the KINGS MEN quartet, we actually won the championship. After we were announced, I walked over to the edge of the stage, pointed at the secretary of the judges, and in a loud voice said, "Are you absolutly sure about the score this time?"

Yes, it's hard to second-guess how the scores will come out. There's just no telling until you hear the final announcement or see the score sheets. Even then it may be a mite hard to comprehend.

One of Reedie Wright's early quartet contests was a tough one to predict:

In my gung-ho days I sang with a quartet called the FOUR ROSES and we thought we were pretty good, so along with about two dozen other quartets, we entered the contest to see who was going to International to represent the District. We bought beautiful white dinner jackets and were really dressed fit to kill. On the contest stage we sang up a storm.

At the end of the contest, the MC named off the top five quartets, starting with the fifth place foursome. It wasn't the FOUR ROSES. Then the fourth place quartet; again not the FOUR ROSES. The third and second place quartets were announced. Neither one was ours. We began to congratulate ourselves and straighten our ties to accept first place honors, as the MC announced the winners. "The first place quartet, ladies and gentlemen, is...the BONANZA FOUR!"

We couldn't understand it. There must have been some mistake, maybe a judge's error. There wasn't. We scanned down the rankings when the final scores came out. Down and down and down. We finished twenty-third out of twenty-five quartets. I'll never forget that sobering moment of truth. We've laughed about it many times since, but not too much at the time.

I'm sure you've heard the expression, "Winning isn't everything, but it sure beats coming in second!" Apparently many quartetters find that indeed, winning isn't everything, and they undergo a strange transformation when they win a contest. It's a shift of perspective. The magnitude of the challenge seems to diminish, the pot of gold seems to tarnish, the achievement seems to lose its aura of awe. Jim Massey felt the sensation when his quartet won the District championship:

The OK FOUR's contest history could be described as somewhat ignominious, because we've been nearly disqualified a good number of times and we always seemed to be in the midst of a controversy. We always seemed able to win the audience, though. When we sang "My Wife the Dancer," the judges called it a dirty song. When we sang "Green, Green Grass of Home," they called it a folk song. We continually scored low until the one time we finally won it. We sang the same numbers we had sung before, but they were finally accepted as straight numbers.

The moment we won I was pleased and terribly excited, but I was also aware that it was suddenly different. It was almost more fun to lose and have everybody say we should have won than to win the contest and know we didn't sing as well as we wanted to, or as well as other quartets we'd heard. We were thrilled to win, but at the same time we had to shift our sights to a new objective. Winning the District was old hat. What do we do for encores?

After the contest winners are announced and the losers have had a chance to lick their wounds and mend their shattered egos, attentions shift to the hospitality rooms, where refreshments and more quartet performances are the order of the day. Such parties are to contests what afterglows are to barbershop shows, and they give quartetters a chance to show off some of their wilder material, while they give other barbershoppers a chance to relax and enjoy a great parade of quartet talent.

My quartet, the BROTHERHOOD, was making the rounds of the hospitality rooms after a District convention in Lake Placid, New York one time. We were using a series of gangster songs, were dressed accordingly, and we opened the bit with a song containing three old and corny jokes. I started them off in a dialogue with Pete Donatelli. "Oh, Godfather, Godfather," I pleaded, "can you help me?"

"What do you want from me?" Pete responded.

"Oh, Godfather," I moaned, "I just can't stand the underworld any longer. Can't you help me get out?"

"What do you want from me?" Pete reiterated.

"Godfather, can't you get me some kind of legitimate business? How about...how about a pizzeria?"

"Well, I don't know," Pete said, "it takes a lot of dough!" The punch line was usually followed by a few laughs (a very few laughs) and a lot of groans, but we would mercifully plunge ahead with the rest of the song and act.

Now after we had done that dialogue a number of times, we began to tire of its sameness and we began to change a word here and there, alter an emphasis, modify an expression. It was fun to see what new twist each of us would insert into the routine as we took our act into the early morning hours. In one room I decided to make a drastic deviation. We went through the dialogue as usual until my line right before the punch line. "Godfather," I said, "can't you get me some kind of legitimate business? How about...how about a hardware store?''

I looked at Pete and saw consternation in his eyes, probably the expression Caesar showed Brutus. It was too cruel a trick to play for long, however, so I continued, ''...or better yet, a pizzeria?''

Contests, hospitality rooms, singing, good times. That's the way it goes at a barbershop competition. The thrill of victory and the agony of defeat are both overshadowed by the delight of the barbershop harmony. Afterwards there are trophies for some, anticipation of next year's contest for others, and memories for all. Winners have their prizes and praises, losers have their plans for the future.

Well, most winners have their prizes. Dick Floersheimer reports that winning a trophy and receiving it are two different matters:

> *My quartet, the MAIN STREET FOUR, had the good fortune to be selected as Mid-Atlantic District Quartet Champions at a contest in Washington's Constitution Hall, and we were presented with four gleaming silver bowls as trophies. Immediately after the jamboree the quartet was asked to surrender the bowls temporarily to allow our accomplishment to be properly preserved by engraving, and we readily acceded. After about three months, when the bowls weren't forthcoming, we got concerned, but of course would't do anything so gross as to ask about our prizes. So we waited.*
>
> *At the time I was a claims supervisor for a large insurance company and across my desk one morning came a claim for reimbursement for the theft of four silver bowls. The policyholder was the man who had presented the trophies to us, so I knew the bowls were ours, but unfortunately that meant the policyholder was not eligible for coverage; the bowls did not belong to him. Paradoxically, I was obliged to turn down the claim for my own trophy.*
>
> *We eventually received duplicates, but I doubt that any other barbershop contest winner was ever faced with a similar dilemma.*

Not all barbershop contests are sponsored by the Society, but Bob Morris reports that even unofficial contests have been and still are popular events:

> *My favorite story goes back to when the* New York Daily

Mirror, *in conjunction with the New York City Department of Parks, held barbershop quartet contests. One year a newly-formed quartet called the FLAT BUSHMEN from the newly-formed Brooklyn Chapter sang in a competition in Brooklyn's Prospect Park. Finishing in a tie for first place, the quartet was invited to compete in a sudden-death singoff.*

Tenor Tommy Chase was hard of hearing, but was vain to the point where he wouldn't use his hearing aid. Lead Frank Mongan, baritone Harry Cames, and bass Brendan Fitzgerald insisted that Tommy not only wear the hearing aid, but turn it up as well. Tommy did as directed, then proceeded to harmonize with the engines of a mail plane that flew overhead. The FLAT BUSHMEN lost the play-off!

Val Hicks has a couple of stories about unofficial barbershop quartet contests. They reveal some of the potential pitfalls of participating in such competitions:

A barbershopper/motel owner in Ketchum, Idaho was instrumental in establishing a barbershop quartet contest as part of the town's annual "Wagon Days" celebration over the Labor Day weekend. It was not a Society-sponsored event, but was designed strictly for barbershop quartets, and some handsome prizes were given away. First place was three hundred dollars, second place two hundred dollars, and third place one hundred dollars. In addition, the competing quartets were invited to stay at the motel free of charge. I was invited to judge the contest.

When I arrived at the first year's competition there were only five quartets signed up to sing, but then at the last minute three of the five backed out. Two hundred townspeople had purchased tickets and were seated in the small elementary school auditorium and the entire contest was over in ten minutes! The audience began to make angry sounds and the barbershopper/motel owner began to show signs of worry. He asked the four of us who were judging if we could sing. We hadn't rehearsed or sung together, but knew a couple of songs, so we said we would in view of the audience's attitude. We sang four or five oldies but goodies for the people and I must say we made a halfway decent sound.

Evidently some members of the chamber of commerce were in the audience and they insisted that we receive a cash prize.

We ended up winning first place and the two competing quartets were furious!

For the second year of the contest I was invited to be chairman of the judges and I had to drive from Salt Lake City all the way to Ketchum, a six-hour trip. Not able to leave work until close to two o'clock in the afternoon, I drove nonstop to get there in time. I even changed into a suit as I drove, knowing I didn't have a minute to spare. It was eight o'clock on the button when I arrived at the school, but I found I was the first judge there. "Where are the others," I inquired of the barbershopper/motel owner.

"Well," he said, "they all cancelled. You're the only judge here. Can you handle it?"

"I guess I can do it alone," I said. "By the way, who's the MC?"

"The MC? Gosh, I didn't think of that," he said. "Val, do you think you could announce the quartets, too?"

By then I was suspicious. "Who's the secretary of judges," I asked.

"I didn't think of that either. If you can't do it, maybe I can find somebody else to total up the scores."

So picture this: I announced a quartet, raced over and sat down to judge it, and oh yes, I was the timekeeper, too. I happened to have my stopwatch with me, so I timed each of the performances. I had to work like a beaver for that contest. Fortunately, a lady was found to act as secretary of the judge, so I didn't have to total the scores.

After the winner was announced and the scores were published, a losing contestant discovered an error in the arithmetic. His quartet should have won the contest. By then we had already given out the prizes. We had to get the quartets back together and tell everybody we'd made a big mistake. Frankly, it was a most unpleasant situation, and I almost needed a police escort out of town!

Ah, yes, it's neat to compete. You may spend six months working on your songs, developing interpretations, creating effective stage presence motions, refining and polishing the sound. You may travel a thousand miles to reach the convention site. You may spend hundreds of dollars for air fare, lodging, and meals. You may spend hundreds more for costumes, makeup, and props. You may find your stomach bounding around like it's doing the twist as contest time grows nigh. And then you may spend only four to six minutes singing your songs on the contest stage.

Even if you don't win, even if you don't score as high as you expect, even if you make some terrible blunders and wind up in the basement of the rankings, it won't be very long before you're thinking and planning and anticipating next year's contest. Don't try to make any sense out of it. There's really only one explanation: It's neat to compete!

CHAPTER 7

The Barbershop International

The Barbershop International

Unless I'm wrong
I but obey
The urge of a song:
I'm—bound—away!

Robert Frost

h boy, it's the International! I've been told by those who have attended all kinds of convention gatherings that nothing in the world compares with an International Barbershop Convention.

My first International was in Chicago, where I went with the Poughkeepsie Chapter to compete in the chorus contest. I hadn't been a barbershopper for very long at the time and as a matter of fact had never before sung with the chorus in competition. The Palmer House in downtown Chicago was familiar to me since I'd stayed there before on business trips, so I was acquainted with the hotel's quiet dignity and its hushed, almost library-like atmosphere in the impressive, spacious lobby, but at the convention when I walked in, I couldn't believe it. The hotel's staid, sedate ambiance had been

229

shattered by a throng of busy and boisterous barbershoppers. The place was jumping!

There must have been two dozen quartets singing. Simultaneously! I later learned the din was typical of all International Conventions. I saw a press of people in the center of the lobby and I squeezed into position to see what the attraction was. It was the ORIOLE FOUR straining to be heard over the discord, and they could indeed be heard with their real sock-it-to-'em sound.

After acclimating to the ninety-six-part harmony that ricocheted endlessly off the black and white marble walls and the high lobby ceiling, I enjoyed watching non-barbershoppers enter the hotel. Stopped short in their tracks and stunned with surprise, they looked about in disbelieving wonder at the barbershoppers enjoying their hobby. "Gawked at" might be a more fitting description.

The International Convention is the summit. It's the top of the ladder for competing quartets and choruses and the annual gathering spot for barbershopping's who's who. From all over North America singers come together for a ritual of harmony and song. It's also a time to meet new acquaintances, hear the latest barbershop gossip, and of course converse, chat, chatter, and discourse at length about all imaginable aspects of barbershopping life. Bob Royce gives a glimpse of these goings on:

When my quartet qualified for its first International quartet competition in Toronto, the other three fellows drove from northern New Jersey, but my wife, Dobbie, and I decided to fly. On the airplane in New York I observed four men sitting immediately in front of us. They wore matching seersucker jackets and dark pants. "I bet they're a barbershop quartet," I said to Dobbie.

Spotting a Society lapel pin, I got up the gumption to lean forward and say something to them. "Excuse me," I interrupted, "are you a barbershop quartet?" My question was answered with four instant smiles.

"Yes," one of them said, "and you must be a barbershopper, too. What chapter are you from?"

I told them Livingston, New Jersey, and then found out they were the CROSS COUNTRYMEN from Massachusetts. I was talking to Terry Clarke, bass, and Wally Cluett, baritone.

"Livingston," Wally said thoughtfully. "Then you're from the Mid-Atlantic District. Tell me, I understand there's a quartet

down there that beat the ORIOLE FOUR in the preliminaries.''
''That's right,'' I said.
''A lot of people tell me that was a fluke,'' Wally continued.
''Well, I really can't say,'' I said. ''I didn't think so.''
''What was their name again?''
''The MAIN STREET FOUR,'' I replied.
''Never heard of them,'' Wally said.
At that point Terry Clarke spoke up. ''Are you singing in a quartet?''
''Yes,'' I said, ''as a matter of fact, I am.''
''What's the name of it?''
I hesitated. ''The MAIN STREET FOUR.''
Wally slid down in his seat and Terry roared with laughter. ''Nice going, big mouth,'' he said.

When you travel a great distance to an International Convention, you want to pack as much barbershopping into your schedule as possible. Don Hewey tells of his chapter's journey to a convention in San Francisco:

When you think of barbershop singing you don't think of Honolulu, Hawaii, but the Aloha Chapter has been ringing chords over here for a long time. Twenty-eight chorus members made the trip to San Francisco and we put on a special ''Barbershop Hawaiian Style'' show at 2:30 in the morning after one of the preliminary quartet contests. Even at the late hour we had over 2000 people in our audience and we wowed them! We called a portion of the chorus forward to sing and they sang in Swedish! They were the Swedes barbershop singers from Stockholm. We had corresponded with them during the year and they learned part of our show package for the performance. We even brought along extra uniforms for them; everything worked out perfectly.

Also during convention week the Aloha Chapter made its first-ever visit to another chapter. The night we arrived we diverted our bus to Palo Alto to visit the Peninsulaires. We walked in singing and really surprised them. It was a great evening of barbershop harmony.

As you can imagine, a trip to International is pretty special and to make it even more so, quartets and choruses often mount elaborate

publicity campaigns. Sometimes the wives participate in the promotional activities by wearing color-coordinated outfits and by becoming dedicated cheering sections with banners, pom-poms, and
screams of encouragement when their husbands compete onstage.

Jed Casey recalls his chapter publicity efforts of a number of years
ago:

> *As something distinctive, the Fairfax Chapter decided to buy*
> *hats for the International Convention in Los Angeles. Everybody*
> *wore a red, white, and blue-striped cap. It was attention-getting*
> *and a good spirit-building idea, too. The hats were so popular a*
> *lot of people in Los Angeles tried to buy them from us, so we felt*
> *we started something. Convention goers could always remem-*
> *ber that the Fairfax Jubil-Aires had been in town.*
>
> *One year, much to the distress of hotel managers, we used*
> *stickers printed with the simple statement, "Fairfax, Virginia*
> *was here." We stuck them all over the place, in the halls, on*
> *elevators, in the men's rooms, on ceilings, everywhere. Unfor-*
> *tunately, the self-stick stickers stuck like Super Glue and we got*
> *complaints from the hotel management because they were so*
> *tough to get off. All chapters were warned never to use stickers*
> *again.*
>
> *The following year the Jubil-Aires had a weak-adhesive label*
> *made. It could be peeled off very easily and it read, "Fairfax,*
> *Virginia is not using stickers this year." We stuck them all over*
> *the place.*
>
> *You'd be surprised where some of those stickers turned up.*
> *One of our members went to Dallas, Texas about three weeks*
> *after the convention and found one on the underside of the*
> *toilet seat on his Eastern Airlines flight.*
>
> *We enjoyed doing all kinds of silly things like that. When we*
> *competed in a District contest one time in Atlantic City, we*
> *sang "Red Head" and each of our wives wore a red wig and a*
> *black dress. All sixty-five wives had red wigs and they were*
> *beautiful. They made a big hit, too.*

Many wives get a kick out of such convention participation and are
thereby able to join in the fun of their hubby's hobby. However,
Reedie Wright reveals that under certain circumstances a wife's enthusiasm can lessen over a period of time:

I should tell you that at the beginning my wife went along with my convention antics in great stride. She thought Internationals were the greatest things since night baseball, but after thirty-three years she cooled a little. It's not that she doesn't like barbershop harmony. She says she never sees her husband at the conventions from the time we get there 'til the time we leave because I'm always off attending meetings of some kind, and it takes the fun out of it for her. She still loves barbershop music, just thinks I should curtail my activities.

One of the funniest things that ever happened to her may be partially to blame for her diminished enthusiasm. My wife's name is Lucille, but I've called her "Dude" for over forty years. I used to call her my little "Doodlebug" when we were first married; now I call her "Dude."

Some time back, the two of us were attending a barbershop gathering at the Huntington Sheraton Hotel in Pasadena, California. It was a big, fancy, dress affair. It seems that Governor Brown was also at the hotel, in another wing, for a political rally. When the two meetings happened to adjourn at the same time, I was asked by one of the governor's aides, whom I know, if I'd like to meet the head of state. Opportunities to meet such nobility do not present themselves very often, so my wife and I leaped at the chance. We tripped excitedly across the lobby for our audience with the political elite. "This is Governor Brown," the aide said, "and this is Reedie Wright, a visiting barbershopper."

"How do you do, Governor," I said, feeling very important, "and this is my wife..." but I couldn't think of "Lucille" to save my soul. I didn't want to say "Dude" because that would sound a little crude. There was a long instant of deafening silence before the Governor chimed in, "How do you do, Mrs. Wright."

Have you ever seen a woman absolutely mortified? Dude, I mean Lucille, was fit to be tied. "That's one hell of a time to try to be funny," she snapped at me. As God is my witness, in all truth, at that critical moment I could not think of "Lucille." She swears to this day I did it on purpose, but I didn't. Honest Injun, I didn't.

"Well," she said later, "if you can't think of anything but barbershopping, if you even forget my name, then perhaps it's better that I bow out of your barbershopping functions."

Lucille no longer attends International Conventions with me.

Even without his wife, Reedie seemed readily able to get himself into trouble, as he himself discloses:

> *Dottie, the wife of past International President John Cullen, doesn't attend our conventions anymore, either. Maybe she and Dude both for the same reason. Anyway, John and I got together and have been roommates over a number of years now. We always get a room at the headquarters hotel.*
>
> *Tuesday afternoon at the New Orleans convention after the Harmony Foundation Trustees meeting, John and I went to our room to get ready for the International President's Reception that night. When it came time to get dressed, I wanted to wear a dickey, but for the life of me I couldn't get the thing buttoned properly. John said he'd do it and he wrestled and tugged and had a terrible time with the pesky piece of apparel. When he finally got it buttoned, the dickey was upside down! Fortunately, we made it to the dinner reception on time in spite of our difficulties.*
>
> *Executive Director Barrie Best introduced each of us on the dais and when John's name was called out, he got up and remarked that he was rather disappointed with his roommate because the guy wasn't even able to dress himself. Moments later Barrie introduced me and I got up. "I have to admit," I said, "that I'm not exactly thrilled with my roommate, either. However, I can tell you he's absolutely the best dickey fixer in the entire Society!"*
>
> *For three seconds you could have heard a pin drop in that big room. Then I thought the roof would go off. Barrie Best's face turned a brilliant crimson from the top of his forehead to his Adam's apple!*

For most barbershoppers, the International doesn't mean meetings, it means singing but not necessarily contest singing. Moments of singing in a massed chorus can be as memorable as any of the chorus or quartet contest sessions. Particularly memorable for Buck Dominy was a convention in Washington, D.C.:

> *Word spread quickly that President Eisenhower was coming to the Statler Hotel, our convention headquarters, for some kind of meeting, and we all gathered together in the lobby in hopes of singing a song for him. He was expected to enter the main*

entrance from Sixteenth Street so we lined up on the wide stair-
way that leads up to the balcony and we filled up the balcony,
too. The place was packed with barbershoppers. Then we
waited.

It wasn't too long a wait before the doors opened and Secret
Service men rushed in, with the President right behind. The mo-
ment he stepped inside we burst into "Keep America Singing"
and President Eisenhower stopped abruptly at the sudden swell
of four-part harmony. We thought he'd pause for a moment and
then quickly continue on his way, but no, he stayed for the
whole song.

I noticed a couple of old ladies on the balcony in front of me.
When the song ended, there were tears in their eyes. It was
such a moving and inspiring feeling to sing with that enormous
chorus for the President. I'm sure everyone there had the same
reaction and will never forget it.

A mass sing is a regular part of International Convention week and
is always impressive. Hugh Ingraham lists such a performance
among his biggest barbershopping thrills:

At the International in Atlanta we had a mass sing in the lob-
by of the Hyatt Regency Hotel. The huge atrium must go up
twenty-five floors and the first seven were rimmed with singing
barbershoppers. Bob Johnson directed everybody from a plat-
form in the lobby and it was a mighty thrilling experience, I'll tell
you.

What really got to me was when they sang "Let Me Call You
Sweetheart." After the first verse the men hummed and Bob
called out, "Okay, gals, let's hear you sing the words now." The
girls sang and it was so beautiful it nearly destroyed me.

Lloyd Steinkamp was handling convention public relations at
the time. After the mass sing, people were rushing to get to the
afternoon show in the ballroom, when a radio reporter ap-
peared with a microphone in his hand. "Mr. Steinkamp," he
said, "I have all the equipment ready to record the giant chorus
that's singing here today."

"It's all over," Lloyd said.

"What do you mean, it's all over," the reporter demanded. "I
came here to record it."

Lloyd was very patient. "I'm sorry, sir," he said, "but you were given information describing the time and place. I'm afraid it's all over.''

The reporter was indignant. "Well," he said angrily, "couldn't you get them all back and do it over again?" I don't think I want to repeat Lloyd's response.

There are big, spectacular convention extravaganzas and there are more quiet moments of pleasant conversation and happy reminiscing. Val Hicks describes an incident in the latter category:

I was coach, arranger, and manager for the OSMOND BROTHERS when they were a young barbershop quartet. They had saved money from some of their singing jobs for a trip to the Intenational Convention in Kansas City and had reserved a room for their entire family at the Muehlebach Hotel.

I was sitting on the mezzanine level with two grand old barbershop gentlemen, Molly Reagan and Doc Nelson, who had sung together in a barbershop quartet in their high school days, probably twenty-five years before the Society was founded. Reminiscing about their old quartet songs, they remarked they'd give anything to hear an old number they used to sing, "Take Me Back to Baby Land."

The Osmonds sang that song with an arrangement I had prepared for them. "Look," I said, "you two guys sit tight. I'll be back in a minute." I got to the house phone and called Mr. Osmond in his hotel room. "George," I said, "can you bring the boys down to the mezzanine for a few minutes to sing for a couple of special people?"

A short time later the elevator door opened and out walked the Osmonds. At the sight of the four boys in their quartet uniforms, nearby convention goers quickly gathered around. We found an empty ballroom and went in. Doc and Molly sat down on some chairs and the boys began to sing "Take Me Back to Baby Land." With tears streaming down their faces, the two old barbershoppers listened joyfully to the song they themselves had sung a half century before!

Barbershop music has a way of reaching your emotions like that. Huck Sinclair has a story about a listener who became a little *too* involved at an International performance:

Part of the enjoyment of singing is the contact and rapport with the audience. I recall a Friday afternoon convention jamboree in Milwaukee. The HARMONIZERS decided to sing a potpourri of song segments, familiar snatches, and favorite swipes. One of them was "My dearie, I'll sigh, my dearie, I'll cry-y-y," and we could see and feel the audience reaching forward to thrill with us in the ring of that great "cry" chord, but Bill Hess of the Gary, Indiana HARMONAIRES extended a little too far and fell right out of the balcony!

Everyone who has ever sung in a competing quartet or chorus at International has some memorable experiences to tell. My first International quartet contest was my biggest barbershopping thrill ever. We sang at the Cow Palace in San Francisco. More than 10,000 barbershoppers attended the convention.

Our trip across country was enjoyable to begin with, and the sights of the city and its attractions were very exciting. Like a tried and true tourist I took hundreds of pictures. Our quartet host was Howard Donley, a prince of a man, who drove us anywhere and everywhere we wanted to go. Then before we knew it, it was Thursday, contest day.

Out behind the Cow Palace are a number of cavernously-large buildings which were sectioned off by curtains into "dressing rooms," with two quartets assigned to each. As we nervously prepared for our appearance, someone came in and asked if we'd mind if network TV people video-taped our preparations and performance. Who were they kidding? Of course we wouldn't mind.

The TV coverage was supposed to be candid. "Don't pay any attention to the cameras and lights and microphones," we were told. Sure thing! All America was looking through that little lens pointed at us. Don't pay any attention to it!

When you reach a certain level of excitement, I think that's it; you can't get any more excited. We had reached that level much earlier in the week.

As it got closer and closer to the time to sing, we were led from one staging area to another. The last stop was a pleasant but small room only a few paces from the stage. At that point I was hoping and praying I could just live through the experience. For people who tend to be nervous, it was an excellent room in which to die.

Out of that last sanctuary we were ushered after a short, fidgety stay. We were still backstage and the TV people scurried about us as if we were presidential candidates. I saw a microphone boom thrust in my direction and felt obliged to make some wise and spontaneous comments. They were certainly spontaneous all right, but I doubt they were by any stretch of the imagination wise. I probably said something worldly philosophic like, "Well, here we go."

Then we were onstage. It was a gigantic stage. We walked forever to get to the middle of it. I looked out at the audience and noticed the entire world had assembled before us for the contest. We sang our first song. It's amazing how many millions of thoughts fly through your cranium at such a time. It's always too bad you only seem able to think about things you shouldn't be thinking about.

Our first song wasn't too good, but it wasn't too bad, either. We used a bunch of magic tricks and they all came off okay, even the "bomb" which sent up a mushroom cloud of black smoke at the end of the number. Our second song was okay, too, I guess, and about six minutes after we walked on the stage, we walked off.

The TV people were waiting for us and they dodged about to get good camera angles and position their microphone to pick up our utterances. We paused to catch our breath and saw a dozen or so people racing down a ramp toward us. They were friends with words of congratulations and we thoroughly enjoyed sharing those happy moments with them. Believe me, that first appearance on the International stage produced some incredibly thrilling once-in-a-lifetime moments!

Jack Hines' first International quartet contest was also a once-in-a-lifetime experience but of a slightly different breed:

We were happy to learn that as alternates from the Northeastern District, our quartet, the ELMCHORDS, was going to be able to compete at the International Convention in Miami, but none of us knew how we were going to pay for the trip. The expenses looked frightening.

Fortunately, the brother of our tenor, Dave Chapman, was with a Ford Agency in town and he got us a used Chevy wagon for the trip. Nemo Lynch's wife couldn't go along, but the other three wives could, so seven of us piled into the car and headed south.

Back in those days the hotels provided rooms for some of the competing quartets and their wives, and also meals, but we didn't realize the wives' meals were included. After looking at the prices on the hotel restaurant menu, we figured it would be cheaper for all seven of us to eat out than to get four meals free and pay exorbitantly for the other three. Consequently, we ate at the hotel only once. The rest of the time we bought hamburgers and hot dogs, the cheapest stuff we could find. The servings were skimpy, awful tasting, but within budget.

By Friday, the day of the big contest, we were really hyped up. Back then the competitions were scheduled in the morning, and since we were lucky enough to draw the first spot, we were due on stage at nine o'clock. At 6:00 a.m. Dave Chapman called my room to make sure I was up. I lifted the receiver and the voice on the other end sounded like the Jolly Green Giant. If that was as high as our tenor could sing, I thought, we're already in deep trouble. It was time to start worrying in earnest.

I was supposed to be the steady guy in the quartet, the one who had all the poise. I had the reputation for nerves of steel, but no food and all the excitement began to take a toll. Nearer and nearer to nine o'clock I felt worse and worse. My head was spinning, my heart was pounding, and my stomach was churning like an outboard motor.

We were waiting backstage and I thought the world was going to end. Apparently I looked like it already had ended, and Bob Hafer, then Executive Secretary of the Society, grabbed my arm and hauled me outside, back of the Miami Beach Auditorium. The sun was shining, huge palm trees were swaying in the gentle breeze, and I made the worst of an already bad situation.

The rest of the convention was anticlimax. I hardly remember going onstage, but that's probably just as well. Of the forty-one quartets in the contest that year, we came in fortieth. We only beat number forty-one, thanks to a whopping-big time penalty they received.

The next time we went to compete in an International quartet contest, at Los Angeles, I was determined we'd do everything right. With our prior experience, how could we go wrong?

Checking in at the Mayfair after our 3000-mile trip, I just couldn't wait to dive into the hotel pool. Just my luck, there was a "Pool Closed" sign on the door. Phooey with that, I thought. There was water in the pool and I was determined to go swimming until they threw me out.

I plunged into the pool and it was wonderful. I swam around, splashed about, and had a jolly good time until somebody saw me and screamed. He waved his arms and shouted at me. "You dummy," he yelled, "we just cleaned the pool with muriatic acid and it hasn't dissolved yet!"

The acid got in my ear and within twenty-four hours I had an infection. Off I went to the doctor's office on Santa Monica Boulevard. He tried to clean my ears but in the process punctured an eardrum. I was in tough shape. When he put peroxide in the ear, it bubbled like mad. My head ached mercilessly. My ear gurgled and fizzed like an Alka Seltzer.

At the peak of my troubles it was contest time. We walked out onstage and bowed. When somebody blew the pitch pipe it sounded to me like it was blown under water. I couldn't even hear the other three guys sing. Another International contest, another disaster!

Some people have all the luck, all the bad luck, but it takes more than good luck to win an International contest. It takes talent, experience, and practice, too.

How do you get to Carnegie Hall? The same way you win contests: practice. Plenty of good, old-fashioned practice. "We worked extremely hard for a year," explained Tom Masengale of the CHORD BUSTERS. "We rehearsed or sang out at least five nights a week, sometimes seven nights a week, and our rehearsal sessions were three to five hours long. So we were in fairly decent shape when we went to the International contest at St. Louis." That's some rehearsal schedule, but it paid off. They won.

Rehearsing, even in large doses, may not be enough, however. The PITTSBURGHERS would never have won their contest had it not been for the quick thinking of their lead. Jiggs Ward tells the story:

After finishing our first number in the Saturday night championship round, we bowed and stepped into the huddle to take the pitch for our second, when bass Bill Conway whispered, "I can't remember the next song." Lead Tommy Palamone blew the pitch, but instead of humming the first note, he sang the first two words. That was all Bill needed to jog his memory. We sang the song, won the contest, and the judges weren't even aware we had teetered on the brink of disaster.

Such quick thinking is not uncommon on the contest stage. Here's a story about Huck Sinclair's quartet, the FOUR HARMONIZERS:

When my quartet sang in national competition, there were no regional preliminary contests, so there were no limits on the number of competitors. As I recall, eighty other quartets competed with us in Chicago in the elimination sessions during the week. At one point along the way, the surviving quartets were awarded small harmonicas as prizes.

We were lucky enough to reach the finals, but when our lead, Leo Ives, tried to blow the pitch, his pitch pipe failed, so resourceful Leo pulled out his harmonica. I don't know if he blew into the thing or sucked out, but I know we found ourselves singing the song so low we sounded like four strangers to each other. I was angry and disappointed with our performance and in my exasperation I resigned, right then and there. I was really upset. However, with the return of the final scores, which proclaimed the FOUR HARMONIZERS champions, I decided charity was a virtue. I forgave the other three and promptly rejoined the quartet!

If you win or if you don't, it's an extra special thrill to walk out on that stage and sing in an International quartet contest. Frank Lanza contends that the contest thrill is not necessarily the greatest at the top of the heap:

Winning the International Championship at the Shrine Auditorium in Los Angeles was a big thrill, but I think an even more exciting time was when the FOUR STATESMEN sang at the International contest in Boston. It was one of the biggest thrills of my life. When we got onstage the ovation was unbelievable. It must have been some kind of hometown phenomenon that happened. The applause went on and on and on and on.

That can do one of two things to a quartet. It can either shake you up and destroy your performance or give you courage to sing your best. We sang way over our heads at that convention. We came in fifth and it was one of the most exciting moments I've ever experienced.

A contest performance can be a great emotional high, but if you think you've got a chance to win all the marbles, then waiting for the results can be agonizing. Jiggs Ward gives us a glimpse of this type of torment:

> *Bear in mind that the PITTSBURGHERS had been together just over a year when we took our first crack at the big prize at the International Convention in Oklahoma City. After the medalist round we were backstage sweating it out. We thought we might have a chance to win, but surely that same thought was in the minds of the other finalists.*
>
> *Charlie Merrill, outgoing International President, was MC. Slowly he announced the fifth place quartet: from Terre Haute, Indiana, the FOUR SHADES OF HARMONY. There was eager audience applause. It subsided and Charlie announced the fourth place foursome: from Pittsburgh, Pennsylvania, the WESTINGHOUSE QUARTET. More applause. The four of us wrung our hands. Charlie announced the third place quartet: from Dearborn, Michigan, the CLEF DWELLERS. We knew then that it was between the MIDSTATES FOUR, a great quartet, and us. The applause slowly died down. I held my breath. At that moment Frank Thorne, past International President and bass of the ELASTIC FOUR, walked by us, turned, and in a whisper said, "Congratulations, champs!"*
>
> *It was as if we had been granted a wish that we didn't believe could come true. Our tenor, Chummy Conte, dropped to one knee, looked up into the backstage ropes and curtains, and speaking for the four of us said simply, "Thanks, God."*

Winning the International Quartet Championship has to be a source of endless satisfaction and pride, yet the aura of that ultimate achievement can be overshowed by simple human gestures and deeds. Here's a story from Ken Hatton:

> *We call Rachael Hackett our "Mother Hen." Although her husband passed away years ago, she has maintained a strong and active interest in the Louisville Chapter and in my quartet, the BLUEGRASS STUDENT UNION. She's always helping out with this and that, participating in barbershop activities, and supporting the chorus and quartet. Of course she went to Cincinnati for the International Convention.*
>
> *Well, she's getting along in years, and on her way to the Friday night quartet contest she fell and broke her leg. Her friends*

wanted to take her immediately to the hospital, but she refused. "No," she said, "I'm going to hear the boys sing." They had to carry her into the Convention Center.

She heard us sing but still refused to see a doctor. She came back Saturday night for the quartet finals and heard us sing and win. Then, only then, would she agree to see a doctor. "Now I'm ready," she said.

It was the most heartwarming incident we've ever experienced. She showed us a kindness and loyalty we'll never forget. With support like that, how could we help but win. She's special; the A-Number-One Mother Hen of all time!

One quartet is finally crowned champion, is presented to the assembled barbershopper multitude, and receives its due in thunderous applause. It performs to screaming enthusiasm, receives the revered gold medals and other trophies of recognition, and spends the remainder of the weekend in a cloud of song and euphoria.

Then it's back home again, where those mighty singers, world champions, cynosures of the barbershop quartetting universe, become simple husbands, fathers, and wage earners once again. At least that's the way I suppose it is for most contest winners. Not so when the SCHMITT BROTHERS were the victors, however. Joe Schmitt says his number one barbershop experience wasn't winning the championship; it was returning home from the convention in Toledo, Ohio the following day:

In those times we rode the train, the Chicago Northwestern Four Hundred, and when we pulled into the station at Manitowoc, Wisconsin, there was a whole crowd of people. There was a band there, too. Wasn't that special, we thought, and we wondered whom it was for.

It was for us! They put us in a convertible like we were conquering heroes, and drove us the seven miles from the railroad station to our hometown of Two Rivers. Central Park was full of people, a temporary stage had been built for us, and we sang for half an hour. They even gave a lovely bouquet of flowers to Mother.

Our hometown reception thrilled us more than I can say. We're fiercely proud of our community's support and recognition, and we have been tremendously honored by the people's actions. Twenty-seven years after that wonderful homecoming celebration, we gave a concert for three thousand people who had gathered in that same park to hear their quartet sing. The people in our city have been affectionately interested in the SCHMITT BROTHERS ever since our quartet was formed, and we've made every effort to demonstrate our warm affection for them.

When chorus and quartet champions have been selected and properly cheered, and the formal contest activities concluded, there's still more time for barbershopping. It may be midnight or after, but barbershoppers dig in for the more informal side of their singing hobby. Dozens of hospitality rooms open up along with the "Chorditorium," a Society-sponsored hospitality room, where all competing quartets are invited to appear and are encouraged to perform their more entertaining material.

Reedie Wright was asked to MC the festivities in the Chorditorium at a convention in New Orleans. He seems to have a unique knack for getting himself into a pickle:

After the finals were over I rushed to catch a cab back to the Roosevelt Hotel where I quickly changed clothes. I was late for my MCing commitment. At the elevators there were wall-to-wall people, and if you've attended a convention you know it's impossible to get an elevator after the Saturday night contest, so I thought I'd walk down the two floors to the Chorditorium. I found an exit sign and pushed open the door. The empty hall led to another door which I opened. I went down a short flight of stairs and all of a sudden it sounded like an air raid. Bells rang and clanged, sirens shrieked, and it scared me half out of my wits. I decided I'd go back but couldn't get the door open. I was locked in.

All decked out in my fancy clothes and convention badges, I was lost somewhere on the third floor of the Roosevelt Hotel and I was late for a very important date. I discovered I was locked in the offices of the Shell Oil Company.

Every exit door was locked tight and I scampered around from office to office for I don't know how long. The air conditioning had been turned off since Friday and it was hotter than an oven. I eventually made my way back to the stairway and sat down on the steps hoping to collect my thoughts. Bells and sirens were still blaring. I hadn't collected too many thoughts before the door above me burst open. I looked up quickly into the eyes of a guard and the barrel of what appeared to be a Gatling gun. "Don't move," the guard commanded.

"I won't even breathe," I quickly replied. Then the door below me flew open to reveal another guard and weapon. The scene was so bizarre I thought it was a practical joke. I prayed it was a practical joke.

"Come on," the officer said authoritatively. "We're taking you down to the Parish Police Headquarters."

I tried to explain. "I'm the past International President of the barbershoppers," I said in a nervous voice. "I had lunch with your mayor today and he gave me the key to the city. He said we could do anything we want to!" I kept glancing back over my shoulder for someone to say it was all a big joke. No one was there.

They took me to headquarters and called the Parish Captain, who was home in bed at that hour of the night. I waited about thirty minutes for him. Then I explained again who I was.

"Oh, yeah," he said, "that's right. We know there's a convention here and we're proud to have you in town. It's all a mistake. We're very sorry. Please forgive us. We'll take you right back to the hotel in the police car."

"No, you won't," I said. "I'll walk back. I don't want anything more to do with that police car."

By the time I got back to the Chorditorium it was close to two in the morning. I was hours late for my MCing job and I couldn't convince anyone of what had happened to me. The story sounded so cock-and-bullish no one believed it. They accused me of fabricating the whole tale. Bob Gall, who was in charge of the Chorditorium, has never forgiven me. "A likely story," he said. "Go down and get yourself thrown in jail just to keep from MCing at the Chorditorium!"

I wasn't booked or thrown in jail, but I'll tell you it was an awfully scary experience. Thinking back now, it's funny. At the time it was a very serious, no laughing matter!

Hal Purdy, barbershop lover and singer for many, many conventions, has a storehouse of memorable experiences:

The first International I attended was in Oklahoma City. Dur-

ing one of the sessions, noncompeting quartets in the audience were asked to report backstage, because a search was underway for groups to sing on a program Friday morning from the steps of the capitol building. Imagine my surprise when our quartet, the RIPPLEAIRES, was chosen along with the famous CHORDETTES of Sheboygan, Wisconsin. We really felt proud of ourselves until we learned no other men's foursomes had brought along their show outfits.

The jamboreé Saturday afternoon was a great event at the International in Buffalo. All nonfinalist quartets—there were thirty in those days—were asked to sing their most popular showstopper numbers. The HARMONAIRES from Gary, Indiana sang ''Barnacle Bill the Sailor Man,'' and bass Bill Hess hit the lowest note I've ever heard sung. It stopped the show. The applause was so sustained, the MC had to break the rule and allow the quartet to sing another song.

At the convention in Omaha, the BUFFALO BILLS won the contest and another great quartet finished second: the CLEF DWELLERS from Detroit. I asked them where they obtained their great arrangements and lead Dunc Hannah said, ''We just 'boondoggle' them. We stand in a circle and start woodshedding to each other,'' he explained, ''and when we hear a chord or progression of chords we like, we leave it in. Eventually we wind up with an arrangement that pleases us.'' Most of their arrangements were outstanding; ''Corabelle'' and ''Wait 'Til the Sun Shines, Nellie'' weren't the only ones. With today's countless written arrangements and high-powered music writers, it's refreshing to remember the great CLEF DWELLERS and their self-created music. They had real arranging talent in addition to a fine set of voices.

In Philadelphia, the year of the SUNTONES, we didn't decide until quite late to attend the convention. Then the only suite available near the headquarters hotel was at the old John Bartram Hotel, about a half block away. At three o'clock Sunday morning my family and I plus a roomful of barbershoppers were singing and visiting as usual, when the hotel fire alarm rang. Bill Lahl and Gordon Hay were packed and ready for an early daybreak departure, so they grabbed their suitcases and ran down the fire escape, as did we. At the bottom we landed in an alley in the arms of a hotel house detective waiting there to see who was running off without paying his bill. He tried to arrest us until he found there had been a false-alarm fire call.

The Dapper Dans were rehearsing for an International contest one night in Livingston, New Jersey, when a busload of barbershoppers from Catonsville, Maryland streamed into our rehearsal room for a surprise interchapter get-together. After songs and socializing, a Catonsville Chapter member entered the hall with a huge roll of paper. It was the words and music to "Keep America Singing." The scroll was four feet high by six feet long and a silver dollar was taped in place of each note as a donation to our International travel fund. At the conclusion of the evening, I walked out to the bus with Freddie King, Catonsville chorus director. "Freddie," I said, "you don't have a very large chapter. This contribution must have really strapped you."

"It's worth it," Freddie replied. "When we get home, our treasury will be depleted except for the cost of our chartered bus, but without a doubt it's worth it!" What a beautiful gesture!

At Los Angeles for the chorus competition, I was standing in the lobby of the Biltmore Hotel talking with Don Donahue, when Ron Riegler, then baritone of the ROARING 20's, happened to walk by. Ron was in charge of promotion for the Gateway Chorus and he said, "Donahue, we're going to swamp you with PR this year!"

Donahue looked at him and said, "Can you beat 6000 copies of handouts weighing 1400 pounds?" Ron turned on his heels and walked away, mumbling.

A few days later, after we walked off the International stage, Jack Condit said, "I wonder what the 'fun' chapters are doing this afternoon." We had been criticized for working too hard on our contest numbers, but you can't imagine the fun we had when we were announced as the new chorus champions!

The highlight for me at the next year's convention was when we sang the "Disney Medley," fourteen nonstop minutes of great music with arrangements conceived by our own chapter members and put together by the famous Renee Craig. I have the last rocket that was shot off at the end of that performance and I intend to raffle it off someday for the benefit of the Institute of Logopedics.

At the convention in St. Louis it was hotter than blue blazes. We had a suite at a hotel far away from the headquarters hotel. Most memorable were the SIDEWINDERS. They sang in our hospitality room, our "Corral," as we call it, at 2:00 a.m., then came back again at 6:00 a.m. and said they wanted to sing another song for us, "From Me to Mandy Lee." As they sang I turned to Ruth Wright, wife of the quartet's bass, Jay Wright, and saw tears streaming down her cheeks. "Ruth," I whispered, "do they still get to you that much?"

"Hal," she whispered back, "when Russ Hosier leaves to catch his plane after they sing this song, that's the last you'll ever hear of the SIDEWINDERS."

I shed a few tears with her in the contemplation of that, but she made me promise not to let on I knew. They sang their quartet swan song for us in our Corral and we were greatly honored. What a super quartet!

At the convention in Portland, Oregon we had a motel room over a mile from the headquarters hotel and were afraid we wouldn't have many quartets visit us, but they showed up nevertheless. At one point Renee Craig came in and said we'd have to speed up the program. "There are five International Championship quartets outside waiting to sing," she said. That I had to see.

Sure enough, five championship quartets were there. Some couldn't stay and sing, but we were thrilled that they stopped by. Those International Conventions are fabulous!

Behind the scenes of every International are a lot of Society people who put in long and tiring hours to make a convention a success. Hugh Ingraham was directly responsible for a good number of conventions but no matter how hard he tried, some completely unexpected development fouled up a portion of each year's proceedings:

There was the hammer in Atlantic City, the pigeons in Atlanta, the rain in Indianapolis, and the tornado in New Orleans, but I think one of the most interesting incidents happened in Kan-

sas City. The headquarters hotel was the Muehlebach, where
O.C. Cash and Rupert Hall first met to found our Society, but at
the time of the convention the building was in rather poor condition. The air conditioning wasn't working properly and there
were lots of other problems.

International President Leon Avakian had the Presidential
Suite which was quite posh, but it wasn't well suited for entertaining, so Leon asked me if he might get another room for the
big VIP party Thursday night after the contest. The party was a
pretty big bash each year for Board of Directors members,
District officers, committee people, a couple hundred barbershoppers in all. I talked to the hotel management and was told
we could use the Tudor Suite. We took a look and it was perfect.
The hotel reserved it for eleven o'clock Thursday night.

The scene is the hotel lobby, Thursday afternoon. By then the
Muehlebach was completely oversold, people were running
about in the un-air-conditioned lobby yelling and shouting that
they didn't have rooms, and I was trying to hide as best I could.

Unbeknownst to me, the Muehlebach Hotel had a contract
with a number of baseball clubs, and whenever a team played
in Kansas City the hotel handled their accommodations. Lo and
behold, the Detroit Tigers arrived at the height of the confusion
and there was no room at the inn. But the hotel had to find
rooms even if it was oversold because of its contractual arrangements. Then the management had an inspiration. Since
the lobby was a madhouse of screaming barbershoppers, the
ball team could go up to the Tudor Suite while lodging arrangements were made at other city hotels. After all, the suite
wasn't going to be used until eleven o'clock that night.

You can guess what happened. At about six o'clock, Leon's
wife, Ruth, decided to run down to the Tudor Suite and make
sure all was in readiness for the party. She wanted to put some
napkins around the room, prepare a few dishes of peanuts, arrange the chairs. When she opened the door she found herself
face-to-face with the entire Detroit Tigers baseball team in
various stages of undress. Beer cans were all over the place
and it looked, sounded, and smelled worse than a locker room!

Seconds later my telephone rang. Ruth was on the other end
and she was not at all pleased with her findings in the Tudor
Suite. The matter was quickly resolved, but it certainly gave
Ruth some trying moments.

At a convention in St. Louis we used the Jefferson as head-quarters hotel. On Monday morning of convention week we had a meeting of Society staff people to make sure everything was under control before registration opened and the deluge commenced. I asked if there were any problems. There was an awkward silence. Then one hand went up, and another, and still another. Three staff members who were staying at the Jefferson, including Bob Johnson, Director of Music, had mice in their rooms.

"Last night I phoned Housekeeping," Bob explained, "but they couldn't help me, so I spoke to a gentleman in the office and told him I had a mouse in the room. He asked what floor and I told him the ninth floor. The guy sounded surprised. 'That's very unusual,' he said. 'They usually don't get up that high.' " Nothing more was done about the problem during the convention, but the hotel has since been torn down.

Going back in time a little, I used to be Director of Public Relations for the Society. During the convention in San Antonio I was introduced to one of the most unforgettable characters I've ever met in barbershopping. Universal Pictures had decided to do a short subject on the Society and they sent Arthur Cohen to make the film. He was the perfect caricature of a Hollywood producer. He was unbelievable. We had meetings with him that were unbelievable. The problem was that because of a skimpy film budget every song sung in the film had to be in the public domain. That meant we could only use songs written before 1906! Arthur couldn't get it through his head that it would be hard to find a quartet that knew those songs. He looked at the song list we had prepared for him. "Well, here," he said, "we'll use this one."

"That's fine," I said, "but now I've got to get a quartet or chorus that can sing it."

"Give them the music and tell them to sing it," he demanded.

"Arthur," I said, "it just doesn't work that way." We went around and around.

One of the songs finally chosen was "In the Shade of the Old Apple Tree." I was lucky enough to find a quartet that knew it. Next, Arthur wanted to find a scene where he could shoot the film. Have you ever tried to find an apple tree in San Antonio? The best we could do was a pleasant-looking tree located in the

San Antonio Zoo.

The convention was held during the last week in June and the temperature in San Antonio was probably a hundred degrees. We knew we were in for a rough afternoon.

At the zoo progress was slow. Finally the camera, the sound equipment, and the quartet were ready. Arthur wasn't. "Wait a minute," he bellowed, waving his arms wildly. "We can't do anything with all that noise," he said in an angry voice.

"What noise," I inquired. We found a soft humming noise coming from air conditioners used to keep the animals cool. We tracked down the zoo keeper and asked him to turn off the units. Everything was in readiness once again. The sun was high enough and in the right place, there weren't any clouds in the sky, everything was ready to start to shoot.

Without air conditioning, however, the animals quickly became unhappy and soon we got yowls and howls from the various cages. Arthur stamped the ground. "We can't shoot! We can't shoot! We gotta shut those things up!"

"Arthur," I replied, "I'm not going to get in the lion's cage. We either have lions roars or we have air conditioners." The air conditioners were turned back on.

After several hours of such nonsense we were finally shooting the picture when a private airplane flew overhead. "Cut! Cut!" Arthur cried. He ran out in the middle of the field and waved his arms madly. "Get that plane out of here," he demanded.

I later met Arthur in New York and visited with him at his home in Greenwich Village. He was a delightful host. He had taken a projector from his office to show me some of his films. Would you believe he couldn't thread the projector? The man had shot films all over the world, knew cameras backwards and forwards, but was unable to thread his projector. His wife and I did it for him!

Well, that's the monkey business International Conventions are made of. If it's wild and zany, it probably happened at International.

Nonbarbershoppers just don't seem to understand. They have the strange notion that nighttime is for sleeping and that singing at 4:00 a.m. should be discouraged. They even have the distorted perception that when they stay at a hotel they have the right to expect a good night's rest. Strange, these nonbarbershoppers!

Russell Malony has a story about such a misguided hotel guest:

The Westfield, New Jersey Chapter competed in the Society's first International chorus contest in Washington, D.C. We had a hospitality suite at the Lafayette Hotel and since most of the quartets were also staying there, we didn't lack for entertainment. Periodically, however, a gentleman in nightshirt and tasseled nightcap came to the door to complain that our noise kept him awake. When we did nothing to quiet the commotion, he called the hotel manager.

The manager was reluctant to interrupt our party, but when the bathtub full of beer, soft drinks, and ice overflowed and the water leaked through the floor onto the registration desk, he felt obliged to take action. He banged on our door and burst into our room with fire in his eyes.

At that time the FOUR HEARSEMEN were in the midst of a beautiful ballad. Politely, the manager sat on the floor with the rest of us to wait until the quartet finished the song. A good half hour later the man in nightshirt came again to complain. "Look, mister," the manager told him, "if you don't like it here, go find yourself another hotel!"

Eventually the first rays of the Sunday morning sun begin to slow down the hospitality rooms, and one by one barbershoppers drag themselves off to bed. The convention settles down gracefully to its conclusion. Then, after minutes instead of hours of sleep, alarm clocks rouse sleepy barbershoppers to the task of heading home. With visions of quartets and choruses still dancing in their heads, these four-part harmony hounds reluctantly respond.

About the last thing anyone wants to contemplate at the end of a busy convention is the trip back home, but it must ultimately be faced. After the International in Chicago there was also an airline strike to worry about. Ernie Matson describes how a Dapper Dan solved that one:

Because of the strike there were no direct flights from Chicago to New York City, but if you didn't mind a stop in Toronto, you could make the trip via Air Canada. One of the Dapper Dans had an important business appointment on Monday, so he had to travel the circuitous route.

In Toronto he had to undergo customs inspection. He had his suitcase with usual overnight items, his garment bag with his chorus uniforms, and he also had a wooden box about fourteen inches square and three inches thick. Such objects are commonplace in competing choruses; they are used by the shorter chorus members so everyone in a row of singers appears to be the same height onstage. They weren't commonplace items at customs.

The agent looked at the box. "What's that," he inquired.

"It's a wooden box," was the reply.

"What's inside?"

"Nothing."

"Would you open it up, please."

"I'm sorry, but it doesn't open."

"Nothing's inside?"

"Just vacant space."

"What do you use it for?"

"Well, I stand on it."

"You stand on it?"

"Yes."

"Why?"

"So it will make me tall."

"You just stand on it to make you tall, is that right?"

"No, I sing when I'm standing on the box."

I don't know how long the conversation continued like that and I surely don't know why the Dapper Dan wasn't thrown in jail. Perhaps the story was just preposterous enough to be believable!

Al Poole has a final anecdote that succinctly sums up the doings at an International Convention:

In Philadelphia the EVANS BROTHERS and I were in a taxi cab on our way to one of the contest sessions at the Convention Hall. Wondering how the taxi business was doing with a city full of barbershoppers, I asked the driver how the convention was going. He looked at me in his rear-view mirror and smiled.

"Well, I'll tell you," he said, "it sure is a noisy convention. But," he added, "it's a damn good noise!"

There *is* a lot of noise, and to go with it a lot of music, mirth, and merrymaking!

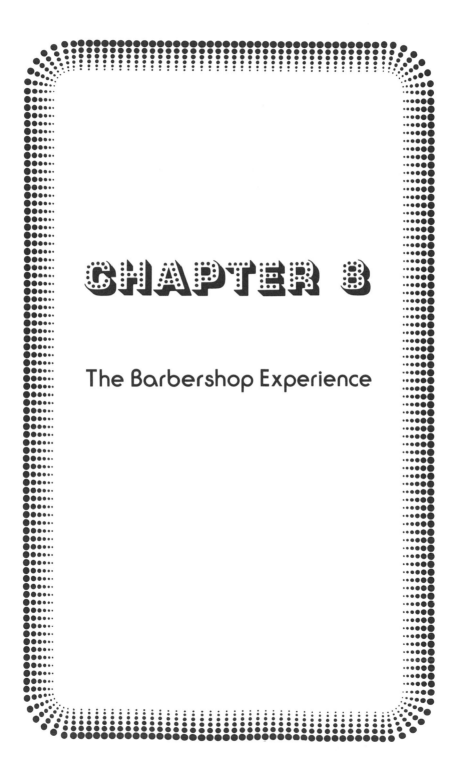

CHAPTER 8

The Barbershop Experience

The Barbershop Experience

None shall part us from each other,
One in life and death are we:
All in all to one another—
I to thee and thou to me!
Thou the tree and I the flower—
Thou the idol; I the throng—
Thou the day and I the hour—
Thou the singer; I the song!

William Schwenck Gilbert

ait a minute! Perhaps I've painted the barber-shop scene with a palette of too many rose-colored hues. Obviously, there is the bitter with the sweet. The world of barbershopping has its share of rain clouds; occasionally tornados, too.

When I think back over the years, I can bring to mind quite a number of frustrations, exasperations, and disappointments. Take the time my quartet had probably a ninety percent chance of winning a $10,000 week-long trip for eight to Monte Carlo, but refused at the last minute to even enter the contest. Then there was the mishandled invitation that prevented us from singing at a special party for Jimmy Cagney. I recall with pain my great wireless microphones disappointment and I wince when I think about the discarded singing robot idea and all the wasted money I invested in it. Our long-running voice lesson battle is another uncomfortable recollection. And to add to the major exasperations are the numerous minor ones. I wish I had a dime for every time I was dissatisfied with the interpretation of a song or its stage motions.

I guess it's inevitable that artistic sensibilities are sometimes ignored, rubbed the wrong way, or on occasion thrashed mercilessly. Equally inevitable, I suppose, are countless instances when misunderstandings, hurt feelings, and personality conflicts between quartet or chorus members flare up like erupting volcanos!

There are indeed times of trials and troubles and if I should choose to ruminate on them I'll get plenty steamed up. But if I step back and take a broader look, those at-the-moment mountainous annoyances and exasperations begin to melt away. They loom large when pride is pricked or feelings are offended, but when viewed in perspective with an entire barbershop career, the unpleasant aspects quickly diminish or disappear altogether within a much larger fabric of satisfaction. Ask a singer who has fully sampled the laughter and love of a barbershop song.

Barbershop Spirit

The show was sponsored by the Scotia Knights of Columbus but was organized by the Schenectady, New York Chapter of the Society. My quartet, the BROTHERHOOD, arrived at the high school at 6:15, found an open classroom, moved in all our props, uniforms, and other belongings, and went out onstage to see the auditorium. There we met the stage manager. He used a hand-held vibrator placed at his neck when he spoke to us. Apparently his larynx had been removed by surgery.

He was an unusually friendly guy, full of enthusiasm, brimming over with spirit, and wore a cap with the letters "SPEBSQSA" over the visor. That puzzled us since he surely could not sing with the chorus. Before the show started he came to our room while we were warming up our voices. He asked for a song and listened intently as we sang for him.

Throughout the evening we wondered about the stage-manager barbershopper who obviously loved the music and avidly supported the cause. We wondered how, with no voice, he had become interested in the hobby and why he had a membership in a singing society. Our questions did not remain unanswered for long.

Following our appearance on the afterglow we were changing clothes in a small back room that was hardly big enough for all the coats and soft drinks stored there. We heard a knock on the door and in walked the stage manager. He wanted to tell us he had enjoyed our performance. He touched the button on his vibrator and said our singing reminded him of earlier days. His eyes lit up as he spoke. He told us he used to sing in a quartet and had many memorable experiences. He told us of singing on shows with the MIDSTATES FOUR and BUFFALO BILLS. What was his quartet? Then he told us. It was the PITTSBURGHERS, International Quartet Champions of 1948! He was Bill Conway, the bass.

The irony was like a slap in the face. He had reached the top of the barbershop ladder, yet a short time later needed a battery-powered mechanism to even utter a sound.

In the few moments he told of his experiences, I gained a new insight into and appreciation of the barbershop spirit. Being able to sing is something very special and beautiful. Just being able to speak is something very special. It's easy to get so wrapped up working for quartet honors and accolades that an appreciation of the basic singing mechanism is missed. Singing is a vocal process not all can enjoy.

Our meeting with Bill Conway brought that realization into sharp focus. He was in no way apologetic for his handicap. He was in no way solicitous of sympathy. He was a dedicated barbershopper who had reached the summit, had enjoyed much of barbershopping's bounty, and then asked only to participate in his hobby as changing circumstances allowed. In his pride, devotion, and love of barbershop harmony I found an inspiration. I also found great strength and courage in his barbershop spirit.

Dick Ellenberger told me more about Bill Conway:

> *You're quite correct about Bill's being a beautiful person and great barbershopper. Once a year he single-handedly manages a barbershop show for the Lions Club in Canajoharie, New York, where he lives. I think he once made efforts to start a new chapter there, but the town is too small to support one. As you know, at Schenectady Chapter shows he willingly accepts the assignment of stage manager and does a fantastic job of it. When he talks with his mechanical voice generator, he is so adept it's hard to realize it isn't his real voice.*

Bill doesn't let the lack of vocal chords bother his enjoyment of barbershopping or participation in it. At our regular chapter rehearsals he sits on the side and spiritedly mouths every word sung. His facial expressions light up the whole room!

Such enthusiasm is a key ingredient of the barbershop spirit. Bill Conway told me his father had the same gusto:

While I was recalling some of those great quartet experiences, I got to thinking about my father's membership in the Society. Pop was an accountant and treasurer of a building-supply firm in Pittsburgh, but he couldn't carry a melody in a twelve-quart pail even if it had two handles on it. Just the same, no one ever appreciated a barbershop chord more than he did. He was always the last one to leave an afterglow or late-night quartet woodshedding session.

He was appointed treasurer to handle the finances for the Pittsburgh Chapter's annual show each year and this he considered his contribution to the perpetuation of barbershop harmony.

If you've sung in a quartet, you know what it's like to be one-fourth of a chord when you "lock it in," and that pervasive harmony gets in your blood. Although I'm no longer able to ring a chord, I can nevertheless avail myself of every opportunity to listen to all the good quartets that can. And the listening is mighty satisfying.

Others, too, come to mind when I ponder the barbershop spirit. Ron Riegler for one. His performance with the ROARING 20's on the International stage in Philadelphia was a testimonial to a barbershopper's courage and determination. The quartet was founded by Ron and his cousin, Tom Schlinkert, but Tom left the group prior to the Philadelphia contest and wasn't even in the audience to see Ron's performance:

I didn't want to be there because I was so close to Ron I knew I'd suffer agonizingly along with him. I knew he'd walk out onstage with so much pride and honor on the outside, yet with so much pain and hurt on the inside. I didn't want to witness that. His singing in Philly was one of the most courageous acts anyone in barbershopping has ever accomplished.

Ron found out he had cancer two years before that contest. I remember the letter he sent to me after he coached at his first Harmony College. He wrote in his usual lighthearted way how much fun he was having and how well his presentations on staging a chorus were received. His letter concluded, "Everything's okay, except I have a stomach ache. Love, Ron." Two weeks later he was rushed to the hospital and told he had cancer of the abdomen. He was given six months to live.

Ron was a brave and determined young man, taken from us at an early age. He was thirty-four when he died and we can only speculate about the contributions he would have made to barbershopping had he lived.

Ron was zany, creative, contrary, argumentative, and thoroughly lovable. He was intensely interested in barbershopping and even more interested in barbershoppers themselves. He studied records of the champions. He knew the champs by name and they knew him. He was also a fantastic showman, fascinated by choreography and the visual portion of quartet and chorus performances. He became a Society stage presence judge, one of the best. He coached choruses and quartets with an emphasis on stage moves and facial expressions he referred to as "energy," the intangible ingredient that makes an audience come alive and feel a part of a performance. Ron Riegler is missed, God rest his soul, dearly missed, on both sides of the footlights.

Part of the barbershop spirit is the drive toward perfection, the desire to make each performance the best. It's a powerful force called pride, and Joe Schmitt reflects on its effect:

I was backstage in Philadelphia thinking about our opening number just before the SCHMITT BROTHERS were to sing on the Saturday night show at one International. Our song started off with the tenor singing an F-sharp "Hello," followed by the rest of the quartet joining him one by one in a bell chord. I tried to sing my first "Hello" note but was unable to coax a single sound out of this big body of mine. Would you believe it? I tried again and again but couldn't produce a tone of any kind.

I guess I was so apprehensive I was physically unable to produce a sound, although the incident occurred twelve years after we had won the Championship. I suppose we had sung 1500 shows in the meantime, yet when the pressure was on, all the shows and experience didn't matter. The sound was scared right out of me, fortunately for just a brief spell.

The fact that you win at International never lets you alone. Although the rules don't allow you to compete again for the judges, you always compete for the audiences and you always try to sing your best. In our many years as champions we've never gone to a convention without practicing extra hard beforehand. Some people are amazed that after dozens of years of singing together we still practice every Wednesday night. It's not a grueling workout, to be sure, but it is a re-hearsal, a time to sing and renew the quartet relationship. Every show has to be top quality. Each time we open our mouths our reputation is on the line.

The challenge of entertaining an audience is matched by the barbershopper's spirit of determination. Freddie King explains it this way:

You always have to reach for something that's inaccessible. There must be that endless drive to do what you have never before achieved, to attain the never-before attained. Only in this way do you improve and grow and succeed. You see, if you don't grow, if you don't reach for the inaccessible, you weaken and ultimately die.

Each year only four men out of 40,000 barbershoppers in our Society win the International Quartet Championship. That's one one-hundredth of one percent, but thousands reach out and stretch and try to snare that golden ring.

It takes courage to keep coming back, to keep battling the disappointments and defeats. I don't mind telling you that quartets like the FOUR RENEGADES and ORIOLE FOUR are monuments to tenacity. They didn't give up when they had more than enough reasons or excuses to do so. But I'd say they're better for the struggle. I know I'm better for it. I learned more and grew more and the rewards along the way were many times more meaningful.

Carl Hancuff describes another facet of the barbershop spir-it—caring:

The SALT FLATS' philosophy is rather simple. If we can entertain people, make them laugh, stir up a little happiness in them, we've accomplished something magnificent. All of us have great pressures and problems in our lives. Maybe you're in debt, maybe you're out of a job, maybe your wife's leaving you, maybe you've had a death in the family. Everyone is touched by one or more tragedies.

If we can appear on a show and put a smile on your face, we feel like supermen. The minute you're laughing at something I do, you're not worrying about those tragedies. I've momentarily taken the pressure off and I believe that's one of the most beautiful gifts anybody can give. It's almost like a religion with us.

Bob Royce has a story about barbershop caring:

One of my most heartwarming barbershop experiences occurred when I was singing with the MAIN STREET FOUR. As District Champions we sang on many shows and were quite successful, but after qualifying for our second International contest, our lead, Dave Mittelstadt, discovered he had a medical condition which required an operation. The doctor advised him to take care of it as quickly as possible and Dave agreed to go into the hospital immediately after the Livingston Chapter annual show. As chorus director, he didn't want to miss that.

Consequently, the quartet had some show commitments we could not honor while Dave was out of commission, and I had the job of trying to find replacements to fill in for us. I called, among others, Freddie King of the ORIOLE FOUR to see if his quartet could sing for us on a show in Brooklyn, New York. That was some years before the ORIOLE FOUR won the International.

Freddie was very sympathetic but his quartet was unavailable since he had another commitment. "You can't afford to be cancelling shows and letting other quartets do them," he said. "You guys need the money for your trip to International. Gosh, if I didn't have another commitment, I'd get myself up there and sing lead for you myself!" We both laughed. "Let me do a little checking," he said. "I'll get back to you."

"Look," he said, when he called a short time later. "I've got

a proposition. Our lead, Jim Grant, said he'll sing with you guys on the Brooklyn show if you want."

"Aw, Fred," I said, "there's no way in the world he could learn all our repertoire—motions, words, music."

"Nonsense," Freddie told me.

Jim Grant made arrangements to drive from Baltimore, Maryland to Livingston, New Jersey one Saturday morning before Dave had his operation. Our quartet met him and spent the better part of the day performing our routines so Jim could see our act, hear it, and record it.

Three weeks later when Jim again drove north, Dave was in the hospital. We had a quartet rehearsal in the late afternoon with Jim singing lead. We drove to Brooklyn and sang the show without a hitch. We didn't announce that we had a replacement lead and nobody knew it. Jim had memorized our material, mastered it, and performed it like he had been trooping with us for years. That was it! One show was all we sang together.

At the afterglow I stepped to the microphone to acknowledge what I consider to be one of the most unselfish barbershopping acts ever. The chapter members were amazed. They couldn't believe he fit in so comfortably and knew the songs so well though we had never sung together before. That's the true spirit of barbershopping, the totally unselfish giving of one's talents.

Of course the quartet paid his out-of-pocket expenses, but Jim refused to accept a penny of profit. He said the money should go in our quartet travel fund so we could make the trip to compete at the International Convention in San Antonio, Texas. What a man!

The barbershop experience is singing and contests and shows, but it's more. It's the barbershopper's caring, dedication, and desire to entertain. Call me sentimental, but I'm telling you those commodities are in splendid abundance at the barbershop store.

Barbershop Music

Barbershop music is by no means an art form of universal appeal, but for those with such a harmony persuasion, there's nothing comparable. At my first International Convention I thought all the quartets sounded alike. After I had heard a dozen quarter-finalists, I got bored! Time has now sharpened my sensitivity to the music and refined my appreciation of it.

To many barbershoppers and show enthusiasts, the music casts an inscrutable spell. I remember a BROTHERHOOD quartet rehearsal with Merrill Callum, well-known coach and Society judge. We were working hard and after many tries sang a song passage exactly as instructed. Merrill bounded out of his chair and let out an enthusiastic squeal of approval. His wife, Stel, looked at him with surprise. "That's more excitement than you displayed when Mother cancelled her two-month visit," she quipped, with a twinkle in her eye.

Strange, but true. Barbershop music works minor miracles on barbershop devotees, sometimes major miracles. Why, it's powerful enough to knock you off your feet! And a Lou Perry experience proves the point:

> *It happened at the Society's Harmony College in St. Joseph, Missouri. Earl Moon and I were walking back from our arranging workshop on our way to lunch, but since there was a long waiting line we stopped for some woodshedding with Jim Miller and Burt Szabo.*
>
> *After a couple of mildly successful attempts, we started in on "Why Don't My Dreams Come True." I don't know if you're familiar with the song, but at the climax the lyric is "But there's no end to my rainbow." When we got to that point, the harmony just gobbled us up. It totally consumed us. The hair on my arms stood up, I got goose bumps from head to toe, and Earl fell over backwards on the ground. I had never experienced such a sensation before. I laughed uncontrollably and couldn't stop. Then my knees turned to Jell-O and I toppled to the ground next to Earl. When I looked up at Jim I saw tears of joy splashing down his face. Only imperturbable Burt was unmoved by it all and stared in amazement, as we rolled about helplessly on the grass!*

The harmony can hit pretty hard, as Hugh Ingraham describes:

> *When the Society first issued its arrangement of "Oh, Canada," the Canadian National Anthem, the music was introduced at Harmony College. During the opening session of the school, Bob Johnson asked the Canadians to assemble on-*

stage while the mass chorus of school attendees sang. There were probably twenty-five of us onstage and six hundred fifty singing barbershoppers in the audience. Being Canadian and hearing my National Anthem sung in barbershop harmony for the first time by that many voices bowled me over. Boy, I'll tell you, it absolutely destroyed me!

At the conclusion of that Harmony College week there was another moment of intense drama, when the music took command. Val Hicks describes what happened:

One of my greatest barbershop experiences occurred at Harmony College on Saturday night when, as you perhaps know, there's a show produced by the scriptwriters' class. The International Championship Quartet flew in to sing, and at the end of the program Bob Johnson called the entire faculty and Harmony College staff onstage for final good-byes and acknowledgement. The program closed with everyone singing the Canadian National Anthem, the U.S. National Anthem, and finally "Keep America Singing."

Well, it was quite an emotion-packed evening. The quartet champs were outstanding, the college attendees sang an in-spired rendition of the Canadian National Anthem, and then we started to sing my arrangement of "The Star Spangled Banner."

Standing to my immediate left was my good friend Lou Perry, along with Burt Szabo and Earl Moon, and as we neared the end of the song, Lou became so emotionally engrossed in it that he broke down and started to sob. I didn't know then he was over-come by the music, so when I heard him gasping I thought for a moment he might be ill. I quickly glanced over and I wish you could have seen the way Earl Moon was comforting him. He had his arms around Lou and was patting him on the back. "That's all right, Lou," he said softly. "That's all right."

Normally I'm a pretty jaded character. I've been barbershop-ping a long time, I've been listening to great barbershop har-mony a long time, and only seldom do I get goose bumps anymore. After all, I'm a trained musician. With a Ph.D. in music, I've reached the point where it takes a truly exceptional performance to excite me nowadays. I looked over at Lou over-come by the situation, I saw Earl Moon tenderly caring for him, and I felt myself slipping over the edge. Then tears flowed out uncontrollably. I couldn't help myself.

The staff saw this, the faculty, the entire audience. As I said, it had been a heavy emotional evening up to that point. Believe me, everyone's feelings seemed to be flowing out! It was one of those times when emotions just couldn't be contained. Then afterward we had to work our way through "Keep America Singing" and that was a tough song to sing under the circumstances.

To me this is what makes barbershopping so great—the camaraderie, the brotherhood, the fraternalism we have. It has taught me much about sharing my emotions with people. Moreover, it has taught me much about the beauty of those emotions.

Lou Perry recalls his feelings during those moments:

I had mixed emotions about that incident. When everyone in the auditorium sang the anthems, I was stunned by the magnificent sound, especially with Val Hicks' arrangement of "The Star Spangled Banner." I don't know how you react to such situations, but I react by completely breaking down. It happens to me occasionally when I hear something that completely overwhelms me.

The sound of "The Star Spangled Banner" rushed up from the singers and swept me off my feet. It might have been a combination of the music and a feeling of patriotism. Whatever it was, I started to cry. I didn't feel I could face the music or the audience, so I turned to the guy who was nearest me, Earl Moon, and cried on his shoulder.

I say I had mixed feelings about it. I know my reaction to the music affected some people in the audience; several told me so afterwards. I felt bad because it spoiled the sound that was being produced. It spoiled it for Bob Johnson, too, I'm sure.

How he is able to stand there in front of everyone with all that sound coming at him, without being overcome, is baffling. He once told me he is affected by it but is somehow able to mask his feelings. I can't do that, so I lost control when the sound was too beautiful to bear.

I was in the audience that Saturday night and I, too, witnessed the heart-warming happening. As the magnificent sound lifted to the heights of the auditorium and reverberated and reinforced in intensity, it seemed to signal a conclusion to the week's activities. The week had been hectic, demanding, exciting, sometimes bewildering, and Saturday night was the last night of the college. I had made heavy emotional investments throughout the week and found a strange set of forces pulling on me as I sang and watched the emotions spill out onstage.

It was a lovely moment. Barbershoppers from throughout the Society were gathered together in the culmination of a week's schooling and work. The next day we would be leaving Harmony College. I looked about. Everyone was sharing in the emotion. My swallowing came hard; tears welled up and overflowed.

It was a happy moment, yet at the same time sad. A myriad of emotions dashed around within me. I was overwhelmed with the harmony,but also overwhelmed with the outpouring of musical devotion I had experienced. Many of the most talented barbershoppers in the world had traveled to St. Joseph, Missouri to share their talents and skills. They didn't come for fame or fortune. They came for love. They so loved their music and fellow barbershoppers that they gladly gave a week of time to coach and counsel in the barbershop art. Love filled the auditorium every bit as much as the sound of "The Star Spangled Banner."

When Lou Perry broke down before us, it seemed a fitting and majestic climax to a powerful experience. It gave sanction to an expression we all felt. It was a sincere reaction to an intensely emotional time, wholly appropriate for the outpouring of love we had witnessed that week!

It is apparently possible for music to rule absolutely, to become omnipotent. The BOSTON COMMON's Terry Clarke describes the feeling:

> *Music is an amazingly intriguing phenomenon. It has been a dominant force throughout the world in all cultures with all people from the beginning of time, yet no one knows how or why it holds such a commanding influence in human life. It works its way into your system like ivy climbing a brick wall. I'm reluctant to give music top ranking in my life, but it's awfully high on my priority list.*
>
> *There's something almost mystical about it. You're drawn to*

its influence and you yield as a thoroughly willing prisoner, but I'd say it goes beyond the mystical. It touches on the edges of psychic phenomena; it may even tread lightly within the realm of the spiritual.

When someone first gets involved with barbershop quartetting, he is impressed with the foursome combination. Creating harmony with four individual voices is an elating experience. As the quartet progresses it eventually reaches the level where the four singers become one. Individual voices merge into a single sound of dramatically improved quality and impact.

There's another step beyond that. We've experienced moments when the four of us actually became the song. It's a strange sensation. We were totally unaware of ourselves and the audience and were so immersed in the song that we literally became its form and substance. At such times we may unconsciously but automatically alter an inflection or intonation. The song changes as it's sung and we're carried along with it. The song itself leads the way. We become vehicles for the song's expression. It's the most extraordinary sensation you can imagine.

It's as if we've drifted into a new world where harmony alone prevails. It's as if we're lifted out of ourselves into a musical Utopia. It's a very high moment. We're removed from ourselves. We're transmitted to another realm.

In describing his ultimate barbershop experiences, Freddie King gives a surprisingly similar account:

I've had any number of barbershop highs during my years of singing, but there have been a few instances when a truly ethereal quality descended about me. Winning the International Quartet Championship was one of those experiences, but even that was surpassed at the Kennedy Center in Washington, D.C., when we performed the "Salute to America" package. I sang solo in "We Shall Meet, but We Shall Miss Him." I was all alone onstage in the center of the spotlight. There was dead silence. Then I sang. I sang better than I had ever sung before, better than I have ever sung since, probably better than I will ever sing again.

You've heard about those experiences. Maslow calls them "peak experiences," and sure enough, I encountered one at

Kennedy Center. On a few other occasions I've also slipped in-to the great beyond. I don't know how to adequately describe the feeling. It's as if I'm being drawn out. I seem to transcend what's onstage and I can stand behind myself and watch the performance happen. That's really the truth. I feel detached, free, in a warm, fluid state where the music dominates and I simply flow along with it.

When it happens with the quartet, I know we've achieved a level of musical perfection. There is no way our performance could be any better. I've experienced the sensation maybe a half dozen times. Some people may never come upon it. During those moments, whatever is divine is breathing on us. We're able to float up over the top of ourselves and look down. I've seen our heads turn from side to side and I've watched us make the right moves. I've been able to see the performance and feel the elation and all the while I'm singing. It's as if I'm singing but I'm not singing. I'm witnessing the crowd, seeing their reaction, and I'm wrapped up in one heck of an encounter. I'm telling you, in terms of emotional and spiritual experiences, such moments are the absolute ultimate!

Barbershop music does strange and wonderful things to people. Here's a story from Jim Massey:

My daughter Marla has a sensitive ear for music and she sings well, too. At the International Convention in Indianapolis we were standing in the hotel lobby listening to the BOSTON COMMON sing and sixteen-year-old Marla got hooked on their sound real fast. The next thing I knew, she was standing in the middle of them, listening intently.

When some friends stopped to chat and asked about Marla, I couldn't resist the temptation to brag a little. "She sure does appreciate good barbershop singing," I said proudly. "The BOSTON COMMON have her spellbound right now. She's a real fan of quartetting, could listen to good old barbershop harmony for hours," About then she joined us. "Well, Marla," I said, showing off again, "how did you like the BOSTON COMMON? They're pretty great, huh?"

"Oh, yeah," she said excitedly, "I guess they're great all right, but golly, is that baritone ever cute!"

*zing to "Keep
n; the eager-
g as well as I
ne face of an
ty Home; the
finale of our
n an unfurled
arbershopper
h great pride
hypnotic ex-
rtets at close
's that warm*

emotions com-
articipation in a
o experience is
o performance.

*about the
ch gave one
ter, at every*

*olumbus, we
for analysis
siological in-
gave a full
were told we
tes onstage
our day!
e same sen-
nce, they're
amounts of*

*olessed with
hen we per-*

*faction, the
ted, and we
e will never*

nderful ways.

*ience do so for the har-
set of benefits from his
into barbershopping and
he music and merriment
nstead to simply sample
approach is better than
id needs vary.
rtain is closed, what is the
he thoughts:*

*ll live forever because it
oves pure harmony will
for all time to come.*

*ore and ten, you have to
ms; we old codgers live
yriad of barbershop ex-
id so many are beyond
anything. I found friend-
ed fun, because we have
ing! When men are sing-
And with themselves!*

*ershopping so special is
life. Barbershopping has
fidence and generated an
vould never have found.
hopping is people relating
excitement, and personal*

dless stream of pleasant

memories: The rich sound of 7000 voices harmon
America Singing" at an International Conventio
ness of a quartet of clean-cut teenage boys singir
wish I could; the toothless smile of gratitude on
invalid the last time my quartet sang at the Cour
thrill of singing "God Bless America" during the
chapter show while the spotlight shone down upc
flag; the sight of a crippled old gentleman b
seated center stage in his wheelchair, singing wi
with his chorus in a District contest; the singularly
perience of hearing one of the Society's best qua
range. That's barbershopping—sights and sounc
the heart and gladden the spirit.

The essence of barbershopping? It's feelings and
municated through song. It's sharing harmony. It's p
great *joie de vivre*. And the intensity of a barbershc
wholly dependent upon the intensity of the barbershc
Vern Reed illustrates:

> *One of the nicest things people ever sai*
> *BUFFALO BILLS was that when we sang, we ea*
> *hundred percent of what we physically had to o*
> *performance.*
> *Once for a concert at Ohio State University in C*
> *were asked if we'd mind being "wired" to record*
> *our pulse rates, breathing efficiency, and other phy*
> *dicators. Electrodes were attached to us and we*
> *forty-five minute performance. After the show we*
> *burned up as much energy in those forty-five mine*
> *as a laborer digging ditches burns up in an eight-*
> *I'm sure many quartetters have experienced th*
> *sation. When they walk offstage after a performa*
> *beat! When they perform, they burn up incredible*
> *physical and emotional energy.*
> *Fortunately, we not only loved to sing but were*
> *an abundance of physical and vocal energy, and v*
> *formed, we never held back.*
> *And that was part of the reward. In terms of satr*
> *return was in direct proportion to the effort contribu*
> *got more than our share of rewards. I think ther*

again be an experience in my life that will compare with my quartetting days. We loved people, we loved working with people, we loved entertaining people! It's the most gratifying and rewarding activity I know.

Here's a final glimpse of the barbershop experience, particularly fitting for these last few pages. It's from Carl Hancuff:

The SALT FLATS went over to Tokyo during the Christmas holidays because we felt if we were going to give of ourselves, that would be the time servicemen would need more cheering up and entertainment. We did our show in all the GI hospitals and performed for all we were worth.

Christmas Eve was very strange. We were eating a delicious dinner with good friends in the beautiful hotel where we were staying, but the mood was not at all happy. Rather, it was sorrowful. Our thoughts were of home. We weren't talking or smiling. Gloom was all around.

Then the door opened and in came a dozen pretty Japanese girls. Each wore a lovely white dress and carried a lit candle, and they sang Christmas carols, but for some reason the singing seemed to depress us even more. After their songs I suggested we sing "Silent Night," and the four of us leaned over the table in a huddle and sang. It seemed to turn everyone on, maybe because it was a familiar sound from home for the many melancholy Americans in the restaurant. Then the quartet got up and did about fifteen minutes of our funniest and fastest stuff on a little stage there. Everybody circled around. Smiles began to appear, and laughs. After our impromptu show we all joined together in song.

Finally there was a festive mood and a feeling of the Christmas spirit. Those people who had been silent and sad were laughing and talking, and I thought to myself we did something good. It was a pleasant, proud feeling.

I had another unique singing experience the same night. A Japanese American at one of the tables asked if I'd be interested in attending a Christmas party at the home of a Tokyo music teacher. I accepted the invitation with pleasure.

Everybody there was Japanese except me, and they were all fine musicians. After we had been served cake, each guest stood up in turn and performed. What a terrific array of talent—piano players, singers, violinists. One was a prima donna from the Japanese opera. Then it was my turn and all eyes looked expectantly at me. "Now we would like you to perform," they said, but I was there alone, without the rest of my quartet.

"I can't sing a solo," I apologized. "I sing in a barbershop quartet. I harmonize with other singers, like the BUFFALO BILLS. I don't sing solos!"

The Japanese guests exchanged puzzled glances. Several collected in a corner of the room for a few moments and after a whispered discussion four of them approached me. "You will now harmonize with us," they said, "and in your honor, because it is Christmas Eve, we will sing 'Silent Night.'"

There I stood in a foreign country in a home I'd never seen before, harmonizing with four, not three, Japanese musicians. We sang "Silent Night" in English. Huge tears flooded down my cheeks and I thought, "Oh my God, this is the way it ought to be all over the world!"

This is indeed the way it ought to be all over the world; men coming together in song, opening their hearts to its harmony, raising their voices for the world to hear. And so, my friend, join the congregation. Sing out loud and strong with laughter, love, and a barbershop song!

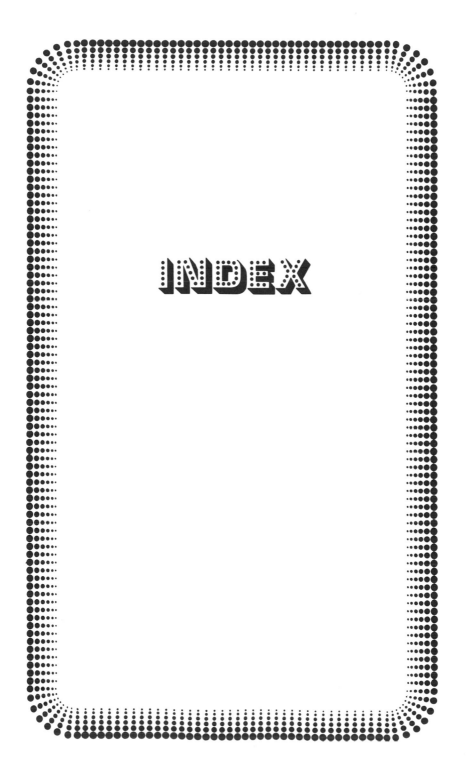

INDEX

Index

Included in this index are the names of barbershoppers, non-barbershoppers, quartets, choruses, and chapters identified in the book. Where the same name is mentioned several times in a story, only the first reference is given here. Also included are references to a number of other organizations, groups, and barbershop activities.

A

B

C

I

J

K

L

m

N

O

P

Q

R

T

Editor and Publisher: Fred Gielow

As a fifth-grader at Edison Elementary School in Detroit, Michigan, Fred Gielow performed in his first quartet at a monthly meeting of the PTA, and that performance was the start of a love affair with singing that has lasted ever since. He participated in glee club and chorus groups in high school and college and accumulated a good many years of singing experience before ever hearing about the Society for the Preservation and Encouragement of Barber Shop Quartet Singing in America (SPEBSQSA).

A Society member and Poughkeepsie, New York Chapter member since 1966, Fred has sampled and savored many sides of barbershopping life. He has sung in International chorus and quartet competitions, worked in chapter administration, served on the Society's Chapter Officer Training School (COTS) faculty, and, as a member of the UNLIKELY HOODS and BROTHERHOOD quartets, performed in shows from St. John's, Newfoundland to Pasadena, California.

Outside of the barbershopping realm, Fred's interests focus on photography and writing. His articles have appeared in local magazines and national publications.

Over the years, as barbershopping became an increasingly important part of his life, Fred decided to combine his writing and singing interests, and he set out to produce a book about his favorite hobby. It took more than three years to complete, but Fred says, "I enjoyed every minute of it!"

Fred has found a special fulfillment in his barbershopping pursuits, a special laughter and love. Through the stories and anecdotes assembled in his book, perhaps you, too, can find a special laughter and love in a barbershop song.

Typesetting: Composing Room
               Subsidiary Company of Community By-Lines
               R.D. 1, Box 157
               Rosendale, New York 12472

Printing: Malloy Lithographing, Incorporated
               5411 Jackson Road
               Ann Arbor, Michigan 48106